SONGS OF THE LISU HILLS

WORLD CHRISTIANITY

Dale T. Irvin and Peter Phan, Series Editors

ADVISORY BOARD:
Akintunde E. Akinade
Adrian Hermann
Leo D. Lefebure
Elaine Padilla
Yolanda Pierce

Moving beyond descriptions of European-derived norms that have existed for hundreds of years, books in the World Christianity series reflect an understanding of global Christianity that embodies the wide diversity of its identity and expression. The series seeks to expand the scholarly field of world Christianity by interrogating boundary lines in church history, mission studies, ecumenical dialogue, and inter-religious dialogue among Christians and non-Christians across geographic, geopolitical, and confessional divides. Beyond a mere history of missions to the world, books in the series examine local Christianity, how Christianity has been acculturated, and how its expression interacts with the world at large. Issues under investigation include how Christianity has been received and transformed in various countries; how migration has changed the nature and practice of Christianity and the new forms of the faith that result; and how seminary and theological education responds to the challenges of world Christianity.

OTHER BOOKS IN THE SERIES:
Krista E. Hughes, Dhawn B. Martin, and Elaine Padilla, eds., *Ecological Solidarities: Mobilizing Faith and Justice for an Entangled World*

SONGS OF THE LISU HILLS

Practicing Christianity in Southwest China

Aminta Arrington

The Pennsylvania State University Press
University Park, Pennsylvania

Library of Congress Cataloging-in-Publication Data

Names: Arrington, Aminta, author.
Title: Songs of the Lisu Hills : practicing Christianity in southwest China / Aminta Arrington.
Other titles: World Christianity (University Park, Pa.)
Description: University Park, Pennsylvania : The Pennsylvania State University Press, [2020] | Series: World Christianity | Includes bibliographical references and index.
Summary: "Explores the history and practice of Lisu Christianity in southwest China, describing how the Lisu maintained their Christian faith through China's tumultuous twentieth century and into the present"—Provided by publisher.
Identifiers: LCCN 2019046996 | ISBN 9780271085074 (cloth)
Subjects: LCSH: Christianity—China, Southwest. | Lisu (Southeast Asian people)—China, Southwest—Religion. | China, Southwest—Church history.
Classification: LCC BR1290.S68 A77 2020 | DDC 275.1/3—dc23
LC record available at https://lccn.loc.gov/2019046996

Copyright © 2020 Aminta Arrington
All rights reserved
Printed in the United States of America
Published by The Pennsylvania State University Press,
University Park, PA 16802–1003

The Pennsylvania State University Press is a member of the Association of University Presses.

It is the policy of The Pennsylvania State University Press to use acid-free paper. Publications on uncoated stock satisfy the minimum requirements of American National Standard for Information Sciences—Permanence of Paper for Printed Library Material, ANSI Z39.48–1992.

For
Chris, Katherine, Grace, and Andrew

You will go out in joy
    and be led forth in peace;
the mountains and hills
    will burst into song before you,
and all the trees of the field
    will clap their hands.

ISAIAH 55:12 (NIV)

Contents

List of Illustrations   ix
Foreword by Brian Stanley   xi
Acknowledgments   xv
List of Abbreviations   xviii
Notes About the Lisu Language and Its Usage   xix

Introduction: Tso Lo Hamlet   1

VOICE: MIE HUI QING   23

chapter 1   J. O. Fraser and the Beginnings of Lisu Christianity   25

chapter 2   Linguistic Borderlands   45

VOICE: A-NA   63

chapter 3   The Evangelization of the Nujiang Valley   65

VOICE: YU PING AN   93

chapter 4   Fixing the Boundaries   95

VOICE: ISAIAH   111

chapter 5   The Easter Festival   113

VOICE: TIMOTHY   133

chapter 6   "Let's Pray for Each Other"   135

chapter 7   Copying the Bible by Torchlight   155

　　　　　　VOICE: JESSE   171

chapter 8   Hymns of the Everlasting Hills   173

　　　　　　VOICE: NAOMI   193

chapter 9   Building the House of Prayer   195

Postscript   205
Notes   207
Bibliography   219
Index   227

Illustrations

Figures
1. The Nujiang Valley   3
2. Two Lisu women walking to church   20
3. J. O. Fraser   27
4. John 3:16 written by J. O. Fraser in the Fraser Script   33
5. Lisu Christian door poster for 2014 (Fugong)   54
6. Fish Four and his wife at Muchengpo   69
7. First page of Carl Gowman's Lisu catechism and hymnal   82
8. A Lisu church in Gongshan County   105
9. The Lisu church stage for the Shee Za Village 2014 Easter festival   121
10. Model of structure-agency balance and imbalance   144
11. "Lord Jesus, My Road" by Pastor Moses   179

Maps
1. Western Yunnan Province   8
2. Lisu villages   30
3. Mission stations   78
4. Location of the Nujiang Valley   87

Tables
1. The roles played by writing in societies along the oral-literate continuum   53
2. Differences in Christian meaning and practice in individualistic and communal societies   142

Foreword

Christianity is a religion of the book. From its earliest days it replicated the Hebrew reverence for sacred text as the medium of the divine word. What made it radically distinctive from the non-Judaic religions of the Graeco-Roman world was in large part the unique place that hearing the Scriptures occupied in early Christian worship. Yet the great majority of the first Christians were themselves illiterate, dependent on an educated few to read aloud the writings that became recognized as the Christian Bible and to teach the faith enshrined in those books. That paradox has been a recurring theme throughout the centuries of Christian history, though from the medieval period onwards it progressively became obscured by the apparent concentration of Christian adherence on European peoples who had rising standards of literacy, an expanding print culture, and a pronounced emphasis on the rational value of individual educational attainment.

However, the remarkable transformation of Christianity over the last century into a religion whose greatest strength lies beyond Europe and North America has reasserted the paradox. Much of this growing non-Western Christianity is broadly evangelical in character, owing its origins directly or indirectly to mission agencies of an evangelical theological character. Protestants, and evangelical Protestants above all, have defined themselves as Christians for whom the Bible is of paramount importance. That priority has usually been accompanied by an insistence on the necessity of individual conversion to a personal belief in Christ shaped and regulated by personal familiarity with "what the Bible teaches." Yet as in the early Church, many of the cultures in which these evangelical varieties of Christianity have taken root are oral and communal cultures. They are societies in which what the West has come to term "religion" is less a matter of individual belief and much more one of communal practice. It is about doing together those acts of ritual and behavior that define the essential moral identity of the people and guarantee its well-being and protection from evil and misfortune at the most profound level of spiritual reality. These cultures may have low levels of literacy, or there may be a marked disjunction between the spoken vernacular and a non-local written language preferred for the strictly

FOREWORD

limited purposes of commerce and education. Or—and this may prove to be increasingly true of Christians even in the West—the individual reading of books may simply not be a natural activity for those of a certain age, whether they be young or old.

Aminta Arrington's fascinating study of the growth and distinctive features of Christianity among the Lisu people of southwest China highlights this paradox with extraordinary clarity. Lisu Christianity derives from a conservative evangelical—some would say, even fundamentalist—tradition. Its pioneer English missionary, J. O. Fraser of the China Inland Mission, faced the challenge of devising a script for a language that had hitherto been entirely oral. That script, perfected in the 1910s, is still in use today, though the Lisu increasingly prefer to use Chinese for written and educational purposes, retaining the Lisu language as a spoken vernacular. Fraser witnessed a movement of collective conversion to Christianity that challenged many of the assumptions of his own theological tradition, yet defended the spiritual authenticity of his converts. His successors, Allyn and Leila Cooke, were graduates of the Bible Institute of Los Angeles, ancestor of the present-day Biola University, but originally an institution of strong fundamentalist and dispensationalist leanings. Nevertheless, the Cookes devoted themselves, not simply, as one would expect, to translation of parts of the New Testament into Lisu, but also to encouraging the use of hymn singing as the most effective vehicle for Christian instruction. In this, they built upon Fraser's own remarkable musical abilities.

Today, the Lisu hymnbook is a constant companion of the Bible in the hands of Lisu Christians. Indeed, Dr. Arrington shows how the devotional life of Lisu Christians is oriented more to the corporate and even individual singing of hymns than to the private study of the Bible, which remains very rare, something of a cultural eccentricity. Lisu piety is recognizably evangelical—many of the hymns they sing are radically indigenized versions of Western evangelical classics—and yet the Lisu Bible is not so much read, as orally performed in public worship, and also venerated as an object carried to church in brightly embroidered Bible bags. The evangelical faith of the Lisu is defined by what they do, and do not do (such as drinking alcohol and smoking tobacco), rather than by formal adherence to a set of Christian doctrines. This left the Lisu church highly vulnerable during the years of the Cultural Revolution in China, since the Christians concluded that state proscription of Christian religious practice necessarily implied the cessation even of individual prayer.

In spite of the apparent historical fragility of a form of Christianity that lays so little emphasis on the need for individual cognitive apprehension of Christian doctrine, the Lisu church has risen again from the near-death experience of those years. It affords a striking example of evangelical Christianity that is neither individualistic nor privatized. Christian faith has become what in Europe it has not generally been since medieval times—an integral part of the entire fabric of quotidian communal existence—while at the same time displaying most of the characteristics of a Reformation and evangelical outworking of the experience of salvation, not least in the commitment displayed to intercessory prayer. This is what makes this book so intriguing, and of such wide-ranging significance.

BRIAN STANLEY
Professor of World Christianity,
University of Edinburgh

Acknowledgments

This is a work centered on relationships, and therefore, I have several people to thank. In Beijing, Huang Jianbo, formerly of Renmin University and now at East China Normal University, met me for coffee to discuss his own fieldwork in the Nujiang Valley, and was kind enough to serve as an outside reader on my dissertation. His insights greatly enriched my work. Li Guirong and Jia Guodong at Renmin University gave me a semester off to focus on fieldwork.

In Kunming, Steve "Fitz" Fitzwilliam, grandson of the Fitzwilliams mentioned in this narrative, was of invaluable assistance as I was coming and going from the Nujiang Valley, always ready to provide a meal, or to buy bus tickets, or to lend a listening ear as I recounted my latest experiences. Rose and Jeff Waligora always had a bed available, as well as encouragement. Lisu linguist Jin Jie enhanced my understanding of the translation of the Lisu Bible and hymnbook greatly. I am very much in debt to his pioneering work, and also appreciate his willingness to answer so many linguistic questions by text message when I was in the valley.

In the Nujiang Valley, I am thankful for the fortuitous bus trip that had me seated next to ethnomusicologist Ying Diao, who shared her own research with me and enriched my knowledge of Lisu Christian pop. I wish we could have met again, but still am thankful for her readiness to answer so many of my emails and text messages. I am also thankful to the Christian workers who opened up their homes and answered my many questions on my first trip into the valley.

In Chiang Mai, Thailand, David and Eugene Morse went above and beyond to explain their family's work and their knowledge of Lisu language and culture to me. I am so grateful that I was able to have an extensive interview with Eugene just a few months before he passed away at the age of 93, a great loss to the Lisu church. David's knowledge of the Lisu language is unparalleled, and his early enthusiasm of my focus on the Lisu hymns was a great encouragement. Moreover, he read through the entire dissertation, validating my study and correcting several errors. Neel Roberts from Chiang Rai took the time to meet me in Chiang Mai with a flash drive filled with valuable archival documents. I also was deeply privileged that

ACKNOWLEDGMENTS

Annabel Rulison, granddaughter of Isobel Kuhn, made time to talk with me in Chiang Mai.

In England, I am very thankful to Mrs. Eileen Fraser Crossman, for a delightful morning tea and conversation, for sharing her old family pictures, and for allowing some of those to be included in this book. Marion Osgood, archivist for the UK headquarters of Overseas Missionary Fellowship in Borough Green, blocked off a morning to show me all of OMF's materials relating to the Lisu work. Finally, I am thankful to Andrew F. Walls for providing timely and meaningful encouragement.

In Los Angeles, I would like to thank Doug Hayward, Rich Starcher, and Tom Steffen for guiding this project during its dissertation stage. Roberta King at Fuller Seminary gave me excellent technical assistance with ethnomusicology, as well as warm friendship. I went through Biola with a cohort of students who greatly enriched my life by their comments on my papers and by their conversations in the cafeteria. For fear of leaving out many I will list none, but they know who they are.

At the Billy Graham Center Archives at Wheaton College, Katherine Graber and Keith Call were immensely helpful in pointing the way to uncatalogued collections. I also appreciate Keith for telling me that Isobel Kuhn's gravesite was nearby, allowing me to pay my respects before I left town.

John Brown University has been a very congenial and supportive place to work and teach, and has also done much to support this book. In addition to providing me with a Summer Scholars Fellowship and a Faculty Development Scholars Grant, I am thankful for several colleagues who were gracious enough to read chapters and proposals, and to answer my many theological questions, in particular, Chad Raith, Rod Reed, and Michael Francis. Rachel Maxson in the JBU library made the connections that put me in touch with Mrs. Crossman, read through the entire manuscript, made incisive and clarifying suggestions, and provided welcome reading recommendations. I am deeply indebted to her. I have also been blessed with amazing student assistants who have been a big part of this book: Mariah Christ (who also produced all of the maps used in the book), Merritt Tully, Kallie Ott Hubbell, and Emma Hunt. Joel Carpenter of Calvin College gave wise counsel that significantly improved the first chapter.

I am very happy that the book landed in the World Christianity series at Penn State University Press. Peter Phan and Dale Irvin, as series editors, welcomed this book that looks at World Christianity through an ethnographic lens. Kathryn Yahner, as acquisitions editor, has embodied professionalism in our every interaction. Two anonymous reviewers also read through the manuscript, giving many helpful suggestions. Any remaining errors, of course, remain my own.

Each member of my family made sacrifices so that I could conduct fieldwork with the Lisu. My husband, Chris, stepped up to single parent for weeks and months at a time, all the while encouraging me and reminding me of the value of this project. Katherine accompanied me on most of my fieldwork stints, hiking up narrow mountain trails and enduring days without showers with surprising cheerfulness. Grace accompanied me for my Christmas / New Year's trip to the Lisu, making many friends in Tso Lo hamlet, but most of the time she, together with Andrew, had to endure their mother's absence. For these reasons, I am dedicating this book to them.

Most of all, I am thankful to the Lisu Christians who opened up their lives to me. Many of them, though pseudonymous, speak through this book. They brought me along donkey trails, into villages, to festivals, at altitudes, into homes—to so many places I was privileged to go, places that required a relationship to get to. More importantly, they showed me facets of Christianity I had never before seen or experienced, and through that, they have transformed and strengthened my faith. I am forever indebted to them and grateful for their friendship.

Abbreviations

BGC   Billy Graham Center
CIM   China Inland Mission
FHT   Frederick Howard Taylor
OMF   Overseas Missionary Fellowship
SOAS School of Oriental and African Studies

Notes About the Lisu Language and Its Usage

The Lisu people living in China, Thailand, Myanmar, or India speak various dialects of the Lisu language, which is part of the Tibeto-Burman language family. While the Lisu language has some structural similarities to Chinese, particularly in terms of tones and particles, it is its own distinctive language unique to the Lisu people.

The basic unit of the Lisu language is the syllable. Each syllable starts with one of many consonant sounds (thirty) and ends with one of fewer vowel sounds (ten). No syllable ends with a consonant. The Fraser Script, the written orthography for the Lisu language used in the translation of the Bible and the hymnbook, uses the syllable as its central organizing feature; it ties each syllable up neatly into its own morpheme bundle. Because of this precise match between the written script and its oral forms, it is easy for most Lisu to learn to read once they are exposed to the Fraser Script.

In the Fraser Script, which is used across all the borders that divide the Lisu people into various countries, all forty letters are written as upper case Roman letters, fifteen of which are inverted. As more syllables end in an "-ah" sound than any other, this sound is omitted altogether in the written form. For example, B is pronounced "bah," B. B: WU-S is pronounced "bah bah voo sah" and means Father God, the name by which the Lisu most commonly address God.

The Lisu language is tonally complex with six tones, annotated by various punctuation marks, and another eight tone combinations. In practicality, tone marks, even in the Bible and the hymnbook, are often not used unless necessary to distinguish meaning.

In the Nujiang Valley, the Lisu use birth-order names. The oldest daughter in a family is called A-na (A-N.,), and the second oldest A-ni (A-NY l). The oldest son is called A-phu (A. dU), and the second oldest A-deh (A-DꞀ.). There are unique terms all the way to the ninth daughter and the ninth son. In the Lisu Christian tradition, Bible teachers and pastors are given a Bible name in addition to their Lisu birth order name. Ma-pa (M. d:) means male teacher in the Lisu language. Ma-ma (M. M.) means female teacher. These appellations are often attached to their Bible names. Now that most Lisu attend Chinese schooling, by school age they are assigned a Chinese name as well. Thus, a Lisu Christian might go by three different names: their birth-order name, their Bible name, and their Chinese name. In this account, I refer to the Lisu by their birth-order names or, if they are a teacher or pastor, by their Bible name. In all cases, unless they are public figures such as Ma-pa Jesse, these are pseudonyms.

INTRODUCTION

Tso Lo Hamlet

> This is my story, this is my song,
> Praising my Savior all the day long;
> This is my story, this is my song,
> Praising my Savior all the day long.

"It's time for church," Naomi said.

I was spending the New Year's holiday in Tso Lo hamlet, high above the roaring Nujiang River in the remote far west of China's Yunnan Province. The home of Naomi, a Lisu Bible teacher, and her family was built in the traditional Lisu style. The house had two rooms, each with a fire pit in the middle, and two beds along the walls. Embroidered Bible bags hung from hooks all over the house, adding splashes of color to the warm brown of the woven bamboo floors and walls. Corn hung from the ceiling. Large bags of rice and burlap sacks filled with corn or cauliflower or radishes leaned against the walls. Beneath the bamboo floor lived the family's animals: chickens, roosters, four pigs, and a donkey.

I grabbed my Bible bag and followed Naomi up the steep hill. In a small, dimly lit room, five women and five men sat on backless benches, men on one side and women on the other. All had brought their embroidered bags

---

Epigraph from "Blessed Assurance," lyrics by Fanny J. Crosby, 1873, hymn #180 in the 2013 Yunnan Lisu hymnbook.

carrying their Bibles and hymnbooks. After singing two hymns and a doxology, and praying, Naomi began to preach.

Directly after church Naomi announced that we were going to a meeting at a neighbor's house for the purpose of intercessory prayer—prayer conducted on behalf of others. Several people were gathered around the fire in the middle of the room. As the fire grew hotter, we pushed our stools back. As it cooled, we inched forward.

The hosts laid out bowls of rice, meat, and boiled eggs, and we all moved from the fire over to a low table to eat. After eating, we moved back to the fire and sang three hymns. There were about ten of us singing in the small dark room around the fire. Still, I could hear the four-part harmony. One of the hymns we sang was hymn #242, "What a Friend We Have in Jesus." This song was very familiar to me, not only from my own church upbringing but because the Lisu sang it often. As we sang the song together in Lisu, the English words drifted through my mind:

> What a friend we have in Jesus,
> All our sins and griefs to bear!
> What a privilege to carry
> Everything to God in prayer!
> Oh, what peace we often forfeit,
> Oh, what needless pain we bear,
> All because we do not carry
> Everything to God in prayer!

This hymn encapsulated two strong interrelated strains in Lisu Christian culture: prayer and troubles. The deeply felt nature of troubles is expressed in the Lisu language in a four-word couplet:

> NI . . . X . . . MY . . . X
> heart . . . worry . . . soul . . . worry

This four-word couplet occurs three times in "What a Friend We Have in Jesus," once in each verse. The missionaries had also used "NI X MY X" frequently in Bible translation. In Isaiah 53:3 this four-word couplet is used to translate *suffering*. In Romans 8:35 it is used to translate the word *hardship*. And when Jesus, before his crucifixion, prayed in the Garden of Gethsemane, his deeply troubled state was translated into Lisu as "NI X MY X."

fig. 1 The Nujiang Valley. Photo: author.

Those who had requested prayer then knelt in the middle; the rest of us stood around them, praying aloud, all at once, in a loud cacophony. After several minutes, the voices gradually died out, until just one voice remained. That voice grew deeper and louder, knowing the responsibility it carried to end the prayer strong and well.

Tso Lo hamlet was a place where the sacred seeped into every space. Unlike the sacred/secular dichotomy that has become a dominant factor in Western consciousness,[1] the Lisu in Tso Lo hamlet experienced desecularization creep, whereby the sacred permeated all aspects of life. Entertainment was line dancing to Christian pop music, learning a new hymn, or sitting around the fire in Christian fellowship with neighbors. Eating was an occasion to thank God for his blessings. Sickness and difficulty were times not to appeal to hospitals, medicine, or any other current remedies, but to petition the Almighty. There seemed no corner of life in this marginalized, impoverished hamlet that was not consecrated and sanctified through a form of Christianity that defined faith through practices.

The Lisu were evangelized over one hundred years ago by missionaries from the China Inland Mission (CIM), and they adopted Christianity in a "people movement" that permeated nearly their entire society. The evangelization of the Lisu is missionary lore, the subject of numerous narratives and even a film.[2] But despite vast knowledge of the Lisu church's beginnings, much less is known about the Lisu church today. In this book I will take the Lisu Christian story from its missionary origins to the present day. I will narrate the story of how the Lisu nearly lost their Christian faith amid China's tumultuous twentieth century—involving war, revolution, famine, and successive government campaigns culminating in the Cultural Revolution, in which all churches were closed for more than two decades. I will also recount how the Lisu, improbably, and entirely on their own initiative, have revived their faith in the years since 1980.

But my primary aim is to explore how Lisu Christians, like Naomi and her fellow Christians in Tso Lo hamlet, have oriented their faith less around cognitive ideas of belief and more around a series of Christian practices that express that belief. Lisu Christian practices, such as attending church, singing hymns, and participating in intercessory prayer, are bodily actions filled with Christian meaning. They are unspoken liturgies. Christianity is, for the Lisu, fundamentally a way of life, not merely a belief system.

Lisuland

I first heard about the Lisu when I picked up a worn copy of Isobel Kuhn's spiritual autobiography, *By Searching*, off a shelf of used books in Oakland, California. I was immediately captured by her narrative voice. Born in 1901 in British Columbia, Isobel retained the vestiges of a Victorian upbringing in her prose. Yet I found her book to be filled with common points of reference, as I, too, had grown up in the Pacific Northwest. After hearing the pioneering missionary to the Lisu, J. O. Fraser, speak at The Firs retreat center in Bellingham, Washington, Isobel was determined to work with the Lisu people. She set sail for China with the CIM.

Isobel wrote captivating descriptions of life in Lisuland—the Nujiang Valley in China's Yunnan Province. She characterized the valley this way: "It is a land of giants—giant peaks, giant winds, giant disease, giant spiritual forces."[3] One could never get away from the feeling of being enclosed by the steep canyon walls. She called it "life on the perpendicular," and said, "there is only up and down here, no level spot."[4] In describing the Nujiang Valley's notorious rainy season, Isobel reported: "The rainy season had begun. Day after day the tent and miserable hut were swept by torrents: clouds and drizzle veiled the grand scenery. All was just cold and mud and wet. 'From Sunday morning until Saturday night, I never had my galoshes off, except to go to bed,' [another missionary] told me."[5]

The Nujiang Valley is named for the Nujiang itself, which in Chinese literally means angry (*nu*) river (*jiang*). The river is aptly named. Unlike China's Yellow River, which picks up yellow-brown sediment on its slow journey to the sea, or Myanmar's fat Irrawaddy, which lazily makes its way through flat landscapes, the Nujiang (called the Salween in missionary narratives) cuts through mountains of rock in its upper reaches, making its aquamarine color just a shade or two from translucence. The river is usually a mass of roiling, foamy anger, rarely placid.

One hundred years ago this river meant life, but it also meant danger. Water was a necessity, but drowning was common, as the river could only be crossed by bamboo raft ferry at certain points and, during the rainy season, hardly at all. The river divided then, and it still does today. Traveling to villages within easy sight of one another on opposite banks required a bamboo raft ferry crossing then, and today, it means trekking out of the way to the nearest bridge.

A few years after first picking up Kuhn's books, I was living in China myself. While conducting some internet research about China's minority groups I came across the Lisu once again. According to the website, the majority of Lisu were now Christians, and the Chinese government was considering declaring them an official "Christian" minority group. I had the sudden realization that there was a direct link with the missionary work of my literary hero, Isobel Kuhn (along with a handful of other missionaries that I had met as characters in her books), and the current religious status of the Lisu ethnic minority in China.

The Lisu are one of China's fifty-five minority groups. Of the over 600,000 Lisu in China,[6] approximately half are Christian.[7] The Lisu live in villages and hamlets across highland Southeast Asia and southwest China, scattered across rugged terrain that now falls under the sovereignty of India, China, Thailand, and Myanmar.[8] In whichever state they have found themselves, the Lisu have been on the margins, geographically, politically, and socially. They occupy mountainous terrain, withstand treacherous monsoon rains, and subsist precariously on the political and physical fringe.

The Lisu have long had a well-defined sense of ethnic identity.[9] Despite Chinese condescension toward the Lisu,[10] J. O. Fraser wrote in the introduction to his handbook on the Lisu language, "No Lisu is ashamed to own his race."[11] The Lisu made every list of the ever-shifting categorical registers of ethnic minorities since the Chinese state began cataloging; by the time of the People's Republic's Ethnicity Classification Project of the 1950s, they were one of only fourteen ethnic groups in Yunnan whose status as a "minority nationality" was presupposed.[12]

The Christian history of the Lisu begins with James Outram Fraser, an engineer, musician, and linguist who began his pioneering missionary work among the Lisu in 1913. For three years he itinerated through the mountains among the Lisu, though he found them unresponsive to his message. In 1916, just as he was about to give up on the Lisu and offer to be reassigned, a great people movement began and whole families, even entire villages, tore down and burned their spirit shelves, declaring their allegiance to Christianity. As the Lisu had no written script, Fraser, together with Ba Thaw from the Karen people, created the script that today bears his name.

Fraser insisted that the embryonic Lisu church follow "three-self" indigenous principles from the very start. It was led locally, supported itself even though the people were poor, and sent out evangelists immediately to spread the good news among neighboring villages and hamlets. Most missions in China used foreign money to build mission stations, churches, hospitals, and schools;[13] in Lisuland the work was entirely self-supporting.

In the 1920s, Fraser was joined in the work by Allyn and Leila Cooke, who lived among the Lisu, working on the translation of the Bible and the hymnbook until Leila died in 1943 and Allyn was forced to leave the country in 1951. Like Isobel Kuhn, Leila Cooke was a gifted and prolific writer. She composed several articles on their work among the Lisu Christians for the CIM periodical *China's Millions*, and she also penned two books, *Honey Two of Lisu-Land* (1933) and *Fish Four and the Lisu New Testament* (published posthumously in 1947). J. O. Fraser himself wrote voluminous correspondence to his mother and the prayer group she established in England, excerpts of many of which are found in his two biographies: a hagiographic portrayal, *Behind the Ranges* (1944), by Geraldine (Mrs. Howard) Taylor, and *Mountain Rain* (1994), by his daughter Eileen Fraser Crossman. Gertrude Morse, matriarch of the Morse family of independent missionaries among the Lisu and other minorities, also penned a memoir entitled *The Dogs May Bark but the Caravan Moves On* (1998). Thus the missionary history of the Lisu is well documented. The recounting of this history presented in this book draws on these published sources, as well as archival materials held by the Wheaton College Billy Graham Center, Yale Divinity School, and the University of London SOAS (School of Oriental and African Studies). The BGC Archives at Wheaton College contain numerous circular letters written by the Cooke and Kuhn families, as well as uncatalogued papers of the Gowmans (fellow missionaries among the Lisu), including translations of the Gospels of Mark, Luke, and John into Lisu, diaries, and an old catechism. In the CIM archives at SOAS, University of London, I found the majority of the interview transcripts and other primary sources used by Mrs. Howard Taylor in her biography of J. O. Fraser. What I was unable to find, however, were the letters Fraser wrote back to his prayer circle in England, letters that Mrs. Taylor quoted from extensively. In searching for these letters I contacted Fraser's daughter, Eileen Fraser Crossman. Sadly, she also did not know the location. Still, the search for the letters led me to a number of exchanges with Mrs. Crossman, including a visit.

Because of the Communist Revolution in 1949, all of the missionaries departed, and the narrative of the Lisu church becomes shadowy and opaque. In 1958 the Chinese Communists began an assault on religion that led to a mass exodus of Lisu Christians—some of the consequences of which were reported by Gertrude Morse from her standpoint on the Burma side. The Anti-Rightist Campaign of 1958 was followed by the Great Leap Forward (1958–61) and other campaigns, most notably the Cultural Revolution from 1966 to 1976. What happened to the Lisu Christians during these difficult years?

With Deng Xiaoping's policy of Reform and Opening Up (*gaige kaifang*), beginning in 1980, Christians in China (including in Lisuland) were allowed to practice their faith once more. But although the Lisu church has been reopened for more than thirty years, few studies exist of Lisu Christianity today.[14]

My first visit to the Nujiang Valley was during the rainy season in 2012. I made the trip from Yunnan's provincial capital, Kunming—a trip that took about thirty days in the missionary period—on the seventeen-hour overnight bus. Several impressions stood out on that first trip. Although I was visiting Fugong, the county with the highest concentration of Lisu in China, Lisu writing using the Fraser Script was largely absent. Large Chinese characters looked down from every storefront. Only Chinese-language books sat on the shelves at the local Xinhua bookstore. Buses announced their destinations with illuminated Chinese characters. Even the local ATM machines required their customers to use Chinese to withdraw their money. I wondered what had happened to the Lisu's precious Fraser Script and why Chinese characters seemed to have eliminated Lisu writing from every public space. It was only in church that I saw the visible presence of Lisu writing, though even in the religious sphere its reign was not unchallenged:

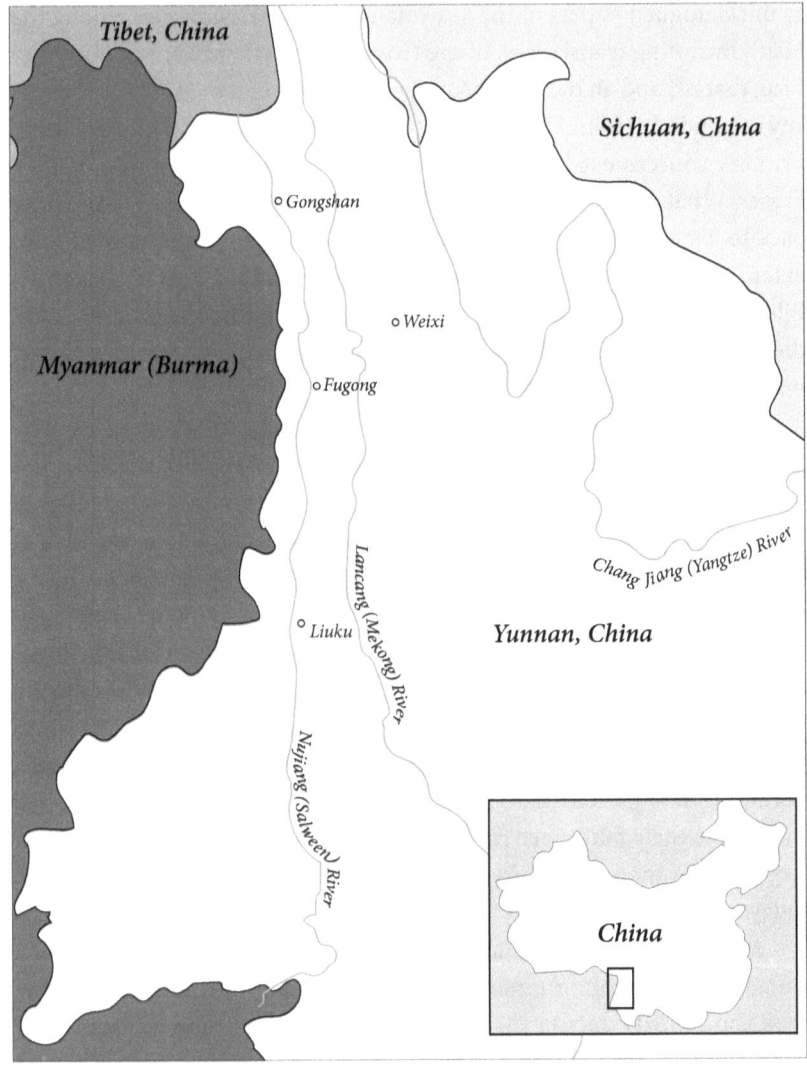

map 1 Western Yunnan Province. Map drawn by Mariah Christ.

many Lisu youth, now educated in Chinese schools, were largely illiterate in Lisu. The Sinicization of the Nujiang Valley—primarily owing to the encroachments of a strong state and its education policies—was bringing the Lisu language back to its original state: an oral language.

While I had seen few vestiges of a particular Lisu identity around Fugong—it seemed rather similar to countless other Chinese towns—this changed when I went to church. In church old women wore traditional clothes and children wore beaded headdresses. Nearly everyone carried an embroidered bag with bright tassels—bags I had read about in the missionary narratives—that contained their Bibles and hymnbooks. Church and ethnicity exhibited a strong relationship.

I made a second visit in February 2013, this time to Gongshan at the northern edge of the Nujiang Valley, a four-hour drive upriver from Fugong. I flew into Kunming and met an American contact who had helped facilitate my previous trip into the valley. I told him my sketchy plan of heading to Gongshan and trying to meet Jesse, a name I had learned from a Reuters article on the Lisu Christians of Gongshan.[15] My American contact told me that Jesse was the leader of the entire Nujiang Valley Lisu church, and as he was a busy and important official who traveled frequently, I had no chance of meeting him. I got on the overnight bus feeling completely blind, going in with no contacts or relationships.

After arriving in Gongshan on a Tuesday afternoon, I found my way to the Zion Church on the hill above town. There were several folks milling around, and they directed me to a church administrator who could speak Chinese. He informed me that there would be a Wednesday evening service. The next day I arrived early for the service and sat in the courtyard of the quiet church. A young woman shortly entered the courtyard, grabbed some laundry from the line, and asked if I had eaten. She invited me to an apartment behind the church and, together with her mother and a few young girls, started making some chicken soup. I spent the evening with them in the kitchen until the church service began.

After the service, the young woman sought me out and invited me upstairs again. This time she walked me past the kitchen, ushering me into a living area where two middle-aged men were sitting. I sat down, accepted the walnut tea she brought, introduced myself, and explained my research. When I had finished, I asked the two men their names.

"My name is Jesse," said the first man.

For the last twenty minutes I had been talking with the head of the Lisu church in the Nujiang Valley.

"And this is my daughter," Jesse added, pointing to the young woman who had first invited me up for chicken soup. My relationship with Jesse enabled my entry along the entire length of the Nujiang Valley. In every place I went, the Lisu Christians knew Jesse; he was my gateway.

I spent most of August 2013 in residence at the Gongshan Zion Church's Bible training center, taking my meals with Jesse and his family. This was where I met Naomi, a Bible teacher at the training center. I came back in

December 2013, attending Christmas festivals in two neighboring villages in Gongshan County.

I returned to Lisuland in March 2014 for my culminating stay, spending most of that time in a village high above Gongshan town with Timothy, a Lisu farmer/pastor, and his family. Ma-pa Timothy taught me Lisu for two hours each morning. The remainder of the time was spent engaged in family, village, and church life. I sat on hard pews in countless church services and sat on low stools around evening fires, eating *baba* (fried bread). I hiked up and down mountains and worked in the fields. I sang hymns, joined in intercessory prayer, and listened to stories.

Altogether, between 2012 and 2014, I conducted five months of fieldwork with the Lisu Christians. I never maintained my own residence at the field site but lived with the Lisu, whether in a bamboo hut, a village farmhouse, or a room at a Bible training center. I participated in the daily rhythm of village life: planting corn, feeding animals, eating food cooked over a fire, washing dishes, playing with children, and after all the work of the day was complete, sitting by the fire and drinking tea. My observation of the Bible training schools was even more intense, as Bible school students were busy with chapel, classes, morning exercises, meals in the canteen, nightly study halls, and music classes.

I attended twelve churches in the Nujiang Valley (five in Gongshan County, four in Fugong County, and three in Lushui County), many for extended periods. I stayed at both Bible training centers—Gongshan and Liuku—that were in operation during my stay. I attended the Christmas and Easter church festivals as well as the New Year's festival, which is more of a family event. I had a research rhythm, in which my time in the field with the Lisu focused intensely on data collection, and my time at my home base in Beijing was spent transcribing, coding, analyzing, and refining my research questions.

In the beginning of my fieldwork, I positioned myself—quite honestly, I thought—as a researcher. However, I soon learned that "researcher" was not a category that existed in Lisu culture, and thus this caused confusion. I then explained that I was there to learn the Lisu language. This made perfect sense to the Lisu, as their advanced linguistic status, with a written script, Bible, and hymnbook, had made learning Lisu a requirement for any local minority who converts to Christianity. In fact, I did spend hours each day studying the Lisu language, either informally through asking questions, or formally through the help of a Lisu pastor. Through daily immersion in the Lisu language and both formal and informal instruction, I became adept at reading Lisu and learned religious terms and phrases, such as those used in preaching and hymn singing. However, Mandarin Chinese remained the primary language I used in my interviews.

In addition to my time spent in Lisuland, I also made three research trips to Chiang Mai, Thailand. During those trips, I attended the Lisu (Borneo) church of Chiang Mai, studied Lisu with one of the church members, had helpful conversations and interviews with David and Eugene Morse, and met members of Overseas Missionary Fellowship (OMF) who currently work with the Lisu in Thailand and Myanmar.

I could see early on that central government and local church research permissions would conflict. The presence of Christian minorities in China's borderlands is a sensitive topic, and gaining official Chinese research permission would have been difficult. Further, formal government research permission and affiliation (if granted) would have entailed the mandatory assignment of a research assistant to monitor my work.[16] Such a situation would not only have brought unwanted scrutiny to the Lisu church but would also have forced a less intimate research encounter. Therefore, I chose not to seek official government permission but to seek the permission of the Nujiang Christian Church *lianghui* organizations within the government-sanctioned Protestant church.[17] At all times during the conduct of my research, I was under the auspices and protection of the local Lisu churches.

Christian Practices

In this book I explore how the Lisu of southwest China have defined faith as a rhythm of shared Christian practices. Christian practices are embodied patterns of activities imbued with a narrative of meaning directed toward faith in Jesus Christ that a community participates in together. They are physical metaphors of the Christian life. Cadenced to the agricultural seasons of the hills, Lisu practices are recurring and regular. Attending to this flow and rhythm means that Lisu Christians affirm what it represents and the togetherness it compels.

As Etienne Wenger puts it, "The concept of practice connotes doing, but not just doing in and of itself. It is doing in a historical and social context that gives structure and meaning to what we do. In this sense, *practice is always social practice*" (emphasis mine).[18] Unlike beliefs, which can be codified into creeds and doctrines and statements, and thus, like artifacts, examined apart from their settings, Christian practices cannot be understood apart from the quotidian contexts from which they have sprung.

Lisu practices are bodily in nature, involving not just culturally situated bodies but physical bodies that eat and drink, breathe and imbibe, work in fields and sing hymns. Lisu practices involve mouths, feet, and hands. Nearly every Christian practice involves the body or occurs close to the body. This is exemplified in the Lisu focus on not allowing smoke or alcohol to enter the Christian body, as well as in the hymn-singing voice emanating from the very core of the body, and the line-dancing body moving in rhythm along with other bodies. Through the actions of their bodies the Lisu configure their worlds.

Practices have long been part of church history. From those of the Desert Fathers, the Rule of St. Benedict, and the ascetic practices of Irish monks to more recent adaptations, all shared the ideal that through habitual practices, virtues would be acquired.[19] Practices do not float freely, separate from belief systems. As Alasdair MacIntyre states, "There is no such thing as 'behavior,' to be identified prior to and independently of intentions, beliefs and settings."[20] Implicit in the Lisu Christian practices are layers of meaning about the nature of sin and God and humanity. But these are not philosophical meanderings, unmoored from the practicalities of daily life. Rather, as Wenger states, "*Practice is about meaning as an experience of everyday life*"[21] (original emphasis).

This meaning is grounded in narratives: communal and individual narratives of experiencing God. Lisu Christians pray because they believe in a God who by nature is loving and caring and answers their prayers. Lisu Christians shake hands and greet each other with "Hwa Hwa" because of the spirit of fellowship and togetherness this Christian greeting implies. Lisu Christians share the Gospel message with others because it is not something for them alone, but for the entire community and beyond: "A social practice involves a narrative, a reason why, a mental horizon within which action is experienced as meaningful."[22] Embedded in every practice is meaning, significance, and worldview; they are not empty. Practices, as Stanley Hauerwas and William H. Willimon state, are theologically significant.[23]

But for this theological significance to be understood, the "semantic domain" of theology—that is, the arena of meaning and the words used to talk about it—must be expanded.[24] Theology does not always begin, as is assumed in Western academic circles, with an articulated philosophical foundation. It does not have to be communicated solely through treatise, doctrinal statement, or commentary. These forms of theology, according to Robert Schreiter, are based on the specific cultural configurations of the West, with its ideal of literacy, its assumption of "sure knowledge," and its rational approach.[25]

Theology for the Lisu follows a different pattern, for an oral, holistic, mountain people would never adopt a Christian faith that is reduced to mere personal, intellectual assent to a set of doctrinal propositions. Theirs will not be doctrine from the commanding heights of systematic theology but rather a theology of the earth, situated in place, culture, and bodies.

It will not be an academic theology but a community theology, centered on the local church. As a community theology, it will necessarily be focused on the exteriority of human experience, assuming that the majority of experiences are done in conjunction with others, in front of others, seen by others, and undertaken with others, for in such cultures, inner experiences are few and relatively unimportant. It will be a theology lived out. And at least with the Lisu, it will be a theology communicated through an enacted script of practices.

And this is where the Lisu Christian story of a faith enacted in practices meets up with one of the oldest theological questions in Christian history: how can sinners be reconciled to a holy God? At the heart of the matter is the question of whether bodily expressions of faith, such as practices, behaviors, deeds, works, or any other human endeavors, have a place in a grace-oriented faith focused on salvation granted by God alone.

Within Western Protestantism, the majority of church traditions have emphasized that salvation comes from faith alone, as a gift of God's grace. They are buttressed by the words of Paul, most notably in his letter to the Romans: "For we maintain that a person is justified by faith apart from the works of the law" (3:28). Such a view emphasizes that humankind cannot earn its own salvation by any form of merit, or, in the words of Alister McGrath, "Faith is not something human we do, but something divine that is wrought within us."[26] Justification by faith alone was a theme for Paul, one he returned to many times in his letters.[27]

Complicating the matter, however, are other biblical passages, such as James 2:14–26, indicating that true faith must show itself through works. In the concluding verse of this diatribe, James declares, "As the body without the spirit is dead, so faith without deeds is dead." James expresses a concern that when faith is reduced to sentiment, verbal profession, or even intellectual conviction, it is in fact no faith at all.[28] James emphasizes that faith is more than a matter of right belief; faith has a practical element, requiring deeds.

This issue took center stage during the Protestant Reformation, when Martin Luther rallied against the works-based righteousness he perceived in the medieval Roman Catholic church, advancing the term *sola fide*—faith alone. Luther went so far as to add the term *allein* ("alone," in English) to his German translation of Romans 3:28, stating that idiomatic German required the addition. If salvation is wholly a matter of God's grace, then salvation is unattainable through human effort or any amount of human striving. Works, however, are inherently human acts. Therein lies the tension. Though the issue remains contentious, Protestants have reconciled faith and works in a variety of ways: as works proving faith, as works subsequent to faith, as works arising from faith. But faith and works are usually placed in a hierarchical relationship, with works playing the role of junior partner.

This is not the Lisu way. In the midst of the flock of Protestant spirituality, in which Luther's "faith alone" still echoes stridently, the Lisu of southwest China have marked out their faith by means of Christian practices. They have made claim to a visceral faith that involves interceding for others in prayer, singing together, line dancing, attending church and festivals, shaking hands in Christian fellowship, keeping the Sabbath, evangelizing, working in each other's fields, and abstaining from practices that have historically been deemed harmful to the community. Lisu Christian practices are more communal than personal, more outward than inward, and more embodied than emotional. The Lisu do not make a fine split between justification and sanctification, as most Reformation theologians do, for their practices include a strong component of moral regeneration. Through their practices, the Lisu have been able to compose their creeds, express their belief, instill their values, and enact their obedience to God. In other words, Lisu practices are theological acts.

World Christianity

In describing the religious practices of an ethnic minority group in China, this book is firmly situated within the field of World Christianity. The center of gravity of Christianity has shifted southward and eastward, toward Latin America, Africa, and Asia. Dale T. Irvin describes the study of World Christianity as seeking to "investigate and understand Christian communities, faith, and practice as they are found on six continents, expressed in diverse ecclesial traditions, and informed by the multitude of historical and cultural experiences in a world transformed by globalization."[29] In a sense, World

Christianity has a subversive[30] or at least revisionist[31] element, as it seeks not just to push out to the geographic edges but also to upend traditional academic categories, decenter Western thinking, and privilege the perspectives of those on the margins.

Though the Lisu were initially evangelized by missionaries of the CIM, the revitalization of the Christian faith after churches in China were reopened in 1980 was a purely local endeavor. While the missionary mark upon Lisu Christianity is certainly discernable, at the same time, their practice-oriented faith conforms nearly completely to Lisu culture. One of the primary contentions of this book—that Lisu Christianity is at its most authentic when its practitioners sing translated Western hymns—demonstrates this complementarity.

Lisu Christianity is a faith that has settled in and taken up residence around the fires in the bamboo shanties on the steep hillsides of the Nujiang gorge. In singing Christian hymns as their sincerest form of devotion, these subsistence farmers declare not just their reverence for their own missionary heritage but also their membership in a communion of faith across borders—into the Lisu regions of Thailand, Myanmar, and India—and even more broadly, their membership in the worldwide communion of faith.

The Ethnographic Imagination

The phenomenon of World Christianity has been studied through both historical and theological lenses. Others have pointed to the polycentric nature of World Christianity[32] or have argued for a more interdisciplinary approach.[33] These are useful frameworks, but my approach will vary slightly by bringing the analysis down to the level of the earth, to the level of lived experience and embodied practice. Inasmuch as World Christianity is concerned with creeds and theologies, reformation and revival, liturgies and sacraments, missions and intercontinental interactions, it is also concerned with hymns sung, liturgies recited, faith uttered, and devotion expressed. In other words, World Christianity is not just themes and topics. It is people and their stories. Given this, my approach to World Christianity is through the ethnographic imagination.

C. Wright Mills, in his 1959 book entitled *The Sociological Imagination*, states that "the sociological imagination enables us to grasp history and biography and the relations between the two within society. That is its task and its promise."³⁴ The sociological imagination holds that these two, history and biography, are interdependent, that neither can be understood without reference to the other.

Borrowing from Mills's sociological imagination, Susan E. Mannon, in *City of Flowers: An Ethnography of Social and Economic Change in Costa Rica's Central Valley*, states that "the ethnographic imagination combines descriptive writing, rich storytelling, and social analysis to make the connection between larger historical forces and individual biographies in particular places and times."³⁵ Drawing upon both Mills and Mannon, I would like to reframe the ethnographic imagination for the study of World Christianity.

To start, let me define my terms. Ethnography refers to a research methodology that places emphasis on fieldwork conducted *in situ* with research participants, usually involving participant-observation, interviews, and archival research.³⁶ Christian Scharen and Aana Marie Vigen define ethnography as "a process of attentive study of, and learning from, people—their words, practices, traditions, experiences, memories, insights—in particular times and places in order to understand how they make meaning."³⁷

Imagination refers not to flights of fancy, nor to conjecture or loose attachment to objective reality, but rather to an ability to find truth that is not readily obvious, to find knowledge in interstitial places, and to synthesize data from numerous locations. It is perhaps in the imagination that we can truly grasp the nature of the communities that we study.

As the sociological imagination links history and biography, broader social movements and milieus with the individuals involved, the ethnographic imagination in the study of world Christianity links church movements with the individuals that participate in them. It links texts and artifacts with oral traditions. It links creeds with practices. And it links key figures and leaders with lay practitioners. It requires the imagination to find knowledge in the connections.

We do not need the imagination to analyze larger social movements and their histories; we have historiographical methods for that. Nor do we need to imagine the lives of individuals and their stories; those lives can in fact be known through ethnography and anthropology. It requires the ethnographic imagination, however, to yoke together the historiographical with the anthropological and seek knowledge in the frayed edges where they meet. What kind of knowledge do we seek in these in-between places? What kind of knowledge does it require the imagination to uncover? The ethnographic imagination aims to reveal embedded theology. It should describe faithful discipleship. It favors the particular over the universal, the local over the global, the lay over the leaders. It requires decentering.

Most importantly, the ethnographic imagination connects the big stories of World Christianity with the small stories. Individual lives are embedded in broader histories, so the ethnographic imagination must delineate the broad historical forces that provide constraints and parameters. At the same time, it must attend to the voices of individual Christians shaped and constrained by these forces while acknowledging the agency these individuals possess. Big stories without small stories lead to research that is removed and distant, focused on abstract social and historical forces, removed from everyday life. Such research usually ends up telling only a story of the elites. Small stories without big stories lack context; they are just anecdotes. The ethnographic imagination must bring these two—the big stories and the small stories—together and find truth in this tension.

Big stories and small stories are often not easily reconciled, if they can be at all. Yet they need each other, for each story, the big one and the small one, by itself, is incomplete. The truth, messy and difficult and incomprehensible as it may be, is in the stories together, caught up in the epistemological tension. The ethnographic imagination requires us to go into these interstices, to sit a spell in this tension, to seek to understand paradoxical and complex truth.

It requires just such an imagination to understand Lisu Christian practices. Lisu Christian practices are carriers of meaning, and these meanings are understood and communicated through stories. The Lisu experience Christian life as narratives. It is through the narrative lens that they interpret reality, even theology. Ideas about what it means to be Lisu are communicated through community narratives, narratives of social ills, poverty, and resilience, narratives of marginalization, independence, and evangelism. These narratives do not merely recount their history; they also communicate what the good, the moral, the virtuous is. It is in the stories that the theological significance of the Christian practices can begin to be grasped, for practices and narratives are inextricably linked. Each Lisu Christian practice, from the prohibition on drinking and smoking to Christian festivals to singing hymns, has a story. Because the Lisu practices are socially consequential, because they are rooted in the community narrative, they are theologically significant.

The Lisu Christians I interacted with all had a story to tell, stories of migration and hardship, stories of family and history, but ultimately, stories of faith. These individual stories blend into the collective Lisu Christian story, a narrative they know and honor.

Through the ethnographic imagination my intention is to give a detailed and careful, yet personal and intimate, portrayal of the Lisu church. While abstract theorizing is a worthwhile end state, and one for which I strove in this study, I also found that doing so chopped up the lives and experiences of the Lisu into so many codes and themes and categories. I hope that by including ample amounts of narrative, the nature of Lisu lived experience can flow in a more continuous, and ultimately more accurate, fashion. Viewed in narrative terms, my research is just the current chapter of the larger and grander Lisu story. I hope in the telling I have done justice to the high regard in which I hold them.

The Structure of the Book

The chapters of this book will alternate between narrations of important stages in the history of Lisu Christianity and close examinations of specific Christian practices that particularly resonate with the Lisu. Big stories and small stories are interspersed throughout this book, their narratives intersecting in each chapter. The big stories recount evangelization by CIM missionaries, the acculturation of Christianity into Lisu culture, the rupture caused by twenty-two years of systematic government persecution, and the improbable revitalization of the Christian faith—all through local agency and initiative—once churches were allowed to reopen after 1980.

Woven alongside are the small stories of individual Lisu Christians, such as Naomi, Jesse, Timothy, and others. While the big stories give us the context for Lisu Christianity, the small stories are equally essential, for they show the meaning the Christian practices hold for those who observe them. Small stories also show how ordinary Christians responded to China's twentieth century: at times showing resilience, but at other times, fragility.

The first-person "Voices" sections sprinkled throughout the book present the small stories of individual Lisu believers in their own voices. These sections are not verbatim transcripts; I found the transcript, as a translation from oral to written speech, to be quite flattening. Rather, I sought to use their own words spoken in the idiom of their own voices, without elements that are common in oral speech but do not read well in written form, like fillers, partial thoughts, and incomplete sentences. Some amount of literary license was involved, but the result is a more true and authentic representation of their personal story. I want the reader to hear their voices and even to picture their faces. In so doing, I hope not only to have embodied them but also to have empowered them. I want them changed from informant to person.

Naturally, as real lives are messy and complex, more details are included in their stories than just those narrowly related to my study. I hope in this way that their own voices come through as a single embodiment, as a whole story, not parceled out into a plethora of pieces in service to theoretical explication or other aspects of the research agenda. As Gabriel Fackre states, "Narrative speaks in the idiom of the earth. Reality meets us in the concretions of time, place, and people, not in analytical discourse or mystical rumination."[38]

The Church Below

"Hurry," Naomi said to me. "We're going to be late for church down below."

For the Sunday noon service, Naomi's family, as well as most of the rest of the village, hiked down the mountain to what I called Patchwork Village. This larger village had its own large church building sitting atop a rounded mountain covered with a yellow and green patchwork quilt of corn and wheat. For morning and evening services, they remained in their own hamlet, holding small services in the storage room. Naomi referred to these two churches as "the one above" (*shangmian de*) and "the one below" (*xiamian de*).

After Naomi and her mother changed into their Lisu finery—pleated skirts, velvet vests, beaded headdresses—we began to walk down the mountain toward the church. Several neighbors joined us. We walked together, single file, through the wooded path that followed the inside of the ridge, descending into Patchwork Village. Church had already started and we had difficulty finding seats—we were late on account of the intercessory prayer service—but we arrived in time for the last hymn before the sermon.

Naomi's mother sat in the front row with the elderly women. Naomi and I sat in the middle of the women's section, one row behind her second-oldest sister. Naomi's older brothers sat in the men's section. Lisu church seating conventions put people of like gender and age together, scattering family members across the sanctuary. The women's section was a sea of hot pink and turquoise, as most of the women wore the plaid head scarves so ubiquitous in Fugong County.

fig. 2 Two Lisu women walking to church. Photo: author.

For the Sunday evening service, we returned to the hamlet storage room. Naomi's father was back from sojourning for a few days to join with others in intercessory prayer, something he did often. We had met him in Fugong town on our way up; he had come down to join others in prayer meetings. He led the preaching for the evening service, teaching the villagers a new song as part of his sermon. Walking back after church, I could see the lights from villages on the opposite bank of the Nujiang.

That evening I could hear loud music and children laughing, and I walked up the hill to investigate. About seven kids, ranging in age from older teenagers to six-year-olds, were lined up, tallest to shortest, practicing a Christian line dance under some lights outside the house on one of the few pieces of flat terrain in the hamlet. Huge speakers had been set up outside next to the pasture. This hamlet was loud because it contained so many children. All generations were present. (So many Chinese villages, with the adults gone out in search of work and the children boarding at school, had a hollow ring.)

All ten of the families of Tso Lo hamlet were in the same predicament: they were returnees from Myanmar and, as a result, had ambiguous legal status within the People's Republic of China. They lacked *hukou* (residence permits), so they could not work, go to school, or own land. Having lived the majority of their lives in Myanmar, they could not speak Mandarin Chinese. They carved out a precarious perch high on this mountain rock.

Without education they could not speak Mandarin—essential for leaving to find wage-earning work. And so they stayed. Without *hukou* the children could not attend school, so they remained in the hamlet with their parents and grandparents, tending the pigs, chickens, and donkey, cooking over the fire, praying, singing, going to church, being raised with the faith of their families and not the values of the state. The very marginalization of Tso Lo hamlet, clinging to this mountain crag, had contributed to its healthy vitality.

But the primary contributor to the vitality of this hamlet was its heartbeat of Christian practices, a rhythm that overlay the agricultural rhythm of tending to animals and planting and harvesting crops. In its traditional lifestyle high above, Tso Lo hamlet was a place not unlike the Lisu villages where the missionary J. O. Fraser first sat around fires and preached his gospel message.

Voice

Mie Hui Qing (Lushui County)

Why are you standing there in front of a dark and locked church? Come on over to my house. Church will start late tonight because everyone in the village is so busy in the fields.

Come on in and have a seat. Here's a stool. And some cola and guazi [pumpkin seeds].

There, I have washed my hands. Now I can shake your hands and give you a proper Christian greeting: Hwa Hwa!

I have two sons. My oldest is 24, and my youngest is 22. The oldest is a Christian. But the youngest is not. He drinks beer and smokes. It's a big problem with the young people these days.

When did I become a Christian? About 27 or 28 years ago. I can read Lisu writing. Many Lisu Christians cannot. But I started when I was ten or fifteen years old, and I can read. I can't read Chinese characters though. I never had the chance to go to school. I came from a big family and always had to walk around with a basket on my back. Always doing farmwork; no chance to go to school.

But my oldest son can read Chinese characters. He went to school up to middle school. Then his father died. That was eleven years ago. After his father died, he could no longer go to school. Now it's just the three of us. My two sons, and me. We plant rice and corn. And we have animals, pigs, and chickens.

Based on an interview from May 7, 2014.

Have another cup of cola. No really, another one! Eat more guazi!

I've never been to Gongshan, or even to Fugong. But I did go to Kunming once. I injured my knee and I had to go there to see a doctor. I could not understand the people in Kunming! Their speech was so strange to my ears!

Such a long day of farming. I'm tired to death. We're so busy planting the rice these days. There may not be too many people at church. It's a Wednesday night and people are so tired from working in the fields. But on Sundays there's always a lot.

Okay, I think we can walk back over to the church now. It should be ready to start. You like my Bible bag? I wove it myself. That was back when I was young. I couldn't do it now. My eyes aren't good anymore.

Let's go. You can sleep here tonight. No really, sleep here! Not next time, come on. Sleep here tonight!

Chapter 1

J. O. FRASER AND THE BEGINNINGS OF LISU CHRISTIANITY

> God be with you till we meet again,
> By His counsels guide, uphold you,
> With His sheep securely fold you,
> God be with you till we meet again.
>
> Till we meet, till we meet,
> Till we meet at Jesus' feet;
> Till we meet, till we meet,
> God be with you till we meet again.

James Outram Fraser was sent to China's Yunnan province in 1909 as a candidate of the China Inland Mission (CIM).[1] He left behind a promising future in England—he was a newly minted engineering graduate from Imperial College, London, as well as a concert pianist—because of the challenge he read in a small tract. Four years before, a fellow student had given Fraser a leaflet. One sentence in it pierced Fraser's heart and challenged everything he had assumed to that point: "If our Master returned today to find millions of people unevangelized, and looked, as of course He would look, to us for an explanation, I cannot imagine what explanation we should have to give."[2] Fraser applied to the CIM and sailed for China.[3] He was twenty-two years old.

Epigraph from "God Be With You," lyrics by Jeremiah E. Rankin, 1880, hymn #278 in the 2013 Yunnan Lisu hymnbook.

Since his youth Fraser was known for his dogged determination. He once walked to London and back in one day, a distance of 44 miles. Another time he rode 199 miles on his bicycle without once dismounting.[4] A favorite pastime was mountain climbing in Switzerland. "There was nothing half hearted in his make up. He ... really lived," his wife, Roxie, wrote.[5] Fraser took this same diligence and single-mindedness of purpose and applied it to his missionary vocation.

Resolve and willpower were not the only aspects to his character. His soul was also quiet and reflective, deeply stirred by music. It was on the eve of his first London piano recital that his strong sense of missionary calling surged.[6] "His love of music made him sensitive and responsive to all that was beautiful in the lands and among the people where he spent his missionary life,"[7] recalled Mildred Cable.

Upon arrival in China new missionaries were assigned to the CIM Language School in Anking, Anhui Province, to begin studies in the Chinese language. The CIM superintendent for Yunnan Province, John McCarthy, visited the language school with the goal of selecting some recruits for work in the remote, mountainous province. "Send me Fraser, and anyone else you like," McCarthy wired back to headquarters in Shanghai.[8]

McCarthy was in need of good workers. The CIM had first opened a mission station in Yunnan Province in 1881. By 1908, the year Fraser sailed for China, the CIM had six mission stations, twenty-five missionaries, and five native helpers, but just thirty-four converts in all of Yunnan. "The lack of visible results," wrote McCarthy in the mission's annual report that year, "is still keenly felt by the workers of this province as a loud call for increased earnestness in prayer. Thank God the doors have been kept open and the regular work has continued, but the workers repeat that they are still looking and waiting for the blessing which they do expect, because of God's gracious promises of a harvest to those who labour."[9]

Assigned to finish his language studies in the city of Tengyueh (today's Tengchong), Yunnan Province, Fraser came across the Lisu on market days when they would come down from their upland homes to exchange goods, often selling incense made from pounded tree bark.[10] He felt burdened for these people—impoverished, disenfranchised, despised by the Chinese—and began earnestly to pray and seek openings into their culture and society. He penned a letter to Mr. Metcalf, who worked among the Lisu in Ta-ku. Mr. Metcalf responded that one thousand Lisu families had made a start toward Christianity. Fraser wrote, "The thought came to me—'If God could do that in East Yunnan, why not in West Yunnan?'"[11]

THE BEGINNINGS OF LISU CHRISTIANITY

fig. 3 J. O. Fraser. With kind permission from Overseas Missionary Fellowship International U.K. and the private family collection of Mrs. Eileen Fraser Crossman.

According to oral tradition, the Lisu come from "the head of the river" and their name means "the people who have come down," which likely places their point of origin in the highlands of Tibet.[12] Hu Yingshu wrote that "Lisu life has been a constant migration, migration, and remigration along a long and tortuous road. Migration and poverty have hovered around the Lisu tribe like a pair of twin brothers."[13] According to Fraser, the Lisu could be divided into two distinct families. The Flowery Lisu, known for their colorful clothing, were clustered near the plains of Tengyueh, Fraser's first mission station, as well as further south near Muchengpo. The Black Lisu, known not just for their black turbans but also their crossbows and poison arrows, were concentrated in the dramatic upper reaches of the Salween (Nujiang) Valley.[14]

When Chinese soldiers from the Yuan, Ming, and Qing dynasties were sent to pacify the frontier, they often stayed and settled in Yunnan Province. They occupied the fertile plains and valleys, leaving the difficult and desolate mountainous regions to ethnic minorities, such as the Lisu. British Consul George Litton, a member of the Royal Geographical Society, explored the Nujiang Valley in 1902–3. His report stressed that the Lisu were not governed by the Chinese and "admit no man as their lord."[15] This was a calculated choice. The Lisu could have remained in the fertile flatlands and gradually become acculturated into the majority Han Chinese ethnicity. Instead, they built their homes on the steep sides and rocky crags of Yunnan province, where clinging to life would be much more difficult, but clinging to independence and ethnic identity would be easier.[16] From these mountains they came to the market towns to trade, where they met Fraser.

Fraser said later, "Much led out in prayer for these people. Not a mere superficial interest. In prayer so drawn out for these people. Couldn't stop!"[17] Despite his prayers, the longed-for opening did not come. Fraser wrote, "The matter is in the Lord's hands. If he wants me to go He will send me. It would be very unwise to attempt to rush things or force a door which He has closed."[18]

After many attempts to penetrate Lisuland had failed, Fraser's cook brought home a Lisu who volunteered to act as a guide. Fraser found himself at a Lisu betrothal celebration. In the midst of the drunken revelry, not too many were interested in his message; still, Fraser managed to copy down four hundred Lisu phrases into his notebook.[19]

One of the guests led him to a small hamlet at 7,000 feet on Trinket Mountain. There he spent a week with the Koh family, teaching them the Christian message. He could not yet speak Lisu, so he explained his message in simple Chinese. Fraser's initial preaching among the Chinese had focused on the crucifixion and resurrection of Jesus Christ, along with an exhortation to repent of sins and a promise that those who believe in Jesus Christ will receive remission from sins.[20] When he preached to the Lisu, however, he simplified the Gospel message to just two aspects: atonement from sin and deliverance from evil powers. Of the two, Fraser emphasized the power to be delivered from spirits, as spirits were greatly feared by the Lisu. Fraser was content for a spiritual understanding of sin to grow through maturity.[21]

Fraser's Gospel proclamation also had an eschatological ring: "Whilst there [at Trinket Mountain] I told them of the second coming of our Lord and the blessedness of His millennial reign, bringing peace, prosperity, and happiness to all mankind. This is splendid!—they think."[22]

Fraser ate as the Koh family did: rice and vegetables twice a day. He slept as they did: on the earthen floor next to the log fire. He found they were naturally musical and enjoyed the Chinese hymns he taught them. At the back of the home was the spirit shelf, what Fraser's daughter Eileen Fraser Crossman called "the garrisons of an alien host."[23] Each Lisu home had a shelf that contained the objects used in spirit worship: "a shelf, bowl, incense burner, a thin strip of red paper with T'ien Ti [Heaven and earth] in the middle on one side."[24] Should sickness or calamity occur, shamans were summoned who required animal sacrifices. Spirits were thought to reside in trees, mountain clefts, and rocks, making life for these mountain people one of fear.

One evening, a week after his arrival, there was an animated conversation between the father and his four sons. Fraser couldn't follow the conversation well, but they soon made their meaning clear. They wanted their spirit shelf to come down. They had heard and understood Fraser's message, and they wanted to give their allegiance to God instead of the spirits. Without a word from Fraser, they tore down the shelf and put its contents in the fire.[25] The Koh family were Fraser's first Lisu converts.

In 1911 revolution broke out in China and the Qing Dynasty was overthrown. Fraser was forced to evacuate to Burma. After four months he was able to return to Tengyueh and was soon joined by Carl Gowman, formerly of Ford Motor Company and a recent graduate of Moody Bible Institute in Chicago.[26] Fraser told Gowman of his drawing toward the Lisu, and Gowman encouraged him, spurring him on to pray and seek ways to make contact.[27]

Fraser and Gowman roomed together while Gowman, who was engaged to Anna, another CIM missionary, awaited the end of the mandatory CIM two-year waiting period before marrying. One day, a Lisu knocked on their door with a gift—a beautiful pheasant—and a request—a ten-dollar loan to help pay wedding expenses. Though it was against CIM policy to loan money, Fraser felt led to do so anyway, and in January 1913 he and Gowman found themselves in the midst of a Lisu wedding in a mountain valley called Six Family Hollow.[28]

When the revelry finally died down, the Tsai family was willing to listen to Fraser's message and made a positive response, led by the mother. The family went through a period of illness immediately after their conversion,

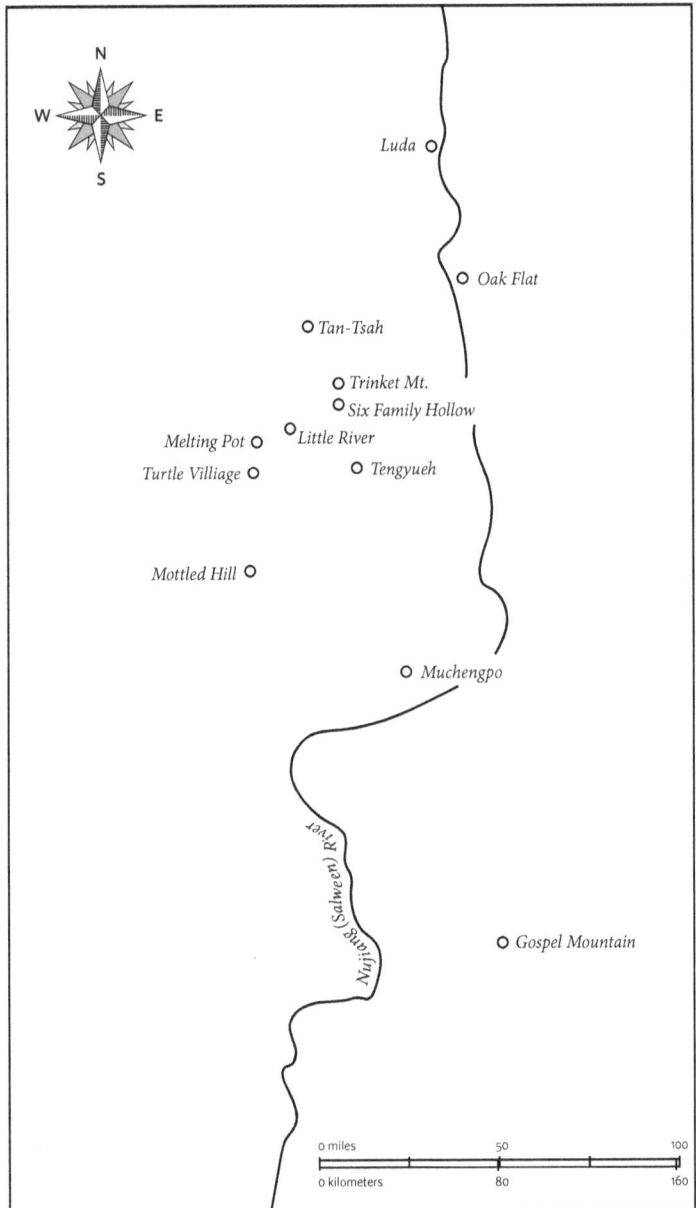

map 2 Lisu villages. Map drawn by Mariah Christ.

and some of the sons recanted their belief. But the mother remained firm. "That old lady was almost the pivot on which our work turned, at that time," Fraser stated. "But for her, I might have given up."[29]

The Tsai family would come at times and visit Fraser in Tengyueh. Each time they visited, he taught them a hymn. The Tsai family reported to Fraser their evening prayer routine. First, they sang all three hymns that he taught them. Then, the whole family stood up to pray. "They tell me they can pray in Lisu now," Fraser reported.[30] On Sunday evenings, they tried to have an extra special kind of service.

In March 1913 Fraser made a five-day visit to Valley of Ease, another Lisu village close to Six Family Hollow. "The response to my preaching was most encouraging," Fraser wrote. "The singing appealed to them most. . . . They showed a readiness to hear and accept the Gospel message which I have never experienced anywhere among the Chinese."[31]

That summer, Fraser wrote a letter to CIM headquarters in Shanghai expressing cautious enthusiasm about the possibilities of work among the Lisu. A telegram arrived from Shanghai directing Fraser to make a survey of the area and conduct a census of the minorities. Still, CIM headquarters did not change Fraser's own designation to work among the Miao people in the eastern part of Yunnan province. Fraser conducted the survey, taking along one of the Tsai family sons who had held fast. Upon his return, Carl Gowman's long-awaited wedding to Anna took place, and an unexpected telegram from D. E. Hoste—director of the Mission—arrived. The contents of the telegram stated that Fraser was free to devote himself to Lisu work, should he feel so led.[32]

Now with an official designation as a missionary to the Lisu, Fraser left on another exploratory journey, accompanied by Rev. J. G. Geis of the American Baptist Union, as well as Ba Thaw, a Karen tribesman from Burma who spoke English and Lisu. Ba Thaw had been educated in Calcutta and converted to Christianity in a Pentecostal mission.[33] The three made their way to what is called the Upper Salween in missionary narratives and is known today as the Nujiang Valley, the site of my fieldwork. Fraser was deeply impressed by the mountain passes, the magnificent scenery, and the concentration of Lisu. "It is Li-su country—the nearest approach to a pure Li-su district. The main part of the valley, both sides of the Salween, the population is Lisu."[34]

Turning back about three days' journey past Luchang (which is near present-day Liuku), Fraser returned to Lisu villages he had previously visited and settled in for the spring of 1914 at the village of Little River.[35]

Spiritual Oppression and Prayer

It was at Little River that Fraser experienced a deep and prolonged depression, a questioning of all that he had previously accepted, accompanied by uncertainty and torment. Fraser wrote that this depression continued until he received by mail a magazine called *The Overcomer*, with which he had not been previously familiar. In Fraser's words, "I read it over and over—that number of *The Overcomer*. What it showed me was that deliverance from the power of the evil one comes through definite resistance on the ground of The Cross. . . . I talked to Satan at that time, using the promises of Scripture as weapons. And they worked. Right then, the terrible oppression began to pass away."[36]

As he came out of his depression, Fraser began to recognize anew the power of prayer. He felt convinced that he would not see the work among the Lisu that he desired without a strong backing of prayer—prayer not just on his part but also on the part of others. "The truth gradually dawned upon me that God wished me not to be the only intercessor but to get others—those upon whom He would lay the burden of this Lisu work—to join me. With His help I started a prayer circle. . . . The Lord was showing me, I believe, that more prayer on the part of the intercessors at home was the *chief need*."[37] Fraser wrote his mother, and she enthusiastically agreed. The prayer circle for the Lisu back in England started with six or seven people but gradually grew to more than one hundred intercessors. Fraser wrote to the prayer circle regularly, keeping them apprised of the needs of the Lisu.[38]

The Fraser Script

Fraser spent the fall of 1914 in the village of Tan-Tsah, deeply engaged in study of the Lisu language. After several weeks he traveled to Myitkyina, Burma, and spent a month with Rev. Geis and Ba Thaw, working on a Lisu script and catechism. Ba Thaw had already been working on a writing system for the Lisu, using a Romanized system, but Fraser did not feel that the phonetics of the Lisu language, which consisted of syllables that all ended in vowel sounds, could be adequately expressed using the alphabet.[39]

Fraser's orthography, still in use among the Lisu and today called the Fraser Script, used twenty-five capital letters from the Roman alphabet and inverted another fifteen letters to produce sounds that English did not

fig. 4 John 3:16 written by J. O. Fraser in the Fraser Script. With kind permission from Overseas Missionary Fellowship International U.K. Photo courtesy of University of London, SOAS Archives.

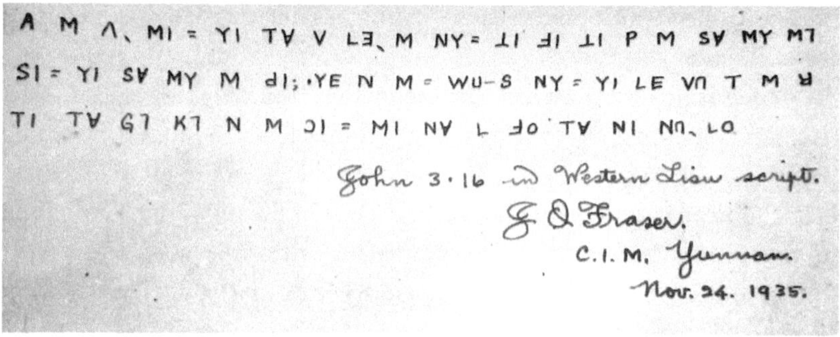

possess (see fig. 4). Tones were marked by punctuation. The Fraser Script also contained a feature borrowed from other nearby orthographies: the vowel *a* was inherent in the previous consonant, so B represented the sound "ba."[40] From the very beginning, the Lisu were able to learn to read using the Fraser Script very quickly; it seemed naturally suited to their language.

The Letter Never Written

After another exploratory trip, Fraser returned to Tan-Tsah for the first half of 1916, preaching there and in the surrounding villages. As he came to understand Lisu culture more deeply, he changed his missionary methods. James C. Scott, in *The Art of Not Being Governed*, makes a convincing case that the hill peoples of upland Southeast Asia chose their difficult geography, livelihood, social organization, ideology, and even their oral culture as a means of avoiding assimilation and takeover by the Han Chinese state. Whether by conscious strategy or not, the Lisu were largely successful at maintaining their independence and evading state control—they were not fully incorporated until after World War I. This collective sense of independence extended to the individual. Isobel Kuhn wrote, "No Lisu likes to be a servant. Poor as they are . . . they love independence."[41]

Fraser noted this independence. He abandoned his attempts to persuade; instead, he just laid out the Gospel with no attempt to "make the sale." He knew Lisu independence meant that they could never feel cajoled into acceptance; they had to make the decision for themselves. Instead of preaching, he sat around firesides, chatting, asking questions, even telling the occasional joke.[42]

Still, his hopes for a great turning in Tan-Tsah were not realized. His journals sometimes report not a single comer to the Sunday services he held.[43] After short stints in Tengyueh and Paoshan over the summer, Fraser began to head back toward Tan-Tsah. He was of the mind that God's time for the Lisu had not yet come. He planned on writing the mission to volunteer for another field of service. "But before I write that letter," Fraser stated, "I will take my final visit round my district. Just one more round."[44]

Fraser spent the night at a village where he had often stayed previously. "We will just preach to them again to make certain that everything is as dead as before—then I will write the letter," Fraser said.[45] The next day, eight families wanted to turn Christian. Fraser and his companions then moved to a village lower down. Five more families. In the next ten or twenty villages, the story was the same. Thus began the people movement of Lisu Christianity.[46] Families, hamlets, and villages converted en masse, burning their idol shelves and declaring their allegiance to Jesus Christ.

"That letter was never written!" said Fraser.[47]

Indigenous Principles

Once the people movement began amongst the Lisu, Fraser found himself no longer a pioneering missionary, street-corner preacher, or itinerant evangelist—all roles he had previously held. Now he was the shepherd of a nascent church, a role that required a new set of skills: discipleship, Bible translation, literacy training, teaching, and organizing a group of uneducated converts into a church. For these tasks, Fraser turned to the writings of Roland Allen. John Kuhn, missionary to the Lisu from the 1920s on, wrote, "The first book that I ever noticed Mr. Fraser reading was Roland Allen's *Spontaneous Expansion of the Church*. From the early days he was persuaded of indigenous development in church growth. The foundations laid in the Lisu church reflect his early conviction of this."[48]

The indigenous principles Fraser employed were originally advanced by Henry Venn (1796–1873) of the Church Missionary Society and Rufus Anderson (1796–1880) of the American Board of Commissioners for Foreign Missions. The ideas were later refined and put into practice by John Nevius (1829–1893), a missionary first to China and then to Korea. Indigenous principles, also known as three-self principles, were given a new, robust reading by Allen in his book *The Spontaneous Expansion of the Church* (a follow-up to *Missionary Methods: St. Paul's or Ours?*). Fraser embraced Allen's paradigm wholeheartedly and applied the indigenous or "three self" concepts—self-supporting, self-governing, and self-evangelizing—exactingly, perhaps too exactingly, to the developing Lisu church.

Self-supporting meant that the Lisu church would receive no money from foreign sources. The Lisu church was supported neither by mission funds nor by individual donors. Lisu evangelists were paid through offerings from the Lisu church. According to Mildred Cable, "He had strong views about the training of indigenous Church workers. When he speaks of paying converts to preach he says: 'It is the line of least resistance but is something like the broad road that leads to destruction. No. Far better let the work go slowly and tread the narrow way of self-support. We shall never regret it.'"[49]

In addition, Lisu believers were required to purchase their own Bibles, pens, and notebooks. Further, the Lisu church was expected to fund the Bible training schools and feed the students. Fraser upheld these standards himself and demanded the same of the following generation of missionaries, as Leila Cooke described:

> Mr. Fraser charged us very carefully not to spoil the Lisu with gifts or money, and that we should not pay even for the services of a language teacher, as the work was to be entirely self-supporting. We got around the difficulty by asking different ones to give a month each to teaching us, and count it as work done for the Lord. We had a few pocket knives worth about ten cents apiece, and gave one of those at the end of each month as a token of appreciation for the voluntary service rendered. When Mr. Fraser heard of this he wrote us saying, "Please do not reward them even ten cents' worth. Let their labor be entirely for the Lord."[50]

Moreover, Fraser did not allow giving the Lisu free medicine; rather, the standard payment was one egg per pill.[51] If the Lisu were unable to pay, no medicine would be given.

Self-governing meant that it was the Lisu church leaders who were in charge, not the missionary. Self-government happened quite naturally in the Lisu areas, for the number of Christian villages was great, and the number of missionaries, few. But this principle applied even to villages that had a missionary in residence. Isobel Kuhn, missionary to the Lisu during the 1930s and 1940s, describes it this way: "The Lisu church, being founded along indigenous lines, was self-governing. The missionary gave advice when asked, and likewise preached only when invited. In each Christian village there was one elected as service leader, and this one wrote down on the blackboard the names of those he wished to preach during the coming week. If the missionary's name did not appear, he did not preach but sat in the audience while the selected national Christian officiated."[52]

Church discipline was also administered by local church leaders. Fraser stated, "The system of church government by a few selected pastor-evangelists, paid by the people themselves for full-time service, acting with the deacons of all the churches in the district, has now been in full swing for some time. The missionary acts only in an advisory capacity, and frequently his advice is not even asked; for in many cases involving discipline the people know themselves so much better than we know them."[53] Further, the Lisu did not naturally separate spiritual and secular matters. Particularly in all-Christian villages, village leadership and church leadership were one and the same, with the church in the middle of the village, serving as both civic and spiritual center.[54]

Finally, self-evangelizing meant that it was the Lisu Christians themselves, not the missionaries, who spearheaded efforts in evangelism. Jennie Fitzwilliam, one of the second generation of Lisu missionaries, recalled that Fraser "taught the Lisu that he had come a long way to tell them about the Lord Jesus and now that they had come to know Him, it was up to them to carry the Gospel to all the rest of their people and so that's what they did. And they went out in volunteer . . . usually two together out into the heathen areas far and wide, up and down that border. I think you could safely say that all of that region to . . . way up to the extreme Salween area has been completely evangelized by the Lisu."[55]

In later years, Lisu evangelists had at least one Bible school session as preparation, but in the early years, Lisu Christians were sent out to evangelize immediately upon their own conversion. As Isobel Kuhn noted, Lisu evangelists only needed to know the plan of salvation and John 3:16.[56] In a letter, Fraser described the results of self-propagation: "They will take you to a village you have never set foot in or even heard of before, and you will find several families of converts there, some of whom can read and write after a fashion, and a chapel already put up! They just teach one another— inviting converts over from neighbouring villages for the purpose. They just want to be Christians, when they hear all about it, and just turn Christian, missionary or no missionary. Who put that 'want-to' into their hearts? If they are not God's chosen, God's elect, what are they?"[57]

Long after Fraser had died and the CIM had withdrawn from China, John Kuhn wrote, "One of the wisest principles Fraser ever laid down was that of the spearhead in native evangelism being native. Missionaries supplied the fuel. And where this principle was followed through the years there was blessing."[58]

The Lisu have taken "self-evangelizing," one of the indigenous principles upon which their church foundation was laid, and made it the Christian practice of evangelism. During my fieldwork I often heard Lisu use the phrase "share the good news" (*chuan fuyin*). In addition, a standard church position was that of evangelist (*chuandaoyuan*). Judging from the large number of first-generation converts I met, evangelism was a priority for the church, and new Christians were welcomed.

When I asked Naomi about her future plans once her teaching stint at the Gongshan Bible School was completed, she informed me that she was going to attend another Lisu Bible training school, this one taught in Chinese, not in Lisu. "I want to be more familiar with the Bible in Chinese so I can better *chuan fuyin*," she told me. And I received an email from Barnabas, a Lisu pastor. He excitedly told me about a short-term trip he was planning to go into Tibet to "*chuan fuyin*." Lisu Christians learned from Fraser that spreading the Gospel was their own responsibility; after nearly one hundred years, evangelism is still a vital Christian practice.

For Fraser, these indigenous principles—self-supporting, self-governing, and self-evangelizing—were not an exit strategy; they were an entrance strategy. He put the indigenous principles into play at once. This was not just a strategic decision. It was a matter of necessity. Once the people movement among the Lisu commenced, it was large, spread out, and impossible to control, even should he have wanted to. He was one man on a donkey, itinerating among the Christian hamlets and villages scattered across the mountainsides in difficult terrain.

In the Lisu work Fraser faced a fresh field, which was perhaps his greatest advantage. In other fields within China, mission work had been carried out for decades; the application of indigenous principles would mean throwing out an old and comfortable method and replacing it with something new and untested. Fraser had a unique opportunity to do something innovative and to do it from the very start. Though most others in his mission—often more senior than he—disagreed with his ideas, Fraser never wavered from his commitment to indigenous principles, believing churches should be self-supporting, self-governing, and self-evangelizing.[59]

Group Conversions

38 The conflict between the Western elevation of the individual and the Eastern primacy of the group affected Fraser's work as well. One of Fraser's earliest decisions was to suspend the requirement for individual conversion. Through his long periods in residence with the Lisu, Fraser had come to understand their social structure, determining that they would come to Christ best through families. In Lisu culture it was nearly impossible for an individual to come to Christ on his or her own; conversion would happen by family, or it would not happen. Fraser stated, "It is because only when the responsible members of any particular family turn to God that the household idolatrous implements may be removed, and until that is done the real commitment has not been made."[60]

Fraser realized that individual families were so tied in to village life that they couldn't tear down their spirit shelf without approval from village elders. Therefore, village leaders were approached first. When one family turned Christian, they were watched carefully by neighboring families. If none suffered retribution from the spirits, other families in the village were encouraged to turn Christian as well. Whole clans, groups, villages, and families converted together—a people movement. Fraser addressed group conversions specifically in an article in *China's Millions*, the CIM monthly publication:

> Many people in our home countries object to, or at any rate question the depth and reality of, such mass-turnings. The writer's experience of aboriginal work is that whereas there may be a very imperfect apprehension of Christian truth, especially in the early days of a movement, it would be quite unfair to label the work "shallow," and still more unfair to question its genuineness. So far as the aboriginal Christians go they are as sincere as we are, and the most "shallow" of them has made a clean cut with his old heathen life, and a definite right-about-face.[61]

Fraser recognized that not every individual had made a whole-hearted commitment; that was why further teaching and discipleship were required. Still, he knew that the major decisions of life were made not individually, but by clan and family, and spiritual decisions had to follow the same pattern.

Many Asian cultures are organized around family and filial loyalty, and the Lisu are no different in this respect.[62] The choice to allow family conversion had wide-ranging effects, far beyond a one-time theological statement about the nature of salvation and conversion. Fraser supported the familism and communalism of Lisu culture, making them the foundation of the Lisu expression of faith. Lisu Christian practices, since they are performed together with others, stem from this affirmation of Lisu group-oriented culture.

In a letter to his mother, Fraser explained what happened when a family turned Christian: "I never, now, try to *persuade* the Lisu to become Christians.... I find that they are quite unstable and unsatisfactory unless they 'turn' with all their heart. When they really do this, I go round to each home and gather the family for a good long talk, explaining the step they are taking. Then we all stand and I pray with them, after which they go around chopping and tearing down all sorts of things and piling them on the fire.... They seem glad to make a clean sweep while they are about it."[63]

At the end of 1916, Fraser counted 129 families who had converted. Ba Thaw, visiting from Burma, stayed to shepherd and teach. Fraser had this to say about Ba Thaw: "This young Karen is quite an exceptional man. He dresses like the Lisu, lives among them as one of themselves, and wherever he goes is greatly loved. He is a better speaker of Lisu than I am, and is more capable in the shepherding of young converts. He is thoroughly spiritual, and I have no better friend among the Christians, tribal or Chinese, than he."[64]

Fraser returned to Tengyueh for Christmas, where he had an attack of appendicitis, necessitating a trip to Shanghai for surgery. After seven months away, Fraser returned to Yunnan bringing a new colleague along with him: Mr. Herbert Flagg, a graduate of both Harvard University and the Moody Bible Institute. When Fraser and Flagg revisited the areas of new Lisu Christians, they found them standing firm and even adding to their number. When Fraser arrived at Mottled Hill village, he found the community a beehive of activity as they worked together to construct their own chapel. The villagers were erecting walls of bamboo matting and preparing thatch for the roof. The dirt was being trodden hard, and a carpet of rushes laid. Materials and labor had been freely given to construct the chapel, which, though simple, surpassed all other buildings in the area. Fraser stayed on for the opening ceremony, in which Lisu from far and wide gathered to see this first chapel constructed in the mountains of western Yunnan.[65]

Although many Lisu had converted, their Christian knowledge was minimal. Most of them simply knew that they had switched their allegiance from spirits to God and his son, Jesus Christ.[66] Though they had chapels, they did not know how to worship in them. It was in this context that Fraser introduced Christian practices. Theology and creeds, for these subsistence farmers living in an oral culture, were communicated through prayers and hymns. They usually uttered this simple prayer, in unison:

> God our Father,
> Creator of heaven and earth,
> Creator of mankind,
> We are your children.
> We are followers of Jesus.
> Watch over us today.
> Don't let the evil spirits trouble us.
> We are trusting in Jesus. Amen.[67]

Fraser loved hymns, especially those by Charles Wesley and other old Methodist hymns.[68] Fraser also introduced hymn singing as an effort to convey doctrine. "The hymns are the jam, and the Gospel is the powder to be taken," he said.[69] Later, as he wrote and expanded the catechism for new Lisu believers, he included several hymns.

Fraser was not immune to the desire to civilize or "clean up" the Lisu according to European standards. There were also times that he rigidly insisted upon Victorian moral values without allowing the new Lisu Christians time to develop their own Christian moral code. He stipulated that the Lisu must give up opium to become Christian; later, he insisted upon banning all whiskey consumption at weddings. In one case he dumped out whiskey that had been brewed for the wedding into the pig troughs, causing the pigs to become intoxicated. The current Lisu practice of abstinence from smoking and drinking does certainly have its origin in the missionary J. O. Fraser and his Victorian sensibilities. But while the *origination* of the practice comes from the missionaries, the *preservation* of this practice, as with the other Lisu Christian practices, relies on its place within Lisu narratives.

Fraser spent the summer of 1918 in Myitkyina living with Ba Thaw and his wife, working on the verandah of Ba Thaw's bungalow overlooking the Irrawaddy River, which was nearly a half-mile wide at that spot. Together, they translated the Gospel of Mark.[70] Later that summer, Fraser baptized twenty-five young people in Turtle Village, the first baptisms recorded for Lisu Christians. Fraser wrote, "Each one promised solemnly, not only to trust in the Lord Jesus for his whole lifetime, but to abstain from any connection with heathen worship, from whisky-drinking, immorality, opium-smoking or cultivation, and to observe the Lord's Day."[71] The sacrament of baptism itself was tied less to doctrinal statements of belief, which would have made little sense in this context, but rather to practices that allowed that belief to find its expression.[72] The Christian life, for these first Lisu believers to receive baptism, was framed by Fraser as a faith that was practiced.

This emphasis on practices would cause later missionaries to the Lisu, who felt the stress on works did not properly underscore the necessity of divine grace, some consternation. Leila Cooke wrote, "Sometimes Mr. Fraser would say something like this: 'I believe in the doctrine of grace as much as any other missionary.' Yet in dealing with the Lisu he was very careful to tell them that they must show their faith by their works."[73]

Unlike indigenous or three-self principles, which Fraser was careful to elucidate at length both through letter and in person, there is little to nothing among Fraser's letters, articles, or interviews regarding his thoughts on the relationship of faith and works, or his intentions behind stressing a life of Christian practices for the Lisu. Fraser was, after all, not a theologian but an engineer. My belief is that Fraser's emphasis on practices was less a matter of well-worked-out theology and more an intuitive response, based on his understanding of Lisu culture gained through hours spent around Lisu fires.

Fraser closed out the year 1918 by inviting about forty or fifty Lisu Christians to his home in Tengyueh for the first Christian festival.[74] The men, with swords, satchels, and bare feet, stayed at Fraser's home, while the women, adorned with colored turbans, tassels, beads, and other jewelry, stayed with a Chinese Christian woman who lived nearby. They held church services, played sports, and studied. Every day, after morning prayers, Fraser taught them to read the new script. In the evening, Fraser taught them hymns: "Jesus Loves Me," "I've Wandered Far From God," "God Be With You Until We Meet Again," and others.[75]

In 1919, after Fraser itinerated the entire year among Lisu villages, Christmas was marked yet again by a Christmas festival—this time hosted by the Lisu themselves at Turtle Village. Hundreds attended. Fraser also brought a new missionary to the Lisu, Allyn B. Cooke, a young American.

Muchengpo

By 1920, there was a great turning among the Lisu in Muchengpo and the surrounding district, much larger than Fraser's original Tengyueh district. Fraser had initially visited Muchengpo five years previously. At that time he was on the fifth week of a planned two-week itineration, and Mr. Embery, his senior missionary, had worriedly sent out runners to find him and bring him back to Tengyueh as soon as possible. On his way back to Tengyueh, a woman from Muchengpo had appeared, calling out, "I've heard about you, Big Brother Three [Fraser's Lisu name], what have you come to China for?" Fraser replied that he had come to tell people about Jesus Christ, the forgiveness of sins, and the hope of heaven. "Well come and tell us then," she said. Conflicted, Fraser told her he couldn't stop at that moment, but he promised to come back later. "Don't say you've come to tell us these things and then say you've not time to tell us," the woman retorted.[76]

Now five years hence, a group of Lisu from Ta-siao-ho village, near Muchengpo, sent a message asking Fraser to come and preach to them. Unfortunately, a group of Kachin tribesmen had sent an urgent appeal for Fraser to help arbitrate, as tribal chiefs had begun to persecute the Kachin Christians. As Fraser had already promised to help the Kachin, Allyn Cooke agreed to head south. Cooke was a green missionary who had as yet scant ability in Chinese and no ability in Lisu, so two Lisu Christian companions were assigned to go with him. The three came upon a Lisu wedding banquet, with all the drunkenness and debauchery usually accorded to such an occasion. In the middle of it, Cooke made an emotional plea for their souls.[77] The people responded. After several days of teaching, Cooke had to return to Tengyueh to focus on language studies. The two Lisu remained to teach the people.[78]

By the time Fraser was finally able to return to Muchengpo district in 1920, a Christian movement had already commenced as a result of this visit. The two Lisu evangelists who remained to teach had been unable to cope with the steady stream of inquirers. The new Lisu Christians had learned to read, taken up a collection, and sent the two evangelists back to Tengyueh to buy them books.[79]

The village of Muchengpo itself had converted, including the woman who had called out to Fraser on his previous journey. The church was eventually built on the spot from which she had called out to him.[80] Fraser was much amazed upon finally returning to Muchengpo and the surrounding villages: "Some things specially please me about this new Eastern district. In the first place, the work was practically begun and has been almost wholly carried on by the Lisu themselves, however raw and poorly trained. . . . Another matter of thankfulness is that the proportion of Christians to heathen is so large. In some vicinities scarcely any heathen families remain."[81]

By 1921, more than four hundred families in Muchengpo district had turned Christian.[82] Fraser and Ba Thaw had long been collaborating on translating the Gospels of Mark and John, a catechism, and a hymn book. Now that some of these were printed and available, they came to Muchengpo district to conduct a two-week Bible school with the new Muchengpo Christians. The Lisu church was moving out of its chaotic people-movement phase and into a period of consolidation and maturation. Fraser was thirty-five years old.

Later that year, Fraser left Tengyueh for good. Together with Herbert Flagg and Flagg's new wife, he relocated to Muchengpo (called Stockade Hill in some missionary narratives). Muchengpo was the first settled mission station of Lisu work. Allyn and Leila Cooke, who later translated much of the New Testament, spent their formative missionary years in Muchengpo. Job, the great Lisu evangelist (discussed in chapter 3), came from Muchengpo. Muchengpo became the mother church, sending out Lisu evangelists not just to the surrounding villages of Flowery Lisu but also to the Black Lisu of the Salween gorge.

Throughout these initial years of the Lisu church, the foundation of many Lisu Christian practices—singing hymns, holding church services five times weekly, evangelizing, abstaining from drinking and smoking, keeping the Sabbath, attending Christian festivals—was laid by J. O. Fraser himself. Later missionaries downplayed the practices somewhat, showing more concern about right belief and expressing fear that the practices led to legalism. But the practice-centered Christianity fit well within Lisu frames, enabling the Lisu to begin the process of identifying their culture with Christianity. The Christian practices are earthy, grassroots, and altogether common. They are more utilitarian than philosophical, more practical than theoretical. They rooted themselves quickly and easily in the soil of this oral culture of subsistence farmers living in bleak and primitive conditions out on the margins.

Fraser went on furlough in 1922. When he returned to China, he was assigned for three years to Gansu province in China's northwest, far from Yunnan and away from work among the Lisu. "Everything about it spelt the wilderness to me," Fraser said.[83] He did not return to work in Yunnan Province until 1927, and then not as a missionary to the Lisu; rather, he was CIM superintendent for all of Yunnan Province.[84] While CIM superintendent, he met and married Roxie Dymond, whose parents worked with the United Methodist Mission in Kunming. "Living, as he had done, away up in the great mountains, he seemed to have absorbed some of their bigness," his wife wrote.[85]

Even as he withdrew from hands-on Lisu work to become the CIM superintendent for Yunnan Province, Fraser watched closely over the Lisu church, mentoring and guiding the next generation of missionaries to the Lisu—the Cookes, the Kuhns, the Fitzwilliams, and others.

Chapter 2

LINGUISTIC BORDERLANDS

> Come, thou Fount of every blessing,
> Tune my heart to sing thy grace;
> Streams of mercy, never ceasing,
> Call for songs of loudest praise.
>
> Teach me some melodious sonnet,
> Sung by flaming tongues above.
> Praise the mount I'm fixed upon it
> Mount of God's redeeming love.

I walked through tall corn to reach the Gongshan Bible School. As I approached I could hear singing of the familiar hymn, "Come, Thou Fount of Every Blessing." I had spent the previous months immersed in history, reading about the lives of J. O. Fraser and the other missionaries to the Lisu, such as Leila Cooke and Isobel Kuhn, as well as the early Lisu Christians Job, Moses, and others. Now, I would have the chance to experience present-day Lisu Christianity. My first stop was the Bible school.

The Gongshan Bible School was housed at the Gongshan Zion Church compound. The physical structure of the Gongshan church was designed for communal faith, with dorms for the Bible training center, a canteen for

---

Epigraph from "Come, Thou Fount of Every Blessing," lyrics by Robert Robinson, 1758, hymn #75 in the 2013 Yunnan Lisu hymnbook.

feeding large groups, and a large courtyard for line dancing. I stayed in a three-story building toward the back of the compound, which also housed the canteen and an apartment for Jesse's family.

The compound was a bustling community. Everyone's door was always open, including my own. People were walking in and out at will. Kids were playing in the courtyard. Older kids and students were playing basketball in the makeshift court that was really just tamped down rocks and gravel. Pigs were being slaughtered. Huge vats of rice were being cooked. Pumpkins and squash were being peeled and sliced. Clothes and dishes were being washed. That which in my culture was usually done inside the confines of the home was done outside here, in the external realm, for all to see and help and participate in and discuss.

Early each morning, students gathered in the courtyard to perform their morning exercises, quickly eat, and get ready for class at 8:00 a.m. Students sat in the cement-floored church sanctuary at long planks that had been nailed atop the pews to form desks. A hymn was sung right at 8:00 a.m. to commence the hour of instruction, and hymns would continue to be sung to begin each new hour of instruction throughout the day. Often, as we sang hymns, several students would practice directing—just as students did in the 1930s and 1940s, according to the missionary narratives I had read.

The Bible school had about one hundred students, most of whom were in their early twenties. However, there were some in their forties and fifties or even older, and a few teenagers as well. The younger group had completed several years of Chinese education, even if they had not graduated. The older group did not speak Chinese, and had only a few years, if any, of formal education. Most students were from Gongshan County, though there were several from neighboring counties. The majority were Lisu, with one or two other ethnic minorities attending as well. For nearly all of the students, whether they had completed any formal schooling or not, attending the Gongshan Bible School was their first experience of formally learning how to read and write their own Lisu language.

Lisuland exists in the borderlands. It lies in geographic borderlands, where numerous ethnic minorities make their living in the shadows of the Himalayas, with historically little concern over the statecraft of China, Thailand, Burma, or India. It also exists in linguistic borderlands. Traveling along the region one can hear many languages spoken, not just Lisu but also Lahu, Dulong, Bai, Jingpo, Tibetan, Yi, Thai, and the Yunnan dialect of Chinese.

Lisuland also exists in the borderlands between orality and literacy. Thanks to the Bible and hymnbook that are printed in the Fraser Script, there is sufficient literacy to sing hymns and read the Bible. But as most Lisu Christians are only familiar with these two books in their own language, the drastic changes in social structure that literacy can foster have not occurred. Even though the Lisu have a script and the Bible translated into their own language, books and texts have not gained a place of prominence in Lisu culture; Lisu social structure, communication patterns, and daily life exist in accordance with the oral milieu.

In societies governed by an oral milieu, words often do not exist if the categories do not exist in one's own lived experience, as I learned during my time with the students at the Gongshan Bible training center. When the students first asked what brought me to Gongshan, I answered: research. Though they understood my Chinese pronunciation, they did not comprehend the idea. Research was a category that did not exist in their world. People in Gongshan did not do research; they were engaged in the more concrete realities of life, such as harvesting corn, gathering firewood, and attending church.

During a break in class, my friend A-cha complained about her house. She said that she, like many people in Gongshan, was poor, and the only house she could have was one she built herself. She would like to have another kind of house—a nice house built by others—but "*mei banfa*," she said resignedly. There's no way.

To console her I told her that in Beijing—where I lived—many people had nice apartments, but because of skyrocketing housing prices in China's big cities, the apartments were so expensive that they had a large debt. A-cha followed me until I said the word *debt*. I typed the word into the Chinese translator on my phone and showed her, but she still did not understand. It was not that she did not know this Chinese word. Rather, it was the concept of debt (along with banks, interest, mortgages, and related categories) that she was not familiar with.

In an oral world, there is no reason to learn (or retain) words if the concept behind the word does not exist in one's world, in one's lived experience. Reading and writing change this, for one's own lived experience ceases to be one's only world; vicarious worlds exist as well.

So, how was one a Christian in this kind of world? How did one understand biblical categories and concepts, when those categories and concepts were absent from one's lived experience? Roland Allen wrestled with these questions as a missionary to China in the early twentieth century. He wrote:

> Religious instruction is thus divorced from understanding; it is also divorced from life.... There is created an unreal world peopled with unreal words, altogether separate from the real world in which our converts act. The world of the Church is outside the world of daily life. The world of the church services is foggy, hazy, misty, full of indefinite unreal words like "grace," "sin," "atonement," "faith"; the world of real life on the other hand is full of very definite, clear, familiar needs, passions, desires, efforts. In the world of the Church the convert attends services, he hears prayers said, he says Amen. He attends, but nothing happens. Outside he sows, and he sees shoots and he reaps. Whatever he does, something happens.[1]

In some cases, biblical culture did conform to the lived experience of the Lisu, in ways much closer than those coming from a Western worldview. Heaven, death, planting, harvest, travel by foot, life in community, fear—these were all easily understood concepts in the Nujiang Valley.

But the Bible, as Allen noted, was also filled with theological abstractions—such as justification, redemption, grace, conscience, and humility—all words the Lisu language did not have before they were evangelized. How can such Christian abstractions translate into an oral world? Isobel Kuhn recalled the difficulty the missionaries had in teaching such abstract theological concepts: "The Pauline letters contain many expressions which the Lisu language does not possess and which have to be coined and carefully taught. Lately I have had to teach 'fellowship' and 'example.'"[2]

Although the biblical canon was largely settled already in the fourth century A.D., the fundamental change in Christian ascetic practices was brought about by the age of print, which was "immediately marked in Protestant circles by advocacy of private, individual interpretation of the Bible."[3] The early missionaries to the Lisu were steeped in a sociohistorical tradition positioned around *sola scriptura*, inerrancy, and the applicability of the Bible in guiding one's life.[4] The missionaries to the Lisu laid primary emphasis on the biblical text. They constructed an orthography. They translated the Scriptures. They conducted Bible schools that focused on improving literacy for the purpose of biblical exegesis. They coined new words for theological concepts and then taught them. They held contests in Scripture memorization.[5] They stressed studying God's Word as a form of personal devotion and as a requirement for spiritual growth. But these practices did not gain a foothold in Lisu society and are rarely practiced today.

In the course of my fieldwork in the Nujiang Valley I rarely encountered a Lisu engaged in personal Bible study. Bibles were carried to church in embroidered bags, read aloud from during services, and then hung from a nail on the wall to await the next church service. Knowledge of Bible characters or well-known Bible stories or sequences often appeared sketchy. The text-based religion of the missionaries had not stuck well in the oral culture of the Lisu. But in this oral culture—which, like most oral cultures, respected tradition, cherished community, and favored the concrete and tangible—Christian practices thrived.

The Nature of Orality

Oral cultures have a different relationship with words than literate cultures. In an oral culture, a word is an event.[6] It is in the process of vanishing as soon as it is uttered. As Walter J. Ong states, "Sound exists only when it is going out of existence."[7] This ephemeral nature of words means that "there is nothing to backloop into outside the mind, for the oral utterance has vanished as soon as it is uttered. Hence the mind must move ahead more slowly, keeping close to the focus of attention much of what it has already dealt with. Redundancy, repetition of the just-said, keeps both speaker and hearer surely on the track."[8]

The taxonomic space limitations in human short-term memory mean that knowledge, once no longer needed, is sloughed off.[9] As Ong notes, "When the market for a printed book declines, the presses stop rolling but thousands of copies may remain. When the market for an oral genealogy disappears, so does the genealogy itself, utterly."[10] James C. Scott puts it like this: "Oral culture has therefore an inalterable presentness—if it was of no interest, if it served no purpose for its contemporary audience, it would cease to exist."[11]

Since words disappear in oral cultures when no longer needed, what continues to exist is tacitly important, just by virtue of its durability. There is no equivalent to a dusty tome sitting on the shelves, containing what was important in yesteryear but no longer imperative today. If the stories are still told, if the words are still used, if the memory of the event still exists, if the song is still sung, it is valuable to the society.

The bottleneck in short-term memory also means that much oral thought occurs in formulaic patterns. Antithetical terms, clichés, genealogies, stories, and set phrases are common.[12] The early missionaries to the

Lisu reported many such mnemonic devices in Lisu speech. Fraser stated that Lisu poetry, of which there was an "abundance," relied on antithesis, even using "dummy" (parallel) words simply for the sake of poetic contrast.[13] Leila Cooke, who together with her husband, Allyn, worked among the Lisu beginning in the 1920s, further explained the parallelism in Lisu poetry: "Lisu poetry is very similar in style to that of the precious Psalms of David. Each thought is repeated with the same number of words, and companion phrases to express it."[14] She gave two examples of Lisu proverbs that show the thesis/antithesis nature of Lisu poetry:

> Those who have money are cold and lonesome;
> Those who have children are warm and cosy [sic].
>
> Melons hang as they grow—
> Children cry as they grow.[15]

Cooke also said that important law cases were expected to be stated in poetry, not prose; prose was not considered properly dignified.[16]

In addition to the fleeting nature of words and the need to use formulas—such as thesis/antithesis—to recapture them, oral societies place great value upon words themselves. Ong observed that "oral peoples commonly, and probably universally, consider words to have great power."[17] When I asked missionary linguist and native-Lisu speaker David Morse if he knew some Lisu proverbs, he gave me the following three. All of them have to do with the power of words.

> Once you spit on the ground you can't put the spit
>   back in your mouth. (Be careful what you say.)
> There is no day when the pig's tail stops wagging.
>   (There is always something to be said.)
> When you pull on a root in the garden, you will find that there
>   are tendrils all over the garden. (Be careful when you speak.
>   Your words can have repercussions that you don't expect.)[18]

Moreover, all three proverbs exemplify another aspect of oral thought patterns that Ong mentioned: closeness to the human lifeworld.[19] These Lisu proverbs—all about spit and pigs' tails and tendrils—are earthy, pungent, and almost profane in their concreteness.

Characteristics of Oral Cultures

The thought patterns of oral cultures described above do not just have profound implications for culture and social structure; they have profound implications for Christian practice. To begin, oral cultures intrinsically buttress the group over the individual. Ong states, "The spoken word forms human beings into close-knit groups."[20] Words are shared. Sustained thought requires communication to be meaningful. An interlocutor—or even better, an audience—is necessary if one's words are to have any meaning at all. Solitary, isolating activities, such as reading and writing, that push people into interiorized states of consciousness are nearly unknown. Words exist in a habitat that is not a text; rather, it is a habitat of "gestures, vocal inflections, facial expression, and the entire human, existential setting in which the real, spoken word always occurs."[21]

In contrast with reading and writing, which "are solitary activities that throw the psyche back on itself . . . oral communication unites people in groups."[22] As Eric Havelock observes, "A general theory of orality must build upon a general theory of society. It requires communication to be understood as a social phenomenon, not a private transaction between individuals. Language of any kind acquires meaning for the individual only as that meaning is shared by a community."[23] In other words, orality reinforces the communal nature of Lisu Christian society. As such, oral cultures would tend to favor Christian practices that can be done together, such as singing, dancing, and praying, over those that are more solitary, such as individual Bible reading.

In addition, oral cultures tend to be more traditional. Literate societies can store knowledge and history in books. Oral societies cannot. Rather, they must invest hard work and mental processes in preserving that which is already known. Thus, that which is old is elevated above that which is new, leading to a more conservative bent. Ong explains, "Knowledge is hard to come by and precious, and society regards highly those wise old men and women who specialize in conserving it, who know and can tell the stories of the days of old."[24] Intellectual experimentation is not prized in an oral culture; rather, the stored-up knowledge of the culture—stories, songs, proverbs, set phrases, clichés, and genealogies—are repeated over and over. The traditional nature of Lisu culture repeatedly struck me, as I would read of Lisu Christian practices of the 1920s—from handshaking to hymn singing to Bible-bag carrying—and then experience them in the 2010s.

These two common features of oral cultures—the reinforcement of communal social structure and the favoring of tradition—have had a profound impact on the Christian practices of the Lisu, a lasting influence on how they have chosen to worship.

The Impact of Writing on Oral Cultures

The introduction of writing into a traditional oral culture has wide-ranging effects. But it does not immediately affect the oral aesthetic. The oral culture may remain vibrant for generations. Writing is not an independent variable. Rather than significantly altering the culture, writing is itself defined and limited, its role demarcated, by the social structure and oral aesthetic.

Susan Niditch, in her analysis of the role of the Scriptures in biblical cultures, proposes that rather than a sharp distinction between oral and literate cultures, the role writing plays in a society falls along a continuum (see table 1). Writing is not simply writing; its function changes based on the nature of the society of which it is a part. According to Niditch, "Literacy in a traditional culture is very much informed by the worldviews and aesthetics of orality."[25] That is, even where a society, such as the Lisu, does have writing, both the function and meaning of this writing cannot be fully understood without reference to the oral aesthetic of the culture, of which the writing is but a minor part. The written words cannot be understood without reference to the oral world. Thought patterns will continue to place more value on concrete items, spoken words, and lived experience rather than the abstractions of a text.

In a highly literate society, writing is used for record-keeping, for legal purposes, for producing works of reference, and for such introspective activities as composing works of literature, whereas writing serves quite different purposes in societies that maintain a strong oral aesthetic. In oral societies, words are considered powerful, with the ability to transform, even to the point of possessing magical properties.[26] Generally speaking, writing in societies on the literate end of the spectrum has a preservative function—preserving records, facts, or thoughts for future use. Writing in societies with a vibrant oral culture performs a more symbolic function—symbolizing sacred space, embodying a shared sense of group identity, and reminding the group of core cultural values. In explaining this symbolic function of writing, I will look at two specific functions of writing in an oral society in greater detail: the monumental function and the iconic function.

table 1 The roles played by writing in societies along the oral-literate continuum

Oral	Literate
Iconic	Records and annals
Monumental	Literary works and compositions
Transformative	Legal documents
Symbolic	Letters
Magical	References
Suggestive	

Note: Based on Niditch, *Oral World and Written Word*, 78–98.

Monumental writing refers to writing, often on monuments, doorways, signposts, or other markers, that conveys symbolic meaning, whether or not the specific text can be fully decoded. According to Niditch, "In exploring the place of monumental inscriptions on the oral-literate continuum, once again we find writing in a sacred-rendering, space-defining context. The writing, an activity on the literate end of the continuum, validates the space in a transformative magical way associated with oral-traditional culture."[27] Monumental writing is not about conveying information; rather, it marks a space with holy words. The writing transforms the space from profane or ordinary to sacred.

An example of monumental writing is the poster stuck to the door of many Lisu Christian homes at midnight on New Year's Day (see fig. 5). On the bottom is written 2 Corinthians 5:17 (New International Version): "Therefore, if anyone is in Christ, the new creation has come: The old has gone, the new is here!"

This poster performed the symbolic function of marking the home as a Christian home. The beliefs of the inhabitants and the prayers of the villagers marked the home as a sacred space. The poster stood as a symbolic monument attesting to these facts.

As a point of contrast, when the test scores of a recent examination at the Gongshan Bible training center were posted on the church door, the entire record was posted not in Lisu, though that was the language of instruction, but in Chinese. Each student's name was listed in Chinese characters. The Chinese name is the only name unique to each person; Lisu names reflect family position, and there were several firstborn sons in the class, making record-keeping difficult. Additionally, many of the students and teachers had spent several years in the Chinese school system, and Chinese words such as 分 (meaning *points*) were familiar from this context. The end result

fig. 5 Lisu Christian door poster for 2014 (Fugong). Photo: author.

was that a Lisu-language Bible class that took a test in Lisu used Chinese to report the scores.

Likewise, at the Liuku Bible School the list of school rules was posted in Chinese (such as Rule #1, "Be patriotic, adhere to the 'Three-Self' principles of independence, and be committed to the harmonious development of the church and society," and Rule #2, "Respect the teachers, be in unity with classmates; do not quarrel during school; if you have comments and suggestions, give them to the teachers to monitor and reflect"). Chinese writing was used for such banal, literate tasks as record-keeping and rule-giving. Lisu writing was reserved not only for monumental functions but for a second use of writing in strongly oral societies: as icon.

In its iconic function, the piece of writing, such as a scroll or a book, serves as an item of reverence or worship more than it functions as an actual text. Niditch explains, "The written text provides a portion of tradition that becomes set, an icon, perhaps a sacred object that may be ritually studied sequentially or read in for special occasions, or copied when the old papyrus begins to succumb to age. The stories, the customs, the rituals, and the proverbs live, however, in the oral culture, in the lives and words of people."[28]

As an icon, there is a respect, even an aura, that surrounds writing. However, the writing does not actually reach down to touch the lives of the people. This iconic function of writing has direct ramifications for the use of Scripture in traditional societies.

Oral Societies and Christianity

The Gospel of John opens by stating, "In the beginning was the Word, and the Word was with God, and the Word was God" (1:1). And in Genesis 1, the creation account, God *speaks* the world into existence. In Isaiah, God *declares* that "so is my word that goes out from my mouth: It will not return to me empty, but will accomplish what I desire and achieve the purpose for which I sent it" (55:11). In the New Testament, Jesus performed many miracles that were activated by his speech. He *rebuked* the wind and the waves (Mark 4:39). He *called out* in a loud voice and raised Lazarus (John 11:43). He *told* the lame man to "get up, take your mat and go home" (Matt. 9:6). He *rebuked* a fever (Luke 4:39). He *ordered* demons to leave a possessed man. After this last miracle, reflecting the oral aesthetic pervasive in much of biblical culture, all the people were amazed and said, "What words these are! With authority and power he gives orders to evil spirits and they come out!" (Luke 4:36).

Jesus chose to conduct much of his teaching through parables, which were stories that could be easily remembered and repeated. A final demonstration of the power of words in Christianity is the practice of prayer, words of direct speech that access the power of God Almighty.

Words thus have intrinsic power in Christian theology. Ong, himself a Jesuit priest, states, "In Christian teaching orality-literacy polarities are particularly acute, probably more acute than in any other religious tradition, even the Hebrew. For in Christian teaching the Second Person of the One Godhead, who redeemed mankind from sin, is known not only as the Son but also as the Word of God."[29] Moreover, Ong writes that, although Jesus could read and write, he left behind only oral tradition. Ong further notes that Paul, in his letter to the Romans, states, "Faith comes from *hearing* the message" (Rom. 10:17; emphasis mine). But while early Christianity was grounded in oral communication, since New Testament times, Christianity has become perhaps the most text-based of religions. Christianity contains an oral-literate duality that mirrors the communal-individual duality I will discuss in chapter 6.

The Lisu Linguistic Situation

In the time before missionary contact, the language situation in the Nujiang Valley was what Ong terms primary orality—that is, the culture of persons untouched by literacy. In their remote valley, the Lisu lived in a completely oral Lisu world. There was knowledge of the existence of the Chinese language world and its pictographic characters. There were a few Lisu who could speak or write some Chinese words, as necessary for trade.[30] But the ordinary lived experience of the Lisu was monolingual orality.

The Fraser Script

Into this oral world, the missionaries introduced writing. As mentioned in the previous chapter, after J. O. Fraser had spent many years with the Lisu, he—together with Ba Thaw, a Karen tribesman from Burma who spoke Lisu—developed a written script that was well suited to the various tones and tone combinations of the Lisu language; later missionaries reported that bright learners could learn to read in one month's time.[31] After perfecting the script in 1915,[32] Fraser translated the Gospel of Mark and wrote a catechism and Lisu primer.[33] The catechism, which contained some selected hymns translated by Ba Thaw,[34] was the first book published using the Fraser Script. Below is an excerpt from the beginning of the catechism:

> Who created the world and all that is in it?
>   God created it.
> If God created it, is it wrong to worship demons?
>   It is very wrong to worship demons.
> Why is it wrong?
>   It is wrong because demons are not our Creator.
> Then who is our Creator?
>   Our Father God is our Creator.
> Ought we to say Mother God?
>   We must not say Mother God.[35]

The Lisu treated the written script with great reverence, and Lisu Christians became known for carrying around their written Scripture portions in brightly embroidered bags, a practice that continues today. In 1940 the Lisu New Testament was made available to the Lisu.[36] While possessing an orthography was a meaningful cultural step for the Lisu, it was the process of Bible translation, according to Chinese linguist Jie Jin, which has revitalized the Lisu language not only in its written form but in its oral form as well.[37]

First, the Fraser orthography has served to mitigate dialect differences among the Lisu. Whereas many Lisu dialects had been nearly mutually unintelligible, the common Bible and the shared base of vocabulary and structures it has given mean that most Lisu Christians can now communicate with one another, no matter their dialect.

In addition, Bible translation introduced new grammatical structures. One new structure is the nominalized *because* structure. While the Lisu language previously had a particle that would attribute reason, this particle always followed a noun, for example, *rain + (because of)*. The Bible translators found this structure too limited. They introduced a new structure that allowed an entire sentence to follow the *because* phrase, for example, *because + it has rained*.[38]

But perhaps the greatest achievement of the Bible translators was drawing upon Lisu oral poetry to coin new words and phrases. Leila Cooke sought out oral poets to aid her in the translation work:

> I was so desperate for suitable words to talk about the Lord Jesus that I persisted, until they told me the names of two Lisu poetesses. The Lisu said that although they used to have no writing, yet in almost every village there are those who can repeat poetry from memory from sunset to daybreak, all night long. Well, these two poetesses were old women. They sought a secret place and, after many blushes and shamefaced giggles, the two started in. "Stop a minute—what did you say?" I asked. The language was so rich that I could not understand it. But alas the two songsters could not repeat. They did not know how to back up.[39]

One cannot back up when one lives in an oral world. Each word is an event, and once spoken, is no more.

Leila Cooke's encounter with Lisu oral poetry led to the discovery of four-word couplets in Lisu poetic language and funeral chants. Four-word couplets form one word by combining together three morphemes, usually in the forms ABAC or ABCB. The three morphemes are concrete terms, but brought together in a couplet, they express an abstract thought. This discovery transformed the work of Bible translation, as the Cookes yoked together the translated texts of Scripture and hymns with the linguistic richness of Lisu oral poetry.

In some cases, these biblical terms were borrowed directly from funeral and other chants.

⊥I: ꓲI; ⊥I: P..
one ... lifetime ... one ... world, for an overall meaning of forever and ever.

Mꓵ: CE; MI.. CE;
place ... make ... earth ... make, for an overall meaning of creation.

ꓶ; JO., XƎ, JO.,
good luck ... have ... fortune ... have, for
an overall meaning of blessing.[40]

To coin the word *Gospel*, the translators made a variation on the above couplet for Blessing:

ꓶ; ΛO: XƎ, ΛO:
good luck ... language ... fortune ... language

In the new couplet, the term ΛO:, meaning *language*, was substituted for JO., meaning *have*.[41]

In coining the word for the book of Genesis, the translators brought together the beginning two syllables from paired lines of antithetical poetry to form a new four-word couplet:

YI. CE.. YI. WU.

The original paired lines of antithetical poetry had the meaning of "In very early times, when there were no people"; the meaning transferred to the new couplet was "In the beginning." This same four-word couplet is also used in John 1:1, "In the beginning was the Word."[42]

The words of God in Exodus 3:14, "I am Who I am," were translated into Lisu using a four-word couplet:[43]

ΛW., Jꓵ: ΛW., MU.,
I ... govern ... I ... make[44]

As mentioned, the four-word couplet uses Lisu poetic forms to bridge the abstract-concrete divide, an essential divide to cross if Christian theology is to be understood by those with oral thought patterns. Each couplet uses three concrete nouns or verbs to express an abstract term. An example of this is the word for *salvation*, a quite abstract term essential to understanding Christian theology. To coin this new word, the missionary translators used a four-word couplet:

ꓕO., CYU. W: CYU
person . . . save . . . person . . . save

In this particular case, the word for person was not the ordinary word (ꓧ) but rather the combination of ꓕO., and W: used in oral poetry. The word for *save* also had to be coined; in this case, it was borrowed from Chinese. These aspects of Lisu poetry, originally based on animism, likely would have been lost as Lisu society encountered communism and modernization. Yet they are now codified in the Lisu Bible as well as the hymnbook.[45]

This conscious effort on the part of the missionary translators to incorporate poetic structures and cultural elements has done much to elevate the Lisu language in both its oral and written forms. However, the literary nature of the Bible translation, and its ability to transcend differences in dialect, has come at a cost. David Bradley calls the Lisu used in the Bible translation "literary Lisu"[46]—a compromise dialect similar to central Lisu but also containing many elements from Northern Lisu.[47] In Nu Ni village, a young woman carried two Bibles with her to church, one in Lisu and one in Chinese. "I find the Chinese translation easier to understand," she told me. In my Lisu language lessons, I would sometimes learn a word in two forms: the Bible form and the local dialect form. The dialect compromise and its literary nature meant that Bible was one step removed from everyday speech; distance was created.

Bradley reports that Lisu language publishing, using the Fraser script, was widespread.[48] Perhaps reflecting the isolated geography of the Nujiang Valley, I saw few Lisu-language books other than the Bible and the hymnal in the course of my fieldwork. Most Lisu homes contained no books at all, save for these two. The local Xinhua bookstores in Fugong and Gongshan had no Lisu-language books on the shelves. And even at the Bible school, Chinese books were sometimes passed out to the students, but other than a singing booklet, I did not see a printed Lisu book as part of the curriculum. Bradley also mentioned newspapers and magazines, but I never once saw such publications in Lisu homes or in the Bible schools. However, the Christian Lisu radio broadcasts he referred to were very popular, listened to nearly every evening.

The distinctive Fraser script and the Bible, hymnbook, and small amount of Christian literature that use it have sustained the Lisu Christian church since its founding. They have helped unite Lisu Christians in the four primary countries in which they live: China, Thailand, Myanmar, and India. The ensuing process of Bible translation has resulted in the coinage of new words, the introduction of new grammatical structures, and the codification of Lisu poetic structures within the biblical text. The Fraser Script and the Lisu Bible are seminal—but the complete picture is more complex.

Linguistic Borderlands

Despite the introduction of the Fraser written script and the ensuing advancement of oral Lisu vocabulary and structures, the Lisu did not make a simple or linear shift from orality to literacy. Orality and literacy exist together, in tandem and in tension. As Paul Soukup states, "Orality and traces of oral expression do not disappear—oral expression remains natural to humans where writing is always something learned."[49] The Lisu church exists in the linguistic borderlands between a culturally sensitive written script and a strong oral aesthetic. In these borderlands, Christian practices have thrived.

Written Lisu was also known as Bible Lisu, which not only reflected its origins but also pointed to the only sphere in which writing was available or useful. Being subsistence farmers, the Lisu had no need for additional books or writing in Lisu. Learning how to read was useful only for religious purposes—attending church, singing hymns, reading the Bible. It had no relevance outside of this sphere. A huge oral residue remained in everyday lived experience. Just having the Bible in the Lisu language was not enough to make more than a shallow imprint on the deeply oral nature of Lisu society; the changes in thought patterns brought about when literacy saturates a society had not occurred.

Moreover, the central government is much more present in the Nujiang Valley than in previous decades. Chinese-language education is pervasive (and compulsory). The Mandarin Chinese world has thus encroached on Lisu culture, reducing the Lisu language to the discrete worlds of home and church.[50] Outside of these Lisu pockets, Chinese is dominant. Chinese is required for all commerce or any conversation with a non-Lisu. In the town centers of Liuku, Fugong, and Gongshan, the Chinese script is omnipresent on shop signs, billboards, and road signs. Activities like banking, shopping, education, and transportation all require the ability to read Chinese. The public world is a Chinese-language world, and Lisu is used for the private world only. Or, to use the words of Paul Bradshaw and John Melloh, the liturgical realm is governed by the Lisu language, while the real world is the realm of Mandarin Chinese.[51]

Thus the Lisu, particularly the younger generation, live in a bifurcated linguistic world. They are literate, but their literacy is in Chinese, the national language. Their mother tongue—the language used by mothers to raise children, the language with direct access to the emotions and the unconscious, the language that can reach the depths of their emotion—exists primarily in the realm of orality. Knowledge learned through the medium of their Lisu mother tongue resides in orally cut grooves in the mind; knowledge obtained from reading and writing Chinese uses different, literate processes. It is in these linguistic borderlands where the Lisu church resides.

Liturgical Literacy

The Lisu Christians are a people who, for the most part, can read and, in certain ritualized circumstances such as church services and Bible schools, they do read. Yet despite the symbolic importance of the written word for Christianity in general, and of the Fraser Script for Lisu Christianity in particular, writing has not become fully interiorized in Lisu Christians. Many traditional cultures have, according to Niditch, "pragmatic literacy"—that is, the ability to read numbers, lists, names, and other commonly used items.[52] But the Lisu, whose literacy has been entirely bound up in their religious rituals, have a variation on pragmatic literacy: liturgical literacy.

Liturgical literacy means that the primary context for Lisu reading and writing is within the context of religious ritual. Lisu writing is rarely used for the most assumed function of writing: communication. For those who are technologically proficient and have at least a primary-level education, communication in the form of text messaging and email is done in Chinese. Communication using the Lisu language is almost always done orally.

Liturgical literacy also means that the Bible is not usually read in a personal devotional context. Rather, Bible reading has been performed in unison, out loud, in the public setting of church ritual. The Lisu have treated the Bible, generally, not as a private, devotional, instructive guide, but as a sacred, revered icon. It is a venerated object. The veracity of its words is without question. But it is held aloft; it is not for everyday or commonplace use.

Moreover, literacy in written Lisu has been so low that the majority of parishioners simply cannot understand the biblical text. Unless a Lisu Christian has attended one of the local Bible schools—and only 10 percent have had the opportunity to do so—they will not have sufficient literacy to comprehend Scripture. Thus the vast majority of Lisu Christians—80 to 90 percent—cannot read their mother tongue sufficiently to understand and comprehend the Bible.

A Final Question

This leads to the question of how Christianity, with its long literate tradition and its focus on the written Scriptures, can be sustained among a people who have the Bible but do not read it, a people whose thought patterns and behaviors are primarily oral. Since the age of print, private, individual Bible interpretation has been prized in Protestant circles as a highly important (even required) form of Christian practice. This practice has never fit well with Lisu culture. Not only have reading and writing not been fully interiorized, but such a solitary form of worship does not fit well within a communal social structure that eschews (and makes no opportunity for) the personal and the private. As demonstrated above, although the Lisu have long had their own Bible translation and read the Bible during church services (out loud in unison) or Bible school (also out loud in unison), personal Bible study has not gained much traction in Lisu society.

The Fraser Script, arguably a purely Christian form, has done much to sustain Lisu Christianity symbolically, and the Bible translated into the Fraser Script provides the overall frame for Lisu Christian society. However, neither the written script nor the Bible sustain Lisu Christianity in the everyday arena: the practical living out of what it means to be a Lisu Christian. Something is needed to fill in this frame, to sustain Lisu Christian faith. While literacy is useful for liturgical purposes, it is Christian practices—singing, praying, dancing, gathering together, and so on—that sustain Lisu Christianity at the level of the common and everyday.

Voice

A-na (Lushui County)

That was the first time I preached a sermon in Chinese!

I've preached in Lisu before, but never in Chinese. And there were so many people there—classmates, teachers, other people—I was so nervous! I know I was talking way too fast.

This is my second Bible training school. When I was nineteen I spent two years at the Gongshan Bible training center. Now I'm twenty-one, and I'm in the Chinese language class here at the Liuku Bible training center.

I'm from a village in Bingzhongluo, north of Gongshan. My village has four or five hundred people, but only about eighty Christians. That's because Lisu are not the majority in my village. Most of the people are Tibetan. We also have Dulong and Nu, in addition to Lisu.

I come from a Christian family. My parents and my grandparents are all Christians. But when I was in primary school and middle school, I didn't have a chance to go to church very much, only during school holidays when I was at home.

In middle school it was the same. I couldn't attend church very much. But even though I couldn't attend church, I still had faith in my heart, because my parents were careful to teach me. In my class of thirty-eight students in middle school, six of us were Christians.

I attended half a semester of high school, but then dropped out. Most Lisu don't attend high school because we aren't used to studying. But in my

Based on an interview from May 8, 2014.

case, my grandmother was sick, and my younger brother—he's two years younger than me—needed to study. So I dropped out and helped out at home.

My younger brother is now also studying in Liuku, not at the Bible training center, but at another institute—he's studying education.

After we graduate next year, I hope to attend seminary, maybe in Kunming. I really want to keep on studying. Or maybe I will look for a husband and get married. I will wait and see what God arranges.

Chapter 3

THE EVANGELIZATION OF THE NUJIANG VALLEY

> Thou didst leave Thy throne and Thy kingly crown,
> When Thou camest to earth for me;
> But in Bethlehem's home was there found no room
> For Thy holy nativity.
> O come to my heart, Lord Jesus,
> There is room in my heart for Thee.
>
> Heaven's arches rang when the angels sang,
> Proclaiming Thy royal degree;
> But of lowly birth didst Thou come to earth,
> And in great humility.
> O come to my heart, Lord Jesus,
> There is room in my heart for Thee.

In 1922 J. O. Fraser went on furlough, never again to return to full-time Lisu work. Thus this chapter shifts focus to the second generation of missionaries to the Lisu, primarily Allyn and Leila Cooke, John and Isobel Kuhn, and the Morse family. This chapter involves a geographic shift as well. While the early work among the Lisu was centered south and west of Fraser's base at Tengyueh, in later years the center shifted to the Nujiang Valley.

Epigraph from "Thou Didst Leave Thy Throne," lyrics by E. S. Elliot, 1864, hymn #19 in the 2013 Yunnan Lisu hymnbook.

The Nujiang is considered the heart of Lisu identity and culture; many of today's Lisu in Thailand, Myanmar, and other parts of Yunnan trace their ancestry back to this very place.

Before Fraser went on furlough, he opened Muchengpo station, the first fixed CIM mission station among the Lisu, in the district south of Tengyueh. Allyn Cooke, now married, and his wife, Leila, were placed in charge. The Cookes both attended the Bible Institute of Los Angeles (later renamed Biola University), and Allyn Cooke graduated in 1918 with a Certificate in Biblical Studies. At the time they attended, the Bible Institute was located at a building on the corner of 6th and Hope in downtown Los Angeles, with two large neon signs proclaiming "Jesus Saves" erected on top. The Bible Institute dean, R. A. Torrey, had opened a church in the Bible Institute's auditorium in 1915 called the Church of the Open Door. The Sunday School of the Church of the Open Door contributed a great deal to Leila Cooke's missionary work with the Lisu, and she wrote to the children regularly.[1]

Just prior to the Cookes' attendance, the Bible Institute published a four-volume set of essays entitled *The Fundamentals: A Testimony to the Truth*. These volumes, "the most recognized defense of conservative Christianity at the time,"[2] staked out the Bible Institute's theological stance: fundamentalism. Their publication marked the beginning of the 1920s anti-modernist evangelical movement, which was characterized by deep commitment to the Gospel message and the inerrancy of Scripture, as well as various forms of defensive isolationism.

The Bible Institute of Los Angeles also subscribed to the more controversial position of dispensationalism, an eschatological view that emphasized the imminent return of Jesus Christ, his subsequent thousand-year reign, and the need to preach the Gospel to all nations before the end would come. These eschatological interpretations made the task of saving souls one of great urgency.[3]

Both Allyn and Leila Cooke displayed such exigency in their letters. They often added "if the Lord tarries" when discussing future plans, and in a conference with other missions about how to divide the work, Allyn stated that his guiding principle was "the time is short and the Lord may come at any minute."[4] In a letter to her parents, Leila Cooke described the Lisu Christians of Kai Ho village: "They can answer questions very well about the doctrine. But oh! How eager they were to learn. They drank in the teaching about the second coming like hungry children. They wanted to know what the passage in Mark meant where it spoke of the false Christs who should arise. They were so interested to hear about the Antichrist and about the Tribulation. They also wanted to know about the Resurrection of the Wicked Dead."[5]

The Cookes spent most of their time at Muchengpo teaching the Lisu Christians. At that time the only books available in the Fraser Script were the Gospel of Mark, a few other Scripture portions, and the catechism. Although they were in residence at Muchengpo, Allyn traveled every Saturday night to a different Lisu village, stayed through Sunday services, and returned on Monday. Both Cookes also went on longer itinerations—a few weeks to a few months—to visit Lisu Christian areas that were further afield. In one of her letters, Leila described one of these visits:

> After the welcome and the meal, they gathered to study. They went through the gospel of Mark asking questions on the parts they did not understand. Of course they could not finish in one evening, but kept at it the three days I was there. And hymns! My! They kept me teaching them hymns until I was so tired I did not know how to keep at it. My throat still hurts. I never saw people have such patience in learning to sing. Many of the hymns they can sing beautifully, but a few they cannot get without much practice and patient teaching. They did not let me stop teaching for even a few minutes.[6]

A few weeks later, Leila described a visit to another village, whose inhabitants impressed her with the vividness of their faith despite few visits from a Western missionary: "Practically all the young people can read and write and sing beautifully. As far as I know there is no one in the village who plants or smokes opium or who drinks."[7] While other positive traits are sometimes mentioned in their letters, such as knowledge of doctrine and church attendance, these two sentences distill the desirable behaviors of Lisu Christians—read, write, and sing—and the undesirable behaviors—drinking or having anything to do with opium.

In addition to informal evening teaching and itinerating, the Cookes wanted to organize short-term Bible schools. Carl and Anna Gowman, who had rejoined the Lisu work after a stint in Sapushan, joined them in this project. Many villages—each with about fifteen or sixteen families—had turned Christian and built a chapel. Whoever was able to read conducted the services, though they had minimal learning and meager training. The missionaries felt that short-term Bible schools would build up the reading and writing skills, as well as the Christian knowledge base, of these Lisu Christians, who could then return home and teach their fellow villagers.

The first two-week Bible school was held at Muchengpo in 1925. On the first day they rang the gong and started with prayer and a hymn. That day they had classes in Bible, writing, and singing. Allyn Cooke also announced a Bible memorization contest on the first day, with a prize of one rupee for the first person able to memorize all forty-seven verses of chapter 15, the crucifixion passage in the Gospel of Mark. The winner was a barefoot Lisu who had never been to school. He was wearing dark blue clothes with white leggings, with a red blanket draped over him for a coat.[8] His name was Fish Four.

Fish Four

Fish Four was a twenty-year-old Christian from a village about two days' journey from Muchengpo. His village had been visited briefly by Fraser during the early days of Fraser's itinerating in the mountains. Later, Lisu evangelists with printed gospel portions and catechisms had visited the village and taught the villagers how to read the Fraser Script. After reading the catechism, Fish Four's family (along with many of the other villagers) took down their spirit shelf and chose to worship the God described in the catechism instead.[9]

During that first Bible school Leila Cooke had played a record on the gramophone that included the hymn "Thou Didst Leave Thy Throne." After a while Fish Four approached her with a paper in his hand. On the paper he had transcribed, after hearing it played just once, the melody to the hymn in number notation.

"Big Sister," Fish Four said, "would you mind translating this song into Lisu?"

Together, Leila Cooke and Fish Four translated the hymn.[10] That was the first of many hymns translated together by the Cookes and Fish Four, most of which are still found in the Lisu hymnbook. This collaboration between Western missionary and local believer lasted until Fish Four checked over the translation of his last Lisu hymn on his deathbed, a collaboration that produced not only the majority of the hymns in the Lisu hymnbook but also an ample portion of the Lisu New Testament.

By 1928 Fish Four was the singing teacher for the short-term Bible schools. Carl Gowman wrote, "He is the best teacher of singing we have in the Lisu work, and conducts beautifully."[11] At a short-term Bible school conducted in March at Half-way Mountain, Fish Four taught singing each

fig. 6 Fish Four and his wife at Muchengpo. With kind permission from Overseas Missionary Fellowship International U.K. Photo courtesy of University of London, SOAS Archives.

day from 11:15 a.m. to 12:15 p.m., and from 6:30–7:30 p.m. During the two weeks of the short-term Bible school, "nearly every hymn of the fifty in their first hymn book was carefully reviewed."[12]

The Cookes and the Gowmans planned the first Lisu Harvest Festival. They suggested that the Lisu bring one-tenth of their crops to the Harvest Festival as their tithe, and that the money be used to support an evangelist.[13] Enough was received to support five full-time evangelists. Carl Gowman, whose natural gifts in organization had been honed during his employment with Henry Ford, suggested that one of the evangelists be designated for full-time support with the Bible translation effort. Fish Four was the natural choice.

Fish Four proved to have a keen mind for linguistics. The missionaries, due to the constant clamoring of the Lisu for teaching,[14] and the complicated and ambiguous nature of the Lisu language,[15] were not making as much progress on Bible translation as they wanted. With the full-time assistance of Fish Four, they soon compiled a Lisu-English dictionary and began work on a book of Old Testament Bible stories. Fish Four had an unsurpassed ability to put a biblical thought into ordinary Lisu phraseology, not too literal yet not too free, keeping the Lisu idiom intact.[16] The book of Old Testament stories was finished just before the Cookes went on furlough in 1927, and they were able to print two thousand copies in the United States.[17] In addition to the stories, the book included around fifty hymns.

Later in his life, Isobel Kuhn wrote, "His breadth of brow betokened the unusual intellect he possessed, but he was so humble and modest, always shirking into the background.... There was an atmosphere of rest about him, the serene peace of a life absolutely abandoned to the Lord and governed by Him. Yet he was a born leader of men. When he conducted the singing in church, there was a grace of movement but a power to inspire that I have seldom seen equaled."[18] Fish Four spent nine years working on the Lisu New Testament, and during that time he also translated many hymns, as well as writing a few of his own.

Bible Schools

At the first Bible school, the Cookes noticed how much the Lisu loved to sing and began to teach them to sing in four-part harmony. Singing and learning new hymns in four-part harmony became a part of every Bible school after that, and they still are today.

Two short-term Bible schools were held in 1925, with students representing eighteen different villages, some as far as eight days' journey away. The first Bible school of 1926 was held in January:

> <u>A Lisu Bible School</u>—just what does that mean? The big brass school gong is ringing now, so come and see. You will find that it is not exactly like the Bible Institute of Los Angeles or the Moody Bible Institute. The roof is made of grass and the walls of woven bamboo. . . . You will have to write on your lap at present for they have not finished the rough board tables which are to be used as desks, but listen! the teacher is explaining the same grand old truths which Dr. Torrey used to unfold to us at dear old B.I., and these brown faced people are listening with the same eagerness which welled up in your heart when you first studied the doctrine of the Holy Spirit.[19]

The short-term Bible schools always had classes in reading and writing. They also included homiletics classes, which were necessary given the goal of sending these students back to their villages to teach what they had learned. Students carried in rice or food for themselves for the duration, or enough money to buy it.

In 1926 Carl Gowman held twelve short-term Bible schools, with a total attendance of 562 men and women. There were also 300 baptisms that year.[20] The missionaries often conducted baptisms in the course of itinerating or at festivals. In order to be baptized, Lisu Christians usually had a waiting period of at least a year after their initial conversion, in which they were to validate their conversion by living an appropriately Christian life. Simply assenting to Christian truths was not enough; evidence of a Christian life in practice was required. Baptism was also a time for the candidates to be trained in scriptural truths and Christian doctrines—a necessary task, for the exam prior to baptism was a difficult one. In a letter describing the baptism of 284 candidates at Keng Ma, Allyn Cooke listed some of the questions:

> Have you any sins?
> Where are your sins now?
> What do you have to do to obtain eternal life?
> Have you obtained eternal life?
> Can you lose it again?
> If you stop smoking opium, drinking wine, immorality, etc., will that save you?
> Is baptism for washing away sins?
> What is necessary for washing away sin?[21]

Examining candidates for baptism was a lengthy and tiring affair. Each candidate was interviewed by a committee of no fewer than four persons, at least one of whom had to be from the candidate's own village. If any member of the committee had reservations, the candidate did not pass. Examinations of baptismal candidates usually extended until past midnight for several evenings.[22]

Reflected in these questions was an underlying theological concern with whether salvation resulted from faith or from works, a concern that persisted among the second generation of Lisu missionaries throughout their years with the Lisu. Although the smoking of opium and the drinking of alcohol were banned behaviors, the missionaries wanted to ensure that the Lisu would not consider abstaining from them equivalent to salvation.

Settling into Christian Community

In 1926, Leila Cooke reported that Muchengpo district had 1338 believers meeting in forty-four chapels, none of which had been built with any foreign assistance. There were 40 village leaders appointed to hold services five times weekly in each of the chapels (though she stopped short of calling them pastors, as most did not have any training). There were also 60 deacons. The Lisu in that district had converted 112 families from the Lahu tribe and 6 from the Liti tribe. Altogether, the church supported 5 full-time evangelists, with each evangelist assigned the task of learning another tribal language.[23] With such substantial numbers, the Lisu field was no longer focused just on initial conversions but on building and shaping a church.

Part of shaping a church was discussing and deciding upon new customs by the Lisu community. At the Christmas festival of 1925, there were many matters under discussion. The Lisu Christians had already done away with the custom of the bride price, but other matters relating to marriage had yet to be worked out. At the Christmas gathering the people decided that the groom's family was responsible for the wedding feast, while the bride's family would provide the trousseau. There was also some discussion about widows and orphans. According to the previous custom, upon remarriage, the children of a widowed mother were sent to live with their paternal grandparents. But at this festival they made a change: the children were permitted to remain with their mother, unless the deceased father's parents had no other sons to support them. "These customs were decided on by the people themselves," Leila Cooke emphasized in a circular letter to her supporters back home.[24]

When reading letters intended for public consumption, such as circulars and articles in *China's Millions*, one gets the feeling that there was a grand strategic plan unfolding, all in a spirit of exceeding missionary joy, as the missionaries worked out in practice the ramifications of helping a newly Christian people build a church. But while the public letters give the appearance of a sureness of step, the private letters contain a different tone, betraying questions and inner turmoil along the way. While J. O. Fraser had articulated an elegant vision for an indigenous Lisu church—self-supporting, self-governing, and self-evangelizing—the missionaries found that working it out on the ground was often confusing and difficult.

Self-support proved an especially beautiful practice in concept but much more difficult to actually enact. "As to the self-support question I agree with you heartily," Leila Cooke wrote to Fraser. "Yet there are one or two things in which I do feel puzzled as to how it will work out." Is it harmful to give a dress to a new baby? Can they give gifts to their language helpers? Should they give medicine, or train the Lisu to expect divine healing?[25]

Another issue was the role of women in mission work. Fraser, deeply affected by the single missionary women of the CIM, had progressive views about women preaching and teaching. However, the question troubled Leila Cooke, who had been raised in a more conservative religious environment in America. In a letter home, Leila wrote in a postscript: "Please Mother tell me what you feel about women teaching men. In Allyn's absence, I have often taught men in the main public service on Sunday, and I am constantly teaching the young men who come to our home. But recently, the Lord I believe has been showing me that I am not keeping my place as a woman."[26] The archives do not detail personal resolution on this issue. However, in later letters she wrote often about her role as a Bible teacher to both men and women without any hint of inner conflict. Later women missionaries, such as Isobel Kuhn, also had ministries that were not confined to the women's sphere but rather were actively engaged in the teaching of the Bible to all Lisu.

In 1933, when Fraser was superintendent and spending some time in residence at Muchengpo, three young Lisu women—Tabitha, Ruth, and Sarah—approached his study to volunteer to serve as evangelists He reported on this development in a letter to Mrs. Howard Taylor:.

> You will be interested to know that for the very first time in the history of this work we are about to send out three *young women* to teach in the villages near here. They are aged 18, 20, and 21. They have themselves volunteered, all together, and seem to be so thoroughly in earnest that Fitz and I and the local deacons have decided to give them a trial. One of them was actually in tears when she pleaded to be allowed to go! . . . They do not know a great deal, but they can all read and write, know their catechism, and can sing about a hundred hymns.[27]

The three women were sent across the Salween into Burma for two months under the guidance of an older evangelist and his wife, and according to Fraser's assessment they performed well, even though two of them were ill for part of the time.[28]

The missionaries also contended with beliefs and practices they found to be in conflict with the Christian doctrines they sought to impart to the young church. Lisu believers held to persistent superstitions, such as maintaining large rocks in their granaries to ensure good crops. There was also some conflict with the neighboring Pentecostal mission, for they had begun emphasizing speaking in tongues, a doctrine that Allyn Cooke felt was harmful.[29] And periodically, they had to contend with a prophet or messianic leader who professed a mixture of Christian doctrines with clearly non-Christian practices, attempting to lead a portion of the flock astray.[30]

Fish Four continued the translation work with the Gowmans while the Cookes were on furlough. Upon their return, the Cookes went to Gospel Mountain, about six days' travel south of Muchengpo. Together with the Gowmans, the Cookes revised the Gospel of Mark and translated the Gospel of Luke. Carl was a gifted linguist, learning Chinese, Hua Miao, Chuan Miao, Eastern Lisu, and Western Lisu. Fraser described him as "the kind of man who wrote down a phrase as soon as he got it."[31] But Carl became suddenly ill and passed away in 1930, eleven or twelve chapters into Matthew. Anna Gowman went on to complete the Gospel of Matthew together with Fish Four, who by now went by the Christian moniker Moses, as the decision had been made to give evangelists Bible names. The Gowmans and the Cookes exchanged and corrected each other's translations.[32]

A persistent stumbling block with the Bible translation was that the Lisu language lacked many essential words that were commonly used in the biblical text. In 1931, Leila Cooke reported that Lisu church leaders had approved the addition of seventy-one words to the Lisu language at recent Bible schools at Muchengpo and at Gospel Mountain. "Among these is the word for 'assurance.' To make the new word they combine the Lisu 'to know,' 'faith,' and 'satisfied.'"[33] With the addition of the new words, the Cookes applied themselves during their time at Gospel Mountain to the translation of the book of Acts. In 1932, together with Fish Four/Moses, they traveled to Chefoo in Shandong Province to bring their younger son Joseph to the CIM school, visit their older son David (whom had not seen in four years), and supervise the printing of the Gospels and Acts.[34]

In describing their pace of life at Gospel Mountain, where they stayed for five years (1928–33), Leila Cooke wrote: "So our days are spent in study and ministering to the people. Our evenings we spend teaching the eager young folks who come to study. They are so anxious to learn that they stay until eleven or twelve o'clock if we let them."[35] Allyn Cooke received this letter from a Lisu Christian while at Gospel Mountain:

January 1, 1931
Gospel Mountain, Big Brother.
    Dear Big Brother, the one whom I can never forget. I love you and I want to shake hands by letter. Big Brother, by God's help, are all well? We are longing to see you, so come, visit us. The hymn which you taught us when you were here, we love so much that when we sing it, the tears come in our eyes. If you cannot come to see us now, come some other time, won't you? By God's grace we are all well. The writer is "Prayer Leader" at Palien.
David[36]

    The affection expressed in this letter illuminates a key difference in the nature of the relationships Christian missionaries were able to forge with the Lisu compared with those of missionaries at work in other parts of China. While in greater China the missionary was viewed as a so-called foreign devil, bringing in alien ideas associated with the great powers that had begun to assume semicolonial status by that point, the Lisu were in an entirely different geopolitical situation.

    For the Lisu, it was not the foreigners they resented but the Chinese. The Lisu were too remote to be personally affected by the Opium Wars, the Boxer Rebellion, or other events of the mid-nineteenth and early twentieth centuries that pitted foreigner against Chinese. The status of the missionaries—who lived among the Lisu—further deepened the bonds. These bonds played a vital role in allowing the Christian message to so penetrate an ethnic group in just fifteen years while missionary work in greater China received no great hearing. Fraser's rigid adherence to the indigenous policy of self-evangelization, self-government, and self-support in the Lisu work was another important factor in the development of the Lisu church.

    By the 1930s, the center of the Lisu work was shifting to the Upper Salween. But the foundation of the practices was laid in the 1920s at Muchengpo, Gospel Mountain, and the surrounding villages.

The Upper Salween

The British explorer Archibald Rose, writing in 1912, stated that the Lisu were "so shut in by their encircling mountains that the Chinese have made little effort to interfere in their affairs, and have left them unmolested in the inhospitable defiles of the Upper Salween."[37] In 1919, Fraser wrote about the Nujiang Valley (called the Upper Salween in missionary narratives): "That district must be evangelized, but I want to find suitable nationals to go first."[38] According to Leila Cooke, in 1923 Fraser sent two Lisu evangelists to the Gongshan region—the uppermost portion of the Nujiang Valley bordering Tibet. One of them stayed for a year and converted around one hundred families. But for years, nothing more was heard from these believers.[39]

In 1927, Carl Gowman wrote to the Lisu church: "We need preachers for the Upper Salween!"[40] In 1929, four Lisu evangelists—Job, Andrew, Wa-si, and La-ma-wu—volunteered. These four evangelists were from the same village that turned Christian following the heartfelt appeal of Allyn Cooke in 1919 described previously in this chapter.[41] Isobel Kuhn wrote, "Job told me, years afterwards, that not one of the four found it easy to say yes. . . . Never had four Lisu evangelists faced such an unknown, distant and bleak parish."[42] Their fears were not unfounded: La-ma-wu died, at the age of twenty-three, of one of the Nujiang Valley's famous fevers. But many families turned Christian as a result of the efforts of the four evangelists—in particular, the evangelist Job.

Job

Job was an unlikely evangelist. He started off in the employ of the Cookes serving as their goatherd, a job he did not perform to distinction.[43] It took him six tries before he was finally able to give up tobacco for good.[44] And unlike most Lisu Christians, Job simply could not carry a tune.[45] He used to say, "I am going to be an evangelist someday," though everyone laughed and told him he was not nearly smart enough to be an evangelist.[46]

But at the first Harvest Festival offering, Job, then known as Fish One, surprised everyone by offering nine rupees, one-third of his annual salary, toward supporting an evangelist.[47] When the appeal came, it was Job who was the first to volunteer for the Upper Salween. He stayed at Luda, the northernmost outpost of CIM work, for years of teaching and evangelizing in the Nujiang Valley. Leila Cooke described him: "Teacher Job had been located in that northern district ever since the beginning of that work up there. His other name is Fish One, the goatherd whom we had met back in Stockade Hill [Muchengpo], the lad who was so stupid that no one thought he could be an evangelist. Sure enough, he had stuck to his determination to be a preacher of the Gospel and had been used to win hundreds of Lisu to the Lord Jesus Christ. He had made his center at the village of Luda, and was one of our best workers."[48]

During his early years as an evangelist, Job's salary was so low he did not consider marrying. But when the church later raised his salary, he thought he might finally be able to support a wife. He was very concerned about making the wrong choice, so he turned the entire matter over to the deacons. The deacons prayed and chose Rhoda, a lovely woman who lived across the river, and who possessed a very loud and beautiful alto voice.[49]

When Job was thirty-two years old and attending Rainy Season Bible School, Isobel Kuhn wrote this about him: "Small, slight[ly] pockmarked, undignified. . . . Perhaps the most insignificant looking member of the class, but as far as we know, the greatest soulwinner Lisu land has yet produced. Job has so few natural gifts, and yet has been so used of God, that to me he is a monument to what God can do with any man who brings Him nothing much more than a heart of purposeful devotion."[50]

Bible Translation

In 1933, the Cookes moved from Gospel Mountain into the Nujiang Valley, initially at Oak Flat (Pade) just north of Liuku. Leila Cooke reported in a letter that they found around one thousand Lisu Christian families when they arrived.[51] The mother churches of Muchengpo and Gospel Mountain continued to send experienced Christians to serve as teachers and evangelists for the new work in the Nujiang Valley.[52]

In 1934 the Cookes moved up to Luda, six days' travel north from Oak Flat (about an hour south of today's Fugong Town), where Job, the incompetent-goatherd-turned-outstanding-evangelist, lived. John and Isobel Kuhn took the Cookes' place at Oak Flat. Describing her new home in Luda, Leila wrote, "In building our home here we feel a bit as though we had stepped off the edge of the map. For the only way to reach this place is to dangle across the Salween river on a rope strung about twenty feet above the water. However, we seem to have plenty to eat and heaps of friends, so I guess it does not matter much even if we are 'off the map.'"[53]

The pattern continued much as before: the Lisu evangelists went out into new areas to evangelize; the missionaries conducted Bible schools, gave counsel to the new church, and worked on the translation of the Bible and the hymns. Ci Lin, a Chinese journalist who spent time in the Nujiang Valley in the 1990s and interviewed the old villagers at Luda, described the

map 3 Mission stations. Map drawn by Mariah Christ.

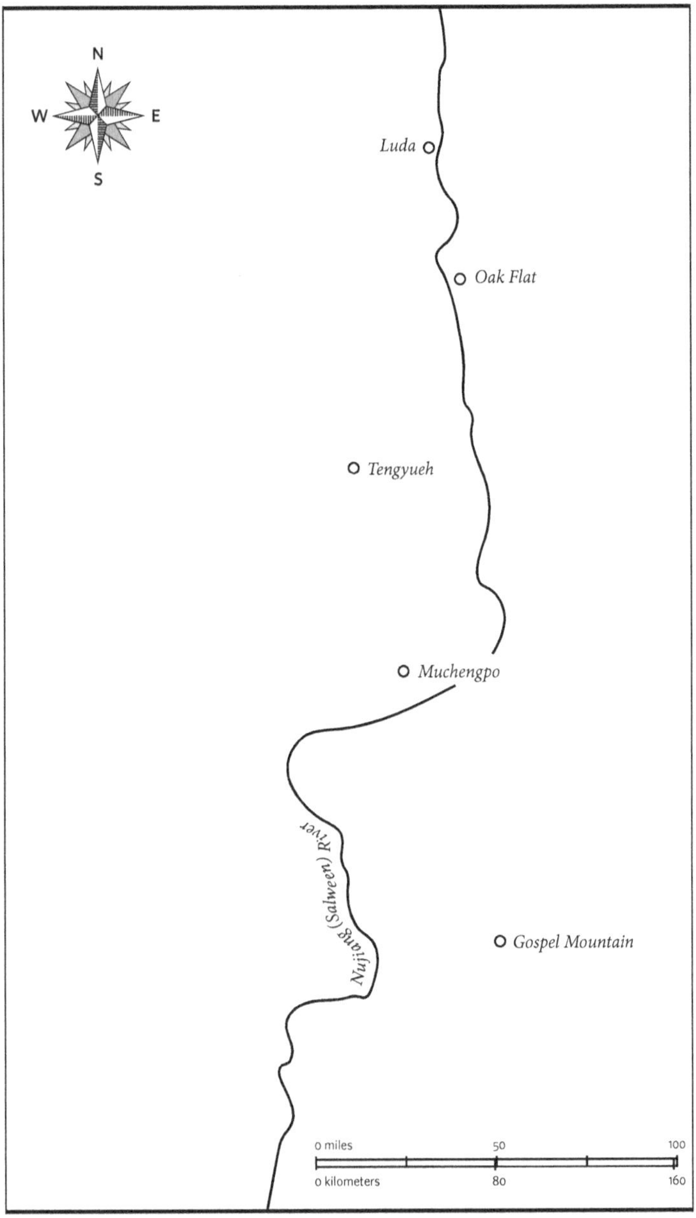

Cookes' life: Their home faced south, the west room was the bedroom, and the middle room doubled as the living room as well as the study. To the east was the kitchen, and outside was the medical dispensary. The spacious living room opened onto a balcony. Opposite the balcony was a large garden surrounded by a bamboo fence. In the garden they grew cabbage, green onion, garlic, spices, spinach, and strawberries. In the corner of the garden was a greenhouse canopy for melons. Because the garden was well cared for and the soil was good, all the vegetables thrived. At that time the Lisu were not used to growing vegetables, and they watched the missionaries' homegrown vegetables flourish. So the Lisu asked them to give them seeds and teach them how to garden. The Cookes generously gave the seeds to everyone, and patiently taught about all kinds of vegetables. Since then, residents of Liwudi [Luda] have known how to grow vegetables.[54]

In the Nujiang Valley the missionaries also had to contend with new and more challenging problems than they had previously seen in Lisu work. They encountered years of conflict with local officials who repeatedly forced the Lisu Christians to tear down the chapels they had built. The officials also collected an opium tax, demanding it even from families who no longer planted opium. In addition, the Lisu were often conscripted as forced labor to build roads. Evangelist Job was put in prison on charges of extortion for collecting the Lisu tithe during the Harvest Festival.[55] Moreover, beginning in 1935, Communist soldiers entered the valley, followed by brigands and looters.[56]

Despite these difficulties, more villages and families continued to turn Christian; Leila Cooke wrote that the church seemed to thrive on persecution.[57] The Lisu evangelists continued in their forward press to spread the Gospel. When the missionaries had moved into the area, there was a cluster of Christian villages surrounding the mission stations of Oak Flat and Luda, but a "heathen patch" stood between them. In her circular of September 29, 1941, Isobel Kuhn told her supporters back home that "your prayers have been pushing back the borders of that unreclaimed land. A contact here, one there; a family believing here, a single believer there—we have reasonable hope now, that in a year's time there will be no 'Heathen Patch.' In other words, although all do not turn, a continual succession of Christian families all the way from here to Luda is fast coming into being."[58]

At Luda, the Cookes continued to work on the translation of the New Testament. Of all the areas of Lisu missionary work since the time of Fraser, Luda—deep in the heart of the Nujiang Valley—was in the narrow belt of land most densely populated with Lisu people. Linguistically, it was close to a pure Lisu environment, unlike the Muchengpo and Gospel Mountain districts in the south, in which the Lisu dialect contained many borrowed Chinese words. According to Shi Fuxiang, who grew up in Luda and knew the Cookes as a young boy, no matter whom they met—young or old, man or woman—they talked with every Lisu they ran into. If they did not understand a word, they would not let it go, asking about it over and over, and then writing it down. Their language was also enriched by the colorful vocabulary of some folk artists.[59]

Fraser, now superintendent of Yunnan Province, came up into the Nujiang himself, spending four months in Luda going over the translation of the New Testament and giving his suggestions for improvements, making it all the way to the book of Hebrews. In 1937 the Cookes moved to Bana, in southern Yunnan Province, to survey this new field and at the same time prepare the Lisu New Testament for printing. Four Nujiang Lisu Christians came along. Luke served as the new translator-helper, replacing Moses, who had passed away. Homay typed the Lisu New Testament, getting as far as the middle of Acts, on a special typewriter that had Lisu characters soldered in. A-chay served as cook so the others could work full-time on translation. Nathaniel helped as well. Paul, a pastor from Gospel Mountain,[60] was able to lend additional linguistic assistance.[61] While Fraser, the Cookes, and the Gowmans have rightly received a great deal of credit for the initial translation of the Lisu New Testament, it was not just a missionary endeavor; it is marked indelibly with the stamp of the Lisu Christians themselves.

While in Bana, the Cookes also translated Handel's *Messiah* into the Lisu language and taught it to Luke, Homay, and A-chay. These Lisu brought the hymn from Bana back to the Nujiang Valley, teaching it to new students at the Rainy Season Bible School.[62] "The Hallelujah Chorus" remains in the hymnbook today.

After nearly a year at Bana, the Cookes left by ship for Shanghai, where they finished typing and proofing the New Testament. They left for furlough, and the New Testaments were printed, bound, and then—along with the hymnbooks—lost in the mail. The hymnbooks finally arrived a year after they had been expected;[63] the New Testaments, not until 1940.[64]

The missionaries who succeeded Fraser in the Lisu work continued to uphold his emphasis on indigenous principles in the Upper Salween. In June 1939 Isobel Kuhn wrote to her supporters about the upcoming Rainy Season Bible School: "Pade-Peter also is trying to find the finances to come for the full time. You understand of course, that *you* may not offer financial help to these boys. The Lisu church is self-supporting, that is its strength and glory."[65] Likewise, Leila Cooke wrote to her supporters about nine new evangelists: "However two or three of them must still pray for their support. (Please do not send money for them, for we could not accept it if you did. The work is entirely self-supporting.)"[66]

Yet this second generation of missionaries was less sanguine about Fraser's encouragement of Christian practices. The faith/works issue caused tension throughout the missionary period, sometimes subtly, but sometimes flashing out into the open—as in the late 1930s, a time when forensic views on justification by faith alone held sway in mainstream Western theological circles.[67] Initially, the issue was the catechism.

The catechism was like many others, laying out the principles of the Christian faith in a question and answer format. However, as the Lisu catechism preceded the translation of Scripture, it was more than just a clear explication of doctrine. It also included some essentials of the biblical narrative, such as creation, the fall, the flood, and the early life and ministry of Jesus. Perhaps more controversially, it went beyond Scripture and doctrine to lay out an appropriate Lisu Christian life, forbidding opium planting and wine drinking, exhorting Christians to study their Lisu books, and advocating gratitude both to God and to the missionaries. In addition to such categories as "Jesus, Birth and Early Life at Nazareth," "The Crucifixion," and "Second Coming of Christ" were other categories such as "Prayer, misc. instructions concerning," "Cleanliness," and "Labor and Trading."[68] In this way, the catechism contained elements of "civilizing mission," or the attempt to spread the ideals of "civilization" or "modernity" along with the Christian message.[69]

Talmadge Payne, an early but brief CIM missionary in the Nujiang Valley, had complained about the catechism, which played a prominent role in Lisu work until the full translation of the New Testament was available. Payne believed the catechism gave an impression of legalism.[70] Another missionary, Charlie Peterson, felt the same. In *China's Millions*, Peterson wrote, "In the very beginning of the Lisu work a splendid catechism was prepared, giving not only doctrinal instructions but also helpful suggestions for 'walking in God's way.' The church leaders took these suggestions and converted them into laws which control and bind at every turn of the Christian life.... Perhaps because of the simplicity of our Lisu people such rules are necessary, but I fear unless we pray constantly that a humble heart be given to our leaders, Pharisaism will manifest itself in our midst."[71]

In 1937, everything came to a head. With the Cookes down south at Bana and the Kuhns on a year of furlough, a new missionary was brought

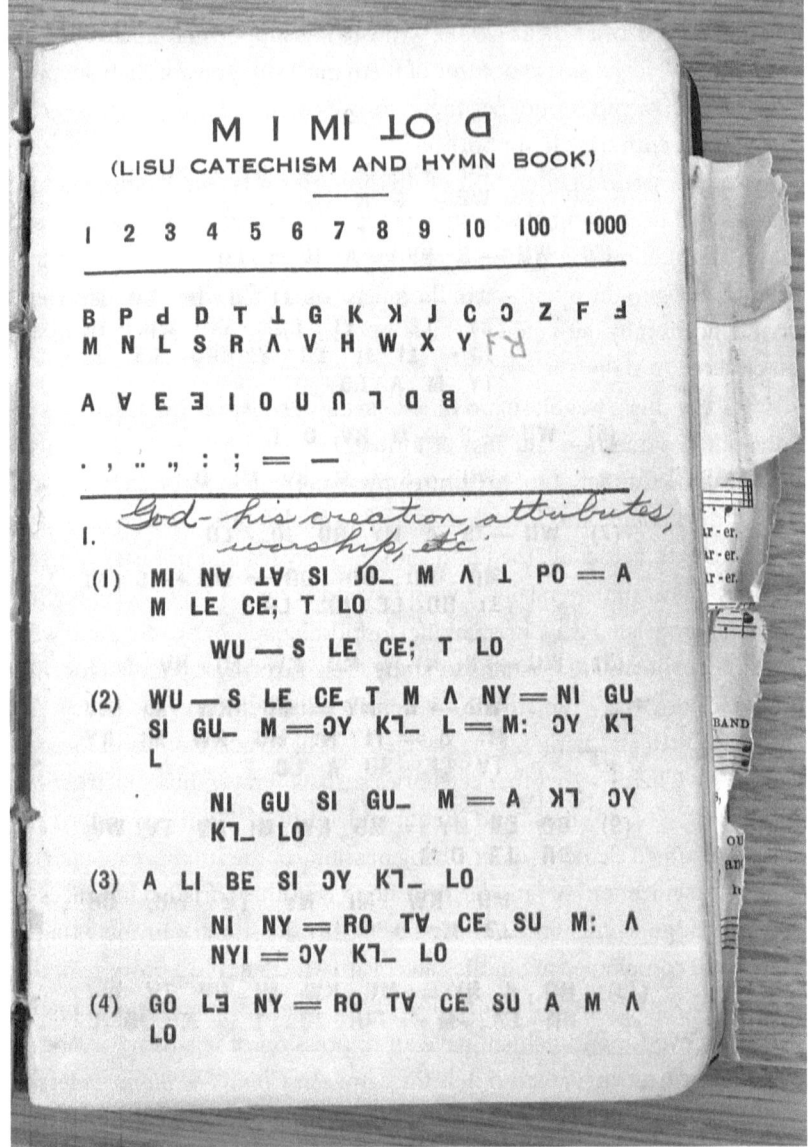

fig. 7 First page of Carl Gowman's Lisu catechism and hymnal (likely circa 1920s). Photo courtesy of the Billy Graham Center Archives, Wheaton College, Illinois. With kind permission from International Ministries, also known as the American Baptist Foreign Mission Society.

to Oak Flat to serve in the Nujiang Valley without the usual guidance of senior missionaries. This new missionary, called Brother Two by the Lisu, was full of zeal, seemingly immune to the hardships of the mountains, and a quick study of the Lisu language. However, he quickly began to object to how the Lisu church conducted its affairs. It started, as usual, with discomfort about the catechism. Isobel Kuhn wrote,

> Mr Fraser had given them a catechism, which long experience with various tribal attempts at catechisms had made us value because its simplicity makes it easy for the beginner to master, and thus encourages him to further study. But Brother Two felt that the catechism, with its simple question and direct answer, had a tendency to produce a "do-this-and-thou-shalt-be-saved" effect for the Lisu mind. In other words he feared legalism for the Lisu church. He was much strengthened in these misgivings to hear that Mr Payne had feared the very same thing.[72]

Brother Two decided to actively combat perceived legalistic tendencies in the church. He started with church discipline. While this had always, because of indigenous principles, been a matter upon which the missionaries did not tread, allowing the local church leaders complete sway, Brother Two began to insist that the church's methods were overly strenuous. He felt it should be easier for a backslider to reenter into church fellowship.

It had long been a Lisu church imperative to keep a great distance from anything related to opium. The Lisu church had faced many difficult trials as a result of spurning opium. It suffered retribution from feudal overlords who could no longer collect an opium tax. Given this context, the Lisu were shocked when Brother Two began to dispense opium as medicine. Further, he challenged the Lisu church leaders on this topic, telling them that there was nothing in the New Testament (which they did not yet possess, as only portions were translated) that forbade smoking, drinking, or using opium. The result was a church schism, with some following Brother Two and the others staying with their local leaders, most notable among them Me-do-me-pa of Oak Flat.

Me-do-me-pa finally wrote to J. O. Fraser, asking him if they had been wrong in how they managed church affairs. Mail into the Nujiang Valley was never quick to arrive, and it took three months for Fraser's reply. Fraser wrote to the Lisu church at Oak Flat: "You have not been wrong in your stand."[73] Fraser arranged to meet with Brother Two in Paoshan at the end of 1937. While Brother Two did not entirely change his views, the meeting did result in reconciliation. Brother Two wrote a letter of apology to the Oak Flat church. He was sent to a different part of China for continued service with the CIM.

Though the immediate crisis passed, the missionaries remained concerned about legalism in the Lisu church, a topic to which they repeatedly returned in their letters. Isobel Kuhn mentioned in a circular letter in 1941, "John Kuhn has been working on a revision of the Catechism, removing legal tendencies and introducing more grace doctrine."[74]

The missionaries had more on their minds than just the faith/works controversy. They were also concerned about "backsliding" and immorality among the Christians. In one particularly frank account, Leila wrote, "And I am sorry to say that the church here is constantly needing discipline; so much so that we hesitate to tell how many Christians there are until they are all safe in heaven. Some of them respond to exhortation. The other day the young folks brought in six Lisu Jews' harps for us to burn. They wanted us to know they were sorry for indulging in their old heathen practices. Others are strong and true, and bring great joy to our hearts."[75]

Finally, the Nujiang Lisu Christians still held fast to their superstitions, such as not serving soup on New Year's Day for fear of making the entire year rainy, or choosing a grave site near an intersection so that those who accidentally walked on it would take the bad luck away from the family.[76] Christianity seemed just a superficial veneer; the missionaries wanted to deepen the knowledge and faith of the Lisu. One of the ways they accomplished this was the Rainy Season Bible School.

Rainy Season Bible School

Rainy Season Bible School began in 1938, largely the idea and subsequent work of John and Isobel Kuhn. The short-term Bible schools provided general teaching and literacy for all Christians so they could understand to what it was that they had changed their allegiance. The Rainy Season Bible School, on the other hand, gave in-depth training for leaders and evangelists in Scripture and doctrine.

Unlike the short-term Bible schools, which were never more than a few weeks in length, the Rainy Season Bible School lasted for the three summer months. The rainy summer months were too dangerous for the missionaries or the Lisu evangelists to travel, and the villagers were too engaged in farmwork to be available for teaching. Thus, it made sense for the missionaries and evangelists to take some time together, with the former teaching the latter. Such practical considerations, however, were not the only motivation for the establishment of the school. According to Isobel Kuhn, "We found the [Lisu] church much confused over the doctrine of Law and Grace and we felt that a longer period of Bible study with church leaders was needed."[77]

For the 1939 Rainy Season Bible School in Oak Flat, the Lisu built a school building out of bamboo. Isobel Kuhn wrote to her supporters describing a number of classes in the Old Testament (despite the fact that it had yet to be translated), to include "the Exodus, Wanderings, Tabernacle, and Conquest of Canaan," as well as classes on the books of Romans, James, Colossians, and Revelation.[78] The 1939 class had twenty-nine students, eleven of whom had been designated as evangelists; the 1940 class had twenty-two students. Most of these students had never attended school before, other than the more informal short-term Bible schools. As Rainy Season Bible School took place during the busy rainy season, and the students were primarily evangelists and not laity, the number of students was fewer than for the short-term Bible schools. The extended time frame and smaller class size allowed for a deeper level of Bible teaching. On the weekends, the students would walk to nearby villages to evangelize or help with church services, as Isobel Kuhn described: "Each weekend the student body scatters (girls included), going into the villages on this side of the river. Some of our boys must walk over twenty-five miles, take three services, walk back the same distance, and do it all between Saturday morning and Monday at 9:00 a.m., when classes start. Our hearts have been touched by the weary but happy faces that run in to shake hands early Monday morning, having just completed such a journey. Every week but one they have had to do it *in the rain*."[79]

In a circular letter, Isobel Kuhn laid out the following schedule for the Rainy Season Bible School in 1941, which had thirty-six students:

> 6 a.m.—The "rising gong."
> 7 a.m.—Gong to call for morning prayers. Another missionary, Charlie Peterson, led short devotionals on First John. This was followed by breakfast of boiled corn.
> 9 a.m.—Gong to announce the start of classes. The three morning classes were the Gospel of Luke (taught by Isobel Kuhn), writing class, and finally a class on the book of Romans (taught by Charlie Peterson).

> After lunch John Kuhn taught a class on doctrine for the older students, which was followed by a class in part-singing led by the Lisu teacher Luke. Finally, a homiletics class (taught by Charlie Peterson), and an English class for older students (taught by Isobel Kuhn).
> 4:15 p.m.—The gong sounds again, and everyone rushes outside to play volleyball.
> 6 p.m.—The whistle sounds for dinner.
> 7 p.m.—Gong sounds for evening worship. First was a half-hour of singing, practicing newly translated hymns. This was followed by a message from one of the missionaries. It was usually growing dark by this time, so the evening service was conducted by the light of pine chips.[80]

In February 1942 Isobel Kuhn started the first Bible School for Girls in the Nujiang Valley. They met in February, as most girls had a break from their family duties right after the lunar New Year.[81] In 1943, despite political instability and looming war, thirty-seven girls attended. In addition to Bible classes, there were also classes in hygiene, obstetrics, "mothercraft," and knitting.[82] And just like students at the Rainy Season Bible School, the girls scattered out on Friday evenings with their weekend preaching assignments.[83]

The Morse Family in Gongshan

The long, thin strip of the Nujiang Valley was divided into three mission districts that roughly correspond with its three counties (see map 4). Today's Lushui County, at the southern end of the valley, was assigned to the China Inland Mission. In the middle, Fugong County was assigned to a Pentecostal mission under the leadership of a certain Mr. Morrison. Very little is known of this mission. Isobel Kuhn mentioned that Mr. Morrison received his Lisu New Testaments before the CIM, and they were able to help each other by exchanging New Testaments for hymnbooks.[84] There was also a Lisu revolt in Fugong County, during which two single women missionaries assigned to the Pentecostal mission fled to CIM's Luda station.[85] By these accounts, it can be inferred that the relationship between the CIM and the Pentecostal mission was a friendly one, and that common Christian literature was used in both areas.

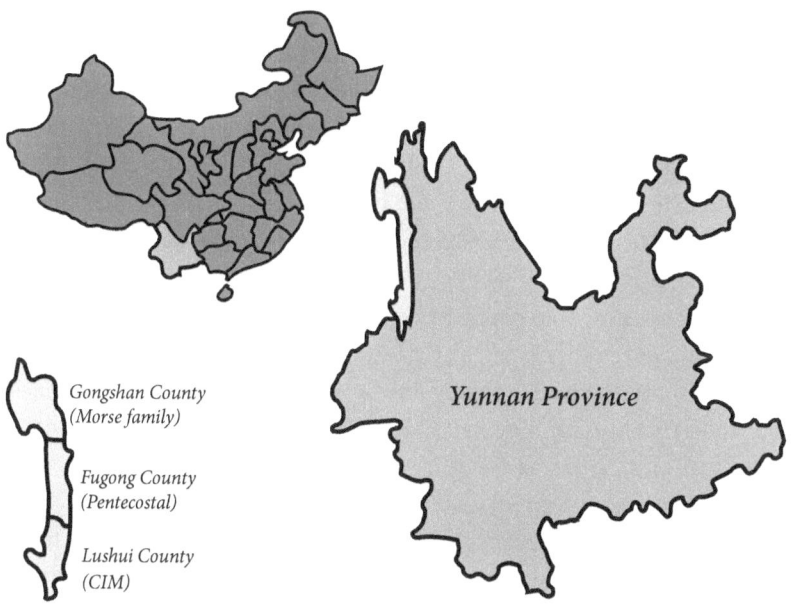

map 4 Location of the Nujiang Valley. Map drawn by Mariah Christ.

Gongshan County, the northernmost county just below Tibet, was assigned to the Morse family—J. Russell and Gertrude Morse, along with their sons Eugene, Robert, and LaVerne. The Morses had started out their missionary career on the borders of Tibet with the United Christian Missionary Society, but by the time they began to work in Gongshan County, they had resigned from their mission and had been working independently for some time. Their work with the Lisu began not in the Nujiang Valley but in the parallel Mekong Valley, where they had moved from Tibet in 1930. Gertrude Morse, who chronicled many of her family's experiences in the book *The Dogs May Bark but the Caravan Moves On*, wrote: "We were surprised and also encouraged when one day, not long after we started our mission work, a Christian Lisu man came from one of the villages near Wei Hsi [Weixi] saying, 'The Lord told me you need me and for me to come and help you preach to the Lisu.' His name was Swa-mi-pa, and he had been a Christian for several years."[86]

By April 1931, Gertrude Morse could report that after six months of work with the Lisu in the Mekong Valley, they had sixty-four new baptized believers and were building a chapel.[87] In December 1932, they held their first Bible school. In 1933 Russell Morse began making evangelistic trips—accompanied by Lisu Christians—over the mountains to the Lisu in the Nujiang Valley. The mountain pass crosses from Weixi in the Mekong Valley and enters the Nujiang Valley in Gongshan County. Russell Morse returned with an enthusiastic report. "Russell said he had never seen people more heart-hungry and earnestly seeking the truth. Fifty-five new converts were baptized on the west side of the river one Sunday and seventy-four more were baptized on the east side the following Sunday. With the thirty-seven baptized earlier in the year that made a total of one hundred and sixty-six. These believers were in two distinct but cooperative congregations."[88]

Another evangelistic trip was made in October 1933. Though their fields were far apart, the Morse family had contact with the CIM missionaries in Lushui County and they shared Lisu Christian literature. David Morse, grandson of Russell and Gertrude, stated that his grandfather and J. O. Fraser were acquainted and that there were "no conflicts" between the two missions regarding the evangelization of the Lisu.[89] Gertrude Morse makes several references to catechisms, hymnbooks, handshaking, Bible schools, singing, Lisu evangelists, and Christmas festivals—all of which were characteristic of the Lisu work under the CIM—indicating a great amount of cooperation between the two missions. Mentioning indigenous principles, Gertrude wrote, "From the time we first starting working among the Lisu, it was our practice to establish self-supporting churches. . . . Church buildings were built and financed by the local Christians."[90] According to Eugene Morse, "We were all on good terms. We used literature and such that they had prepared and then we expanded on that and so we, as far as the literature, Bible and primers and all that sort of thing, well we got it from them."[91]

The Morse family continued to work with the Lisu in the Mekong Valley throughout the remainder of the 1930s, while making several itinerations per year to the Lisu of the Nujiang Valley. In 1937, according to Eugene Morse, "things really began to take off." He continued:

> And my goodness, there were so many answers to prayer for healing and casting out demons and all the signs and wonders. I mean, if the apostle Paul did all his works in thirty years, we had ninety years, we probably had three times as much as were recorded in the book of Acts. It was really an all out manifestation of God's presence in our midst. At one of the conventions, why, people were confessing their sins. Out of four hundred people there at Christmastime over 350 people were crying and confessing their sins and angelic

singing heard overhead and people stopping and listening to angelic singing. And they'd all rush and confessing of sins and it went on for five hours at Christmastime. So I mean it was really an all out moving of God in that area for the equal with Pentecost and Acts there. And then from there of course the work just, at that time there were about 2000 Christians. From there the work just exploded all across the whole country.[92]

Evangelism proceeded at a great pace, using, according to Eugene, the "each one teach one" method. At the Christmas festival of 1939, Eugene, barely nineteen years old, preached his first sermon in Lisu.[93]

On October 3, 1940, the Morses' house in the Mekong Valley was washed out by flood, and they made the decision to relocate to the Salween side.[94] According to Gertrude, "As we were moving into that new home we began to understand God's wisdom in allowing our home in Tobalo to be destroyed. Had it been saved, we would no doubt have remained in the Mekong Valley instead of moving over the pass to be nearer to those thousands of people who were so eager to study the Bible."[95] The Morse family immediately began conducting short-term Bible schools around Gongshan. In 1941, Russell sent fourteen Gongshan Lisu Christians to the Rainy Season Bible School held by the CIM missionaries in Luda.[96]

Throughout the 1940s, the Morse family set about their primary work of holding short-term Bible schools and attending the Easter, Harvest, and Christmas festivals. According to Eugene Morse, about half their time was spent conducting Bible schools. They went through the whole Bible, also covering its history, background, and doctrines. Music was also taught. These Bible schools were used "to really establish them in the faith."[97] Gertrude Morse explained the importance of Bible schools this way: "People with centuries of heathen background cannot hear the Gospel just once and instantly accept the Lord. They must be taught constantly, with much love, patience, and wisdom. Bible schools must be held frequently in order to train leaders and teachers for the new churches."[98]

In 1942 the Morses began hearing from Lisu Christians in the Irrawaddy Valley in Burma. Members of the family began itinerating over the Gaoligong Mountains from their home base in Nujiang into Burma, just as they had done earlier from the Mekong Valley into the Nujiang Valley. Lisu evangelists from Gongshan went across the passes, establishing many Lisu churches in northern Burma. These churches later became the receiving point for Nujiang Lisu fleeing into Burma in the 1950s.

In 1947, while the entire Morse clan was in the United States on furlough, the two older sons, Eugene and Robert, spent several months in Los Angeles with Allyn Cooke, working on the printing of a new edition of the Lisu hymnbook, which contained over three hundred hymns.[99] The nature of the Fraser Script required Eugene and Robert to spend hours manually turning the letters that needed to be upside-down or backward. According to Eugene Morse, "We just literally transformed the whole thing from sort of a cheapie cheapie tryout thing into a real proper hymnbook."[100] Gertrude said, "On our evangelistic tours we were often told of people who became interested in Christianity through hearing and learning to sing the wonderful messages. The demand for hymnals was always greater than the supply."[101]

War, Death, and Departure

The Japanese had invaded China already in 1937, but the war was in the east, far from Yunnan in China's southwest. But when Burma fell, the Japanese were able to penetrate Yunnan Province from Burma. By 1942, there were rumors that the Japanese were crossing the Nujiang River. The construction of the Burma Road greatly shortened travel times; at the same time, military traffic made travel more congested and difficult. American pilots flew over the Nujiang as part of the "Hump" route from India to China. Eugene and Robert Morse helped the war effort by aiding in the search and rescue effort for American pilots whose planes went down over the Nujiang Valley.[102]

On May 7, 1943, Leila Cooke passed away in Luda.[103] Allyn Cooke, the Kuhns, and the other missionaries in the Nujiang carried on with Rainy Season Bible Schools and translating the Old Testament, but supplies were difficult to come by, and there was no possibility of reprinting New Testaments, hymnbooks, or catechisms, all of which were in short supply. The missionaries continued to conduct Rainy Season Bible Schools through 1948. By 1949, many were being forced to leave China. In 1950, the last missionaries to the Lisu—John Kuhn and Charlie Peterson—departed.[104]

The Morse family came back to China after furlough in 1948, but they were never able to continue their work in the Nujiang Valley. Eugene and his new bride, Helen, reached Lijiang in 1949 but were turned back to Kunming. They sent word to Robert, who escaped over the passes into Burma. Gertrude left for Hong Kong, and shortly thereafter Russell was put in prison, where he remained for the next year and a half. By the time they left, Eugene Morse estimated that there were about ten thousand Lisu Christians in the areas in which they had worked in the Mekong and Salween Valleys.[105]

In 1950 the Morse family regrouped among the Lisu congregations in north Burma, continuing work among the Lisu Christians. In July 1972, they were forced to leave by the Burmese government. After a brief time in the United States, six family members went ahead to northern Thailand to begin reaching out to the Lisu in that region. The rest of the family joined the work in July 1973. Several members of the Morse family remain in northern Thailand, continuing their work with the Lisu church.[106]

Conclusion

If the 1910s were the great period of evangelization of the Lisu, the 1920s were a time of working out on the ground the shape of the Lisu Christian church. During that decade, the nascent Lisu church, together with the missionaries, discussed and decided upon new customs. Many of the Christian practices still seen in today's Lisu church were first begun in the 1920s: singing in four-part harmony, participating in Christian festivals, attending church services five times per week, keeping the Sabbath, sending out evangelists, giving up smoking and drinking, and so on.

The 1930s saw major shifts in the Lisu work. From short-term Bible schools designed to teach the basic fundamentals of Christian faith, the work shifted to Rainy Season Bible Schools, providing in-depth training to Lisu Christian leaders. From Gospel portions and Old Testament stories, the work progressed to the translation of the complete Lisu New Testament. This caused the center of the work to shift as well. From the mother church at Muchengpo, the center of Lisu Christianity moved to the steep walls and inhospitable terrain of the Nujiang Valley.

But in addition, the 1930s were the decade where the gap between the Western missionaries and the Lisu Christians began to show itself. While the Lisu desired to change some behaviors and add others to reflect their new Christian convictions, the missionaries were apt to view these as evidence of a legalistic and empty faith. While the missionaries were concerned with defending doctrinal purity, the Lisu were focused on constructing a Christian identity. This faith/works issue remained an area of tension for the remainder of the missionary era, when the missionaries were forced out at the end of the 1940s.

I would be remiss, however, if I gave the impression that the primary mission legacy was one of theological tension between Western missionary and local believer. When I was reading in the archives, the tension was palpable. But when I was immersed in ethnographic fieldwork around fires in Lisu homes, the tension was nonexistent, long extinguished by the departure of the missionaries, the trying decades of post-1949 Chinese history, and the rebuilding of Lisu Christianity at the behest and initiative of the Lisu. For the Lisu I met in the Nujiang Valley, the mission legacy is the Fraser Script, the hymnbook, the moral requirements to not drink or smoke, the translation of the Bible, the Bible schools, and a religious faith that has buttressed the togetherness that has long been at the center of their culture.

Voice

Yu Ping An (Gongshan County)

My name is Yu Ping An, and I am an engineer. I am forty-five years old, and became a Christian eight years ago.

I was not raised in a Christian family. In fact, my parents are still not Christians. Once I became a Christian, I began sharing the good news with my family. My wife became a Christian one year after me, and now my mother-in-law is a Christian as well. Also, my older sister became a Christian after I told her the good news.

My wife and I have two daughters, one lives in Kunming, and the other in Shanghai. They are both university graduates. They don't know Lisu very well. My wife and I speak Lisu with each other, but our daughters speak Chinese with us. They can understand Lisu and speak it, though not perfectly. And they cannot read or write it.

As for me, my first six years of education were in my home village. We learned Chinese in school and spoke Lisu at recess. But in middle school that all changed, and we just spoke Chinese.

There is a big gap between the government school's education, and the education in the home (*jiali jiaoyu*). Often, the school education affects the thinking of the students, and they are not interested in Christianity. In fact, this has happened with my own daughters. I talk to them and tell them: You are in Shanghai, there are so many churches! She tells me she will go to

Based on an interview from August 16, 2013.

church, but then does not. So I can only pray. This is a big problem facing our church.

The church up here in Gongshan is different from the Lisu church in Fugong. In Fugong, because Lisu are the only minority, the church is entirely Lisu. Here in Gongshan, we have a different policy. We are the primary minority, but not the only one. In addition to Lisu, there are Dulong, Tibetan, Nu, and Han. All of these are members of our church, except for the Han. So our Gongshan church encourages its members to read, write, and speak Chinese as well as Lisu. This is important if we are to propagate (*chuan*) the faith. Also, there are many Christian books published in Chinese, many more than in Lisu. This is a good policy of our Gongshan church.

Also, while everyone in Fugong is considered Christian, in Gongshan, because of the many different minorities, there are four religions: Protestantism, Catholicism, Buddhism, and Islam. This has made us take our own religion less for granted.

In Fugong, many of the Christians don't drink and don't smoke, and think they are now Christians. But they don't have belief. This is a problem. Actually, these two things—no drinking and no smoking—has been the great fortune (*fufen*) of our Lisu people. It has strengthened our health. It has strengthened us as a people.

Chapter 4

FIXING THE BOUNDARIES

> Holy, holy, holy! Lord God Almighty!
> Early in the morning our song shall rise to Thee;
> Holy, holy, holy, merciful and mighty!
> God in three persons, blessed Trinity!

In an effort to understand the role of practices in Lisu Christianity in a general sense, this chapter will dig into one particular practice—abstinence from smoking and drinking—and examine it from multiple angles. Theologically, I explore this practice though the biblical categories of purity and pollution. Anthropologically, I attempt to tease out the meaning of this practice in light of the specific context of the Lisu people. Historically, I look at the development of the practice, specifically the interplay between the missionaries and the Lisu Christians, and how the practice then evolved in both form and meaning.

In the frontier towns of the Nujiang Valley, almost everyone knows the reputation of Lisu Christians for not drinking and not smoking. In many Protestant circles, authentic spirituality has long been thought to reside primarily in the realms of the personal and the private, leading to the belief that such external marks are signs of a legalistic and empty Christianity.

Epigraph from "Holy, Holy, Holy, Lord God Almighty," lyrics by Reginald Heber, 1826, hymn #83 in the 2013 Yunnan Lisu hymnbook.

Yet the Lisu Christian practice of abstention from smoking and drinking can best be understood through theological categories that, though present in the Old Testament as well as the New Testament church, have been all but discarded by Western Protestantism: purity and pollution.

Purity and pollution reflect ways of ordering the world. This is the thesis of Mary Douglas, whose classic study *Purity and Danger: An Analysis of the Concepts of Pollution and Taboo* examines some traditional societies, such as the Lele of Douglas's anthropological fieldwork, in light of the purity regulations in the Old Testament book of Leviticus. Douglas takes dirt as her starting point: "Dirt is essentially disorder. There is no such thing as absolute dirt: it exists in the eye of the beholder. If we shun dirt, it is not because of craven fear, still less dread or holy terror. Nor do our ideas about disease account for the range of our behaviour in cleaning or avoiding dirt. Dirt offends against order. Eliminating it is not a negative movement, but a positive effort to organise the environment."[1]

The Western missionaries' concern about the meaning of Lisu practices points to a problem with the categories they used to understand them: they substituted a category with which their own religious tradition was preoccupied (legalism) for a more appropriate category for describing the practices they observed (purity and pollution). This prevented them from discerning that the apparent Lisu fixation with not smoking and not drinking reflects a much wider and more profound concern: a deep-seated need, as both a religious and an ethnic minority, to consolidate their members into a coherent group, to constructively organize their milieu and make it "conform to an idea."[2] Moreover, as with most Lisu Christian practices, it reflects a spiritual need to manifest externally a deeply meaningful internal faith. How eliminating dirt, filth, and pollution helps the Lisu Christians meet these needs is the subject of this chapter. But the Lisu are not alone in their stress on purity and pollution. Societies, in particular ethnic enclaves, have stressed purity and pollution since biblical times.

Biblical Concepts of Purity

The Old Testament book of Leviticus is filled with dietary laws that reminded the Israelites every day that they were separate. Leviticus contains regulations about which animals are clean and which are unclean. It prescribes rituals to restore cleanliness after childbirth, disease, or various excretions. It mandates proper rules for conduct on the Sabbath. It requires circumcision.

It also proscribes ethical violations, such as sexual immorality, stealing, hatred, and revenge. The purpose of the purity laws is to mark the boundaries of God's chosen people: "You are to be holy to me because I, the Lord, am holy, and I have set you apart from the nations to be my own" (Lev. 20:26).

These various purity laws not only reminded the Israelites that they were separate; they also declared this distinctiveness to those all around. According to E. P. Sanders, "There is, however, something which is common to circumcision, Sabbath, and food laws, and which sets them off from other laws: they created a social distinction between Jews and other races in the Greco-Roman world. Further, they were the aspects of Judaism which drew criticism and ridicule from pagan authors. Jewish monotheism also set Jews apart from Gentiles, but it seems not to have drawn the ridicule of pagans in the way that Sabbath, food laws, and circumcision did."[3] Purity and pollution regulations are external. Because of this externality, social distinctions could be made (and ridicule endured). Internal marks—such as belief—have no such ability.

The Jews felt that their way of life was threatened during the Babylonian exile and adopted an even more stringent reliance upon purity and pollution regulations. There arose a class of ordinances derived not from Scripture but from sayings of scribes and rabbis that were either positive or negative in character. These ordinances were designed to prevent any breach of the Mosaic Law or Jewish customs and thus to serve as a "hedge around the Law."[4] To be a Jew was to observe the law.

During the intertestamental period, Antiochus IV (ca. 215–164 B.C.) attempted to wipe out the Jews, not by means of physical destruction but by attacking their very symbols: the purity and pollution laws. The Book of Second Maccabees recalls the heroic death of seven brothers and their mother who died rather than ingest a mouthful of pork.

The purity laws had come to symbolize the Jewish nation itself and were considered worthy of political and military defense. According to N. T. Wright, "Purity (in its very different manifestations such as food laws, handwashing, and so on) was not, in this period, an end in itself, if indeed it was ever really that. It was the symbol, all the more important for a people who perceived themselves under threat, of national identity and national liberation."[5]

It is upon these symbols of the Pharisees that Jesus continually tramples.[6] But although he heals on the Sabbath (Matt. 12:9–14), he touches those with leprosy (Mark 1:41–42), and his disciples do not ritually wash before eating (Mark 7:1–5), it is the specific purity map of the Pharisees that Jesus abrogates, not the idea of using purity and pollution to structure the world.[7] Jesus does not discard the concept of defilement. Rather, he redefines it:

> "Are you so dull?" he [Jesus] asked. "Don't you see that nothing that enters a person from the outside can defile them? For it doesn't go into their heart but into their stomach, and then out of the body." (In saying this, Jesus declared all foods clean.)
>
> He went on: "What comes out of a person is what defiles them. For it is from within, out of a person's heart, that evil thoughts come—sexual immorality, theft, murder, adultery, greed, malice, deceit, lewdness, envy, slander, arrogance and folly. All these evils come from inside and defile a person." (Mark 7:18–23)

Jesus redefines purity and pollution in terms of the internal, rather than the external. Yet the language and concept of purity, he retains.

Given the Jewish system and its preoccupation with purity, the teachings of Jesus that redefine purity, and the momentous consequences of Christ's death on the cross and resurrection and his mandate to make disciples of all nations, it is not surprising that purity concerns are among the first that the New Testament church has to contend with. In Acts 10, Peter falls into a trance and has a vision of a large sheet containing all kinds of animals, reptiles, and birds being let down to earth, as well as an admonishment to kill and eat them. When Peter refuses on account of ritual purity, a voice speaks to him, saying, "Do not call anything impure that God has made clean" (Acts 10:15). Directly thereafter, Peter is led to the home of Cornelius, a Roman centurion and Gentile. To the large gathering of people outside, Peter declares, "You are well aware that it is against our law for a Jew to associate with or visit a Gentile. But God has shown me that I should not call anyone impure or unclean" (Acts 10:28). Peter is announcing a new purity/pollution schema, one necessary for the redefinition of the Kingdom of God. In the announcement, both the language and concept of purity are retained as valid.

The New Testament church continued to reevaluate purity regulations in light of their previous experience with Judaism, as well as Jesus's teachings on purity and mandate to "make disciples of all nations" (Matt. 28:19). A second issue related to purity soon arose: the question of circumcision. Certain people were teaching that believers must be circumcised or they could not be saved. Paul and Barnabas were appointed to go to Jerusalem and meet with the apostles and elders about the question. At the ensuing council, as reported in Acts 15, Peter declares, "[God] did not discriminate between us and them [i.e., Jews and Gentiles], for he purified their hearts by faith. Now then, why do you try to test God by putting on the necks of Gentiles a yoke that neither we nor our ancestors have been able to bear? No! We believe it is through the grace of our Lord Jesus that we are saved, just as they are" (15:9–11).

No longer is purity tied to the Law of Moses and its circumcision regulations and dietary laws. Rather, purity is achieved through faith. Paul later reiterates to the Galatians, "For in Christ Jesus neither circumcision nor uncircumcision has any value. The only thing that counts is faith expressing itself through love" (5:6).

Still, a few requirements are retained: "You are to abstain from food sacrificed to idols, from blood, from the meat of strangled animals and from sexual immorality. You will do well to avoid these things" (Acts 15:29). In further letters to the new churches, Paul urges refraining from drunkenness and debauchery (Rom. 13:13), grumbling or arguing (Phil. 2:14), greed or sexual immorality (Eph. 5:3). Rather, believers are exhorted to give thanks in everything (Eph. 5:20) and above all, to love (1 Cor. 13).

In essence, the ethical core of the Old Testament Levitical laws is retained, forming the basis for the new purity/pollution system of the New Testament church.[8] Moreover, Paul specifically links purity/pollution language with a proper Christian pursuit of holiness. To the Corinthians, Paul states, "Therefore, since we have these promises, dear friends, let us purify ourselves from everything that contaminates body and spirit, perfecting holiness out of reverence for God" (2 Cor. 7:1). Likewise, Paul counsels the Thessalonians: "For God did not call us to be impure, but to live a holy life" (1 Thess. 4:7).

As Sanders states, "Paul often draws on the purity language of the Bible in describing behavior appropriate to being Christian, and he can also discuss that behavior as the 'fruit' of living in the Spirit."[9] Purity/pollution regulations are not, in Pauline discourse, separated from a spirit-filled life. Rather, observing such rules is the outcome of a spirit-filled life.

The System

In light of Mary Douglas's contention that "Where there is dirt, there is a system,"[10] one cannot understand the Lisu ban on drinking and smoking as an isolated imperative. According to Douglas, "Defilement is never an isolated event. It cannot occur except in view of a systematic ordering of ideas. Hence any piecemeal interpretation of the pollution rules of another culture is bound to fail. For the only way in which pollution ideas make sense is in reference to a total structure of thought whose key-stone, boundaries, margins and internal lines are held in relation by rituals of separation."[11]

Consequently, the Lisu ban on smoking and drinking must be understood as embedded in the overall Lisu social order. One aspect of that social order is that the Lisu are a minority people living in close proximity to other ethnicities: Dulong, Bai, Nu, Tibetan, and Han Chinese. Another aspect is that the Lisu are a communal society. This group-orientation was reflected in their initial conversion not as individuals, but as families, clans, and villages. Lisu today convert as individuals, but once converted, they practice Christianity as a group.

Drawing on *Natural Symbols*, a later work by Mary Douglas, I classify the Lisu as a strong group/low grid society.[12] The Lisu are a communal society and their group orientation is strong. As a group-oriented society, religious matters are necessarily public, not private.[13] Faith is not just a matter of individual conscience; it affects all of one's social relations. But in contrast to the majority Han Chinese and many other hierarchical group societies, the Lisu are low grid. Mary Douglas defines grid as "the scope and coherent articulation of a system of classification."[14] In other words, grid is the degree of rigidity of societal roles. Although the Lisu experience a strong degree of group pressure, the structure is egalitarian. There is a specific distaste for hierarchy.

For the Lisu (as a strong group/low grid ethnic enclave), symbols, rituals, and purity regulations assume heightened importance in maintaining group cohesion in the absence of the hierarchical and bureaucratic structures of a high grid society. According to Jerome Neyrey, strong group/low grid societies display a robust concern for purity for both the physical and the social body, both of which are bounded systems, tightly controlled from the fear and threat of pollution. Rituals serve to maintain group boundaries.[15]

The Lisu drinking/smoking ban must be understood as an embedded aspect of their overall system: the Lisu are surrounded by other ethnic groups, live within the bounds of a powerful state, and need to support their strong group orientation by means of symbols and rituals in the absence of hierarchy and bureaucracy. Within such a system, the Lisu purity regulations—namely the drinking/smoking ban—serve this structure by (a) maintaining holiness, distinctiveness, and set-apartness, (b) identifying with the historic conversion, (c) strengthening the group and reinforcing the boundaries, and (d) protecting from danger.

Maintaining Holiness, Distinctiveness, and Set-Apartness

The primary reason for the Lisu ban on smoking and drinking is holiness. When I asked Lisu laypeople, ordinary parishioners, about the reason for the ban, they tended to categorize drinking and smoking as sin. "Because God said so," some Bible school students told me, as if it were self-evident. When I probed more deeply, mentioning Jesus's first miracle of turning water into wine, these particular students seemed unfamiliar with the story. Regardless of the details of Bible stories, with which the students generally seemed to lack a deep fluency, abstaining from smoking and drinking was a way to honor Christ publicly.

When I asked church leaders about the ban, sin was not mentioned. Rather, they mentioned its importance to the history and cultural unity of the Lisu. The church leaders knew that the ban was a distinctive feature of Lisu Christianity, whereas the average Lisu Christian believed it was a rule for all Christians. There was a distinct gap between the clergy and the parishioners. While they both held to the same ban, their theological reasons were different.

When I asked A-chee about the ban, her answer was, "It was God's idea." I asked if there were Lisu who did not drink, did not smoke, and therefore called themselves Christians but in fact had no belief. While she admitted that for a few this might be the case, she stressed that, for the majority (*dabufen*), not drinking and not smoking was synonymous with belief. Frankly, the question seemed a strange one to her: the idea that one's inner self and outer self could be separate was foreign to her.

Jesse, the former head of the Gongshan church, put it like this: "A change in your heart should manifest itself in an exterior change as well (*Xinli de gaibian yiding yao waibian de gaibian*)." Yet Jesse was less sanguine than Ruth about the problem of some Lisu following the ban but not having belief. "It's a big problem," he said. Some Lisu have adopted the no-drinking / no-smoking lifestyle because they feel it is a good habit and beneficial for their health, but have no belief. As Jesse put it, "Just not drinking and not smoking does not make you a Christian. You have to have belief."

It is useful here to recognize that the Lisu drinking/smoking ban is a theological ideal. Empirical reality will not live up to the ideal; it never does, no matter which theological ideal is chosen. My point has not been to prove, empirically, that the Lisu fully live up to any certain ideal. Rather, my point is to demonstrate that it is this ideal—and not another—for which they strive. For the Lisu, withdrawal from ethical vice is viewed simply as the external expression of internal belief, a commitment to holiness.

But what exactly is holiness? Jewish scholar Baruch Levine states that "holiness is difficult to define or to describe; it is a mysterious quality. Of what does holiness consist? In the simplest terms, the 'holy' is different from the profane or ordinary."[16] Throughout his commentary on Leviticus, Levine equates holiness with distinctiveness: "You shall be holy—'You shall be *distinct (perushim tiheyu)*,' meaning that the people of Israel, in becoming a holy nation, must preserve its distinctiveness from other peoples. It must pursue a way of life different from that practiced by other peoples."[17]

David deSilva pursues this theme as well, noting, "The people commanded to be holy to their God will be different from the peoples around them. Holiness and distinctiveness go hand in hand in Torah and in Judaism, and the pursuit of holiness must be worked out in the practicalities of every life."[18] In other words, the abstract ideal of holiness—in daily existence—becomes the more concrete benchmark of distinctiveness.

Like the early Israelites, the Lisu Christians of Gongshan County lived in a multicultural and multireligious area. Distinctiveness from those surrounding was an expression of holiness. John, a Lisu Christian teacher, told me the drinking/smoking ban was important because it showed that Lisu Christians were different from the Muslims, Tibetan Buddhists, and Catholics as well as those with no belief. In a world where everyone drank and smoked, to refrain from such was truly distinctive. This ban marked the boundaries between Christians and others.

Purity laws also work to prevent association with those who hold to a different purity standard. The ban on smoking and drinking, in effect, promoted separation between Christians and others. Even today, kosher food laws prevent an observant Jew from sitting at a Muslim table. The Lisu no-drinking / no-smoking laws had similar social ripples. To no longer drink or smoke set them apart from their former pre-conversion lives. It was a daily reminder that they had changed.

The Lisu did not consider the hands unclean, as the majority Han Chinese did. Corn, their traditional food, was eaten by pulling off individual kernels and collecting them in the right hand until there was an approximate mouthful. Beans and peanuts were eaten by hand, shucking the husks or pods and popping them into the mouth. The Lisu ate rice and other foods with chopsticks, as the Chinese did, but they did so out of convenience, not to avoid the inherent dirtiness of one's hands. The Lisu concern with purity lay not with external surfaces; rather, it lay with what was inhaled and imbibed within. Alcohol and smoke were substances swallowed and taken into the body; they were invasive; they penetrated the bodily boundaries and were absorbed. In so doing, they affected the purity, health, and function of the entire body.

Here there is biblical precedent. According to deSilva, while contact with unclean substances was assumed in Leviticus, pollution coming in through the mouth was put in a class by itself. While in the former case one had simply to ritually cleanse, in the latter case the abomination was so severe the possibility of purification was not even envisioned. In other words, a Jew who ate pork was simply no longer a Jew.[19]

The situation was similar in Lisuland: a Lisu who drank or smoked was simply not a Christian. During the Anti-Rightist Campaign of 1958, some Lisu made a point of drinking and smoking, publicly, to demonstrate that they had renounced their faith and to avoid the persecution being meted out to Christians.[20] That particular danger had now passed, but the drinking/smoking ban as Christian marker continued.

Moreover, just as socializing with smokers obliged one to inhale smoke, being with polluting persons likewise polluted oneself. This was similar to the biblical *leaven principle*—put in a small amount and the whole batch was corrupted. The Lisu, as a group-oriented society, had a fundamental understanding of the leaven principle, as illustrated by this story from Leila Cooke:

> At length some of [the Lisu] came to my husband with a queer request. "Big Brother," they said, "almost everyone wants to give up his tobacco, but he cannot, because one and another tempts us and we find it hard. Won't you set a date, and we'll all give it up together. Then our villages will be rid of the filthy stuff." Big Brother paused thoughtfully for a minute before answering, then said, "No, I hardly think it best to set a date to break off. That would make it a matter of law, and I think it ought to be a matter which every man decides for himself with his own conscience."
>
> The Lisu did not want to take no for an answer, so they went to Mr. Gowman and asked him for his opinion. He felt differently about it and thought their first plan was a good one. Eventually the date was set, and everybody stopped chewing at once. After that, the deacons refused baptism to anyone who either chewed or smoked it,

and they would not allow anyone to shake hands with a person who had once promised to give it up but afterwards chewed or smoked.[21]

In addition to the leaven principle, this passage, in which the Lisu referred to tobacco as "filthy," demonstrated the Western missionary tendency to view a group ban as legalistic and the communal Lisu understanding that change would only be efficacious if the entire group made the change. Finally, this passage demonstrates the historic discontinuity in Lisu culture when they embraced Christianity.

Identifying with the Historic Conversion

Smoking and drinking were the historic vices of the Lisu. The Lisu word for wedding literally meant "drinking-wine affair."[22] As a historical act, not drinking and not smoking purified the community and separated it from its drunken, lascivious past. It externally marked the major discontinuity in Lisu history: Christian conversion.

For the first generation of Lisu Christians, remaining unpolluted by smoke and drink was an external manifestation of their new, clean state. Upon their baptism "each one promised solemnly, not only to trust in the Lord Jesus for his whole lifetime, but to abstain from any connection with heathen worship, from whisky-drinking, immorality, opium-smoking or cultivation, and to observe the Lord's Day."[23] For the following generations of Lisu Christians, continuing to ban these vices was a remembrance of and identification with that historic conversion of the Lisu people. I discussed the drinking/smoking ban with a Lisu gentleman at his home as we shelled and ate peanuts. He stated that, historically, the outright ban was necessary because drunkenness and opium smoking were rife in Lisu culture at the time of their conversion. But, he concluded, mentioning its beneficial effects, the ban has proven to be their *fufen* (good fortune).

When I asked Jesse about the ban, he immediately began to discuss Lisu history. He told me that before the Lisu were Christians they were drunks and opium addicts, that even children would drink beginning at a young age. The Lisu had a lot of "*bu hao de xiguan*" (bad habits). When they converted, it was such a massive change, a redirection for the entire people. That is why this ban is still important to the Lisu people, he concluded.

The Lisu have chosen not to define their church by ethnicity. They have long viewed their Christianity as a missionary Christianity and have sought to bring the Christian faith to other minorities. I often heard Lisu

FIXING THE BOUNDARIES

fig. 8 A Lisu church in Gongshan County. Photo: author.

use the phrase "*chuan fuyin*" (share the good news). In addition, a standard church position is that of evangelist (*chuandaoyuan*). Judging from the large number of first-generation converts I met, evangelism was a priority for the church, and new Christians were welcomed. The Lisu church has not strived for cultural or linguistic purity; cultural and linguistic boundaries are permeable. During the time of my fieldwork, the recently installed head of the Gongshan church was not a Lisu but a Tibetan. The 8:00 a.m. services at both the Gongshan and Liuku churches were conducted in Mandarin Chinese. But the church was not a Tibetan church, nor was it a Chinese church. Despite its increasingly multiethnic character, it maintained its identity as the Lisu church. Within the Bible schools I attended, about 15 percent of the students were non-Lisu. Moreover, not all Lisu were Christians; one was not a Christian simply because one was Lisu. Thus Lisu Christianity required a reframing, a redefinition that was not about ethnicity.[24]

I contend that this reframing has been accomplished by redrawing the purity map. By accepting the drinking/smoking ban, one was symbolically identifying with the historic Lisu church. Thus the unique ethnic history of the Lisu church was not lost after all. By not smoking and not drinking, new converts were not just accepting Christ; they were grafted into the historical identity of the Lisu church and inducted into its community. Not smoking and not drinking allowed other ethnic groups in the Nujiang Valley to join the Lisu church without becoming Lisu. The ban maintained the historic identity of the Lisu church without compromising its missionary resolve. No drinking / no smoking solved the identity paradox of the Lisu church: how to be multiethnic, and yet still be the Lisu church.

Strengthening the Group and Reinforcing the Boundaries

Mary Douglas writes, "The body is a model which can stand for any bounded system. Its boundaries can represent any boundaries which are threatened or precarious."[25] She asserts that those cultures that are concerned with the orifices and excretions of the body are also cultures concerned with the margins and boundaries of their social group. "The anxiety about bodily margins expresses danger to group survival."[26]

The logic goes something like this: those groups concerned with their own survival are preoccupied with their boundaries; to protect the same, they enact purity and pollution regulations over the physical bodies of their members as a means of social control. According to Douglas, "There can be no natural way of considering the body that does not involve at the same time a social dimension. Interest in its apertures depends on the preoccupation with social exits and entrances, escape routes and invasion. If there is no concern to preserve social boundaries, I would not expect to find concern with bodily boundaries."[27]

The linking of social group and physical body is contained in Scripture as well. In 1 Corinthians, Paul compares the church to a body: "Just as a body, though one, has many parts, but all its many parts form one body, so it is with Christ. For we were all baptized by one Spirit so as to form one body—whether Jews or Gentiles, slave or free—and we were all given the one Spirit to drink. Even so the body is not made up of one part but of many" (1 Cor. 12:12–14).

Neyrey asserts that, in many passages, Paul places higher value on that which strengthens the group over that which gives the individual freedom.[28] Concomitantly, Paul understands bodily controls to be appropriate: "Your body is not your own; you were bought with a price" (1 Cor. 6:19).

By carefully guarding the physical body of the individual Christian, the gates of the social body, the church, were guarded as well.[29] The Gongshan Zion Church compound was a sacred space, a space free of pollutants. A sign in bold red Chinese characters stated, "No Smoking Inside the Church."

When I asked some church members why they had such a sign—seemingly unnecessary, as no Lisu Christians smoked—I was told that the sign was for visitors.

The church compound had one entry and exit point and distinct boundaries. All were welcome, but entrance required adherence to the standard of purity. I well recall finishing up breakfast with Jesse and his family one morning. Jesse's house had open doors and open windows—as did everyone's home in the church compound—and various people were constantly walking in and out. Suddenly, all conversation and eating stopped; all eyes focused on a gentleman standing outside the door. "Can we help you?" asked Jesse. The stranger turned, and I was jarred to see a cigarette in his hand. "I think you're lost. This is a church," said Jesse's wife. The smoke exhaled from this man's lips marked him as a stranger, an Other, someone who did not belong. In the Old Testament, the purity laws distinguished Israelites from non-Israelites, and for the Lisu, the no-drinking / no-smoking rules distinguished those who were Christian from those who were not. Purity laws acted to preserve community by clearly marking who was in and who was out.

Most Christian churches use the rite of baptism to mark or commemorate one's new status as a believer. However, baptism is an internal church ritual, one witnessed by church insiders but invisible to outsiders, as it is usually performed in a baptistry within the church compound. One's baptismal state is unknown to the outside world. As Lisu Christians lived in the midst of many Others, who were all aware of the ban, refraining from smoke and drink declared one's Christian affiliation publicly. In so doing, it reinforced identity and strengthened the boundary, making it high and visible.

In Gongshan town, I could recognize Lisu Christians immediately. The frontier outpost seemed to operate continually in a haze of smoke. Bus drivers, street vendors, construction workers, bank tellers—all had their expected cigarette. In that environment, choosing not to smoke or drink was to make a public declaration about who one was, which group one belonged to, and even what one believed. Not smoking and not drinking was a matter of identification.

Finally, the drinking and smoking ban strengthened the community by providing a common ethic, an ethic that promoted communal wholeness by prescribing abstinence from destructive vices. Smoking and drinking were not private but social activities. They both involved the mouth, which was also used for talking or singing. When one smoked in the presence of others, the smoke was inhaled by the entire group. Therefore, smoking and drinking did not just pollute the individual; they polluted the whole group.

"Purity has to do with drawing the lines that give definition to the world around us," according to deSilva.[30] The Lisu ban on smoking and drinking drew a bold, fixed line around Lisu Christians, demonstrating unequivocally who belonged and who did not. It marked the boundary in a clear manner, and that was key, for ambiguity was a danger.

Protecting from Danger

Danger has been a dominant theme for Lisu Christians in the Nujiang Valley. They were on the margins. In a modern China rushing headlong into global commerce and power, the Lisu were poorly educated, geographically isolated subsistence farmers. Other minority groups in a similar situation, such as the linguistically related Lahu, had disintegrated into alcoholism, drugs, and trafficking of women and children.[31] A strong and intact social structure was all that protected the Lisu from a similar fate; fragmentation of their community was perhaps their greatest danger. It was therefore not surprising that purity regulations had arisen to preserve community wholeness.

The social system centered on the Lisu church was a hedge against poverty, alcoholism, isolation, and marginalization. The Lisu had come under pressure from the Chinese state. Education policies required all youth to attend school, which was conducted solely in Chinese. Because the Nujiang Valley provided little in the way of employment opportunity, some Lisu migrated out in search of work. These two factors—education and migration—pressured the Lisu toward assimilation into the Han Chinese majority. And assimilation is danger, even death, for a minority group.

But as has been mentioned, not all Lisu were Christians. Non-Christian Lisu were particularly threatening; too much contact could be dangerous, for they were a bridge to the pre-Christian past, and to go back to drinking and smoking would be dangerous for the Lisu community, as the case of the Lahu demonstrated.

The church's ambiguous position within China's highly regulated political system also posed a kind of danger. There was explicit danger during the Anti-Rightist Movement (1957–59) and the Cultural Revolution (1966–76), but the Public Security Bureau (*Gong An*) still watched to ensure that the church was not overstepping its bounds. Lisu Christians have faced danger from government persecution and danger from those who might tell. In such an environment, where danger was still lurking, ambiguity over who was in and who was out was hard to tolerate.

Thus the Lisu church faced danger from the outside and danger from its own margins. The church and its structure were critical for group survival. As deSilva states, "The life and death of the culture was indeed at stake in the constructions of the purity regulations."[32] Disintegration of the Christian culture would be dangerous to the Lisu, for they would be left with external marginalization and no internal recourse.

A Christian Social Order

Renouncing drinking and smoking was efficacious for individual Lisu Christians. It provided them a means by which to express their belief, to publicly announce their loyalty. It allowed them to worship God by a commitment to holiness. It protected them from the historic vices of their ethnic group, thus keeping them safe from potential danger.

But each Lisu Christian was an individual embedded in community. Not drinking and not smoking allowed them to declare their affiliation with the Lisu Christian community to those within and without. It marked members and removed ambiguity. Far from pursuing legalistic righteousness, through their practice of refraining from drinking and smoking, the Lisu had created their own Christian social order.

Voice

Isaiah (Gongshan County)

I was the first Tibetan Christian in Gongshan County. Now there are about ten or so. I became a Christian when I was about twenty years old after I met my wife, because her father was a Lisu evangelist. I can speak Tibetan, Lisu, Dulong, Chinese, and Nu. But I can only write Chinese and Lisu.

I learned to read and write Lisu in about three months, by attending Bible training schools after I became a Christian.

Later, I became an evangelist myself. I crossed the Gaoligong Mountains several times to evangelize the Dulong people in the Dulong River canyon [about 20 miles west of Gongshan through mountainous terrain]. The annual rainfall there is more than 4500 mm [177 inches], and the mountains are filled with leeches, snakes, and mosquitoes.

There is also something called a red deer louse, which climbs into and, without your knowing or feeling it, bites hairy places. After it's drunk enough blood it heads into the skin. At this point, it cannot be pulled out, because if its head breaks while inside, it will cause skin ulcers and festering boils, which are very painful. But with ointment (*qingliangyou*) or eucalyptus oil balm (*fengyoujing*), or by rubbing saline solution in the area around the louse, after a while it will fall out, leaving a bloody open sore.

This kind of leech also climbs up from the foot, sucking blood without your knowing or feeling it, until when you're warming yourself by the fire

Compiled from an interview on August 14, 2013, and a biographical entry in Zhu, *Dianxi jidujiao shi*, 404.

scratching your feet and you realize that your feet are covered with fresh blood.

It rains there every day, without ceasing, sometimes you can go two months without ever seeing the sun. I traveled to every village in the Dulong River canyon, and many churches were established.

Chapter 5

THE EASTER FESTIVAL

> Low in the grave He lay—
> Jesus my Savior!
> Waiting the coming day—
> Jesus my Lord!
>
> Up from the grave He arose,
> With a mighty triumph o'er His foes
> He arose a Victor from the dark domain,
> And He lives forever with His saints to reign.
> He arose! He arose!
> Hallelujah! Christ arose!

On Good Friday we headed single file down the mountain trail from Nu Ni village. We were in good spirits, for we were going to the Easter festival, we were walking downhill, and the sun was shining after several days of rain. On our backs were baskets and bedding, a change of clothing, and for one grandfather, his grandson. I also carried my laptop computer, video camera, audio recorder, and notebook.

A Lisu Christian festival is a concentrated experience in culture and religion, making it an ideal situation for the participant-observer. For the

---

Epigraph from "Low in the Grave," lyrics by Robert Lowry, 1874, hymn #34 in the 2013 Yunnan Lisu hymnbook.

past several weeks I had been immersed in the family and church life of Ma-pa Timothy. Ma-pa Timothy instructed me in the Lisu language for two hours every morning, and for the rest of the day we settled into the rhythm of caring for the animals, working in the fields, cooking meals and washing dishes, and trekking down the mountain to the Nu Ni village church for Sunday services. This Easter festival, however, would widen my exposure, giving me access to a large gathering of Lisu Christians from villages all around our northern portion of the canyon. The festival turned out to have an added benefit: I was finally able to fill in a portion of the big story of Lisu Christianity that had been eluding me—the events of the Quiet Years from 1958 to 1980. Not only did interviews with elderly Christians who converted before 1958 provide firsthand information about those years, but the communal character of Lisu Christian practice that I witnessed and took part in during the festival helped illuminate the response of Lisu Christians to the period of government suppression. As the next chapter will discuss, togetherness is a vital feature of Lisu Christianity. When the communal practice of their faith was rendered impossible, Lisu Christianity virtually disappeared.

Festivals have been a part of Lisu Christianity since the time of J. O. Fraser. They started as spontaneous gatherings of Christians to celebrate Christmas together, but already by the 1920s, the festivals had a formalized structure with a welcoming hymn and an offering taken to support evangelists. Festivals were times when key community decisions were made, such as accepting candidates for baptism or approving newly coined religious terms for the Lisu language. In the missionary era, festivals brought Lisu Christians out of their isolated villages and into a larger body, building up not just Christian identity but also ethnic identity. Festivals serve much the same purpose today.

There were fifty-four Christians in Nu Ni village, but only eleven of us could attend the festival. All households needed to leave a few behind to feed the pigs, chickens, donkeys, and goats, morning and evening, and to tend to the other work of the farm. One household had a family member suddenly go to the hospital the previous night. Another Christian villager had recently endured a long hospital stay. On a Wednesday a few weeks back, all the Christians had gone to his fields so that his corn would get planted. Some were busy planting and could spare no one; others were not devout enough to make festival attendance a priority. Ma-pa Timothy said that most of these villagers had only been Christians a little over ten years. Their faith was not that strong.

We left the village of wood plank houses and walked past the terraced fields. The villagers had been planting corn when I first arrived a few weeks back. Now the corn was just starting to sprout. Across from us we could see the opposite bank of the Nujiang River, with low clouds fastened to the mountainside like babies clinging to mothers. As we neared the bottom, the roar of the Nujiang met us.

At the bottom of the hill, a bread truck (*mianbaoche*), a private conveyance (usually a small van) commonly used to supplement taxi service and public bus service up and down the Nujiang Valley, picked us up and brought us first to Gongshan town to buy some supplies and then further north. We turned west, away from the Nujiang River, and followed one of its tributaries into the mountains, around curves, past falling rocks, through small villages of huts perched on steep inclines, until finally a village opened up before us.

Unlike most Lisu villages, which are perched on steep inclines, Shee Za village lay on a large, gradually sloping plain, on which were built a scattering of wooden plank houses surrounded by shallow terraces. Near the bottom of the village, the only spot of color that differed from the natural green and brown hues, was a peach-colored church with a cross on top.

A villager invited us in for tea while we waited to find out our sleeping assignments. His home was nearly identical to every other Lisu village home in the Nujiang Valley. We sat in the kitchen building on low stools around the fire. The walls were charred black from smoke. Black smoky webs hung down from wires and poles and bamboo nets. The dark room had no windows, save some escape hatches near the roof for the swirling smoke to seep out. This kitchen/smoke room cured and kept insect-free the dried corn that hung below the roof as well as the cuts of pork that hung from wires near the fire. On nails around the walls hung large Lisu knives and crossbows, plastic bags filled with tea leaves or medicine, and anything else that must be stored and kept above the chickens or small pigs who tended to find their way into kitchens when no one was looking.

Our host served us familiar foods: hot water with large tea leaves along with flat pancakes made of pounded rice. The pancakes were usually either deep-fried in lard in the wok over the fire or cooked over the hot coals. He poured some cola for the children in our party. A yell from outside told us to pack up, so we donned our baskets and backpacks and walked down the hill toward the church. Just before the church we were directed into a home and brought into an upstairs room with two single beds, where Timothy's wife, two daughters, and several other women would stay. Just as in other villages, the beds were homemade, with wooden headboards and footboards and woven hemp mattresses. A few hemp mattresses were on the floor as well.

Timothy then directed my daughter Katherine (who often joined me for fieldwork) and me to a different house. We walked past the church courtyard, down some steps, and through a dense cluster of homes and buildings. A small woman with a serious expression unlocked a door into a windowless room with two double beds, one for Katherine and me, and the other for her and her granddaughter. I found out later that her family helped manage the church. In the room above slept her husband, Timothy, and the other pastors and teachers. In the kitchen building on stilts across the way, we took our meals around the fire.

Over the fire I chatted with Ma-pa Barnabas, whom I had met the previous year during my stay at the Gongshan Bible training center and again at last year's Christmas festival. Barnabas said that Shee Za village had about four hundred people, of whom more than a hundred were believers. The village was multiethnic, with not only Lisu but also Dulong, Nu, and Han people. Two village church members were currently studying at the Liuku Bible training center.

Later, I sat with the other villagers from Nu Ni and discussed the new village. There was much to talk about. This festival brought together people who otherwise would tend their farms, attend their village church, and every once in a while go to town to buy things they needed. Festivals put them in a wider sphere, connecting them with a larger group of believers. While most Lisu Christian practices were part of the daily fabric of life, festivals were times set apart. They ran on sacred time. They were a ritual of intensification, immersions in Christian practices. All work and income-generating activities were set aside. Daily routines of village agricultural life were left behind for four days of attending services, singing hymns, line dancing, and fellowshipping with other Christians. As with most Lisu Christian practices, the festival was meaningful because of its communal nature. All the various activities—even mundane ones, such as eating and sleeping—were done together with others, as a group.

We sat outside the host home, where Timothy's wife and daughters would be staying, and compared Shee Za village with their own village. Unlike Nu Ni village, which was at a high elevation and on a steep incline, Shee Za village lay close to the river tributary. One could hear the water continually flowing through the village in miniature channels, channels that could be directed into rice paddies to flood them with water. Shee Za village produced so much rice that not only did they have enough for themselves but they actually produced a surplus that they could sell. Rice had replaced corn as the staple food for the Lisu of the Nujiang Valley. Every meal I ate in a Lisu home involved several bowls of rice. But in Nu Ni, the village was too far above the Nujiang River to produce rice. Rice, in 25 kilogram sacks, had to be paid for in cash—which was always in short supply—and carried up the mountain on donkeys. In Nu Ni, corn was still the most common crop. The villagers rarely ate corn; it took too long to prepare. Still, most fields were planted with corn, which was harvested and hung to dry from the rafters to provide food for the livestock throughout the year.

"And hardly anyone speaks Chinese here," commented Timothy's wife, who was from the Lahu people. I had noticed the same. In Nu Ni both Timothy's wife and I were accustomed to being able to communicate in Chinese with virtually everyone. But in Shee Za the situation was different. The road to Shee Za village had only been built about ten years ago; before that, Shee Za lay in isolation, closed off even from Gongshan town by the steep mountains. As a result of such transportation barriers, the Chinese language had not seeped into the village.

At dinnertime the church courtyard turned into an outdoor canteen. Huge vats of rice, grown locally, were brought up from the kitchen, along with large aluminum bowls filled with pork and vegetables. Everyone made their way to fill a paper bowl with food and then grab a seat on the cement benches that lined the courtyard.

Around 7:00 p.m., the opening church service began. A small local choir gathered at the entryway and serenaded festivalgoers with hymn #117, "Welcome to the Feast," as they filed in, shook hands with the pastors, and found seats in the sanctuary. The sanctuary filled quickly. The back doors were taken off and removed and another three rows of pews were set outside, with people standing behind them.

Some people from Nu Ni village beckoned to me, and I sat in the balcony with them. Altogether, there were over four hundred people attending the festival from seventeen different villages. In Gongshan County there were five separate Easter festivals that year, with a total attendance of around two thousand.

A large local choir sang an opening song. I had seen many of the choir members in the kitchen, bringing serving tables to the courtyard, and manning the sound system. Then the congregation sang hymn #264, "And Are We Yet Alive." This Methodist hymn, written by Charles Wesley, was by now quite familiar to me; we had sung it in church services in Nu Ni village at least three times since I arrived. The first verse went like this:

> RO: NY SᐯV. TY_ SE: LO=
> And are we yet alive,
> A JᑎN. MO LᐯV ᑐO W=
> And able to meet together.
> YE-SU RƎ ƆE: TᐯV RO: X. MO=
> We thank Jesus for his grace,
> YI NYI J MU J TY=
> His kindness and his care.

After the hymn came several line-dance numbers that people from different villages had prepared specially to perform at the festival. Line dances to Lisu Christian pop were a mainstay at the various festivals. Lisu church dancing was a post-missionary period development, one of the few aspects of the church service that did not directly resemble the church in the early missionary times.

Lisu church line dancing did not use hymns (called MU-GW, pronounced moo gwah). To facilitate the dancing, a new genre of Christian music had been developed, Lisu Christian pop—in Lisu, MU: GW: ꓹ: (pronounced moo gwah zah), adding the diminutive ꓹ: to give the literal meaning of small songs or tunes. According to Ying Diao, "The term is mainly used in the Christian communities, referring to any Christian music that is small-scale, short, not complicated, and usually has only one part."[1] Such Lisu Christian pop usually contained just a melody line and was accompanied by a range of electric guitars and sometimes drums. Most Lisu Christian pop was written for line dancing. DVDs, with music, choreography, and subtitles in the Fraser Script, were sold in markets up and down the Nujiang Valley. Many of them had been produced across the border in Myanmar, but some were locally produced as well.

From these DVDs, villages and hamlets could organize groups to practice the choreographed moves. They provided a Christian practice for villagers once the farmwork for the day was complete. Once they were ready, the dancers would perform on the stage at church, usually in ethnic dress.

Lisu Christian pop should not be viewed as a replacement for the Lisu hymns. They performed different functions during church rituals. While the hymns were sung together loudly by everyone, the dance was a performance watched quietly by the congregation. The communal aspect of the dancing came in the hours of evening practice in the village, not in the performance on the church stage. But this was not individual expression;

the beauty was the symmetry of everyone moving to the same choreography. Nor was there a generational preference among the two. Elderly ladies seemed to be particularly fond of line dancing, though all age groups took part.

After the performances, Ma-pa Barnabas got up to preach, using John 11:25–26 as his text: "Jesus said to her, 'I am the resurrection and the life. The one who believes in me will live, even though they die; and whoever lives by believing in me will never die. Do you believe this?'"

The balcony where I was sitting was packed. Our pews were long boards on top of cinder blocks. Pieces of cardboard had been nailed to the boards to make them slightly more comfortable. Around me were young mothers with babies on their backs, ladies in velvet Lisu costume with beaded headdresses, old men in ill-fitting polyester army surplus uniforms, men wearing pin-striped Lisu shirts with borders and Chinese buttons, and old women with their long black braids wrapped inside gray, blue, or khaki-green caps. Children were playing in the courtyard during the service, wandering in once in a while to get something from their parents. Almost everyone carried a Bible bag, colorfully woven with hot pink or bright red tassels, worn crosswise across the torso or with the strap across the forehead and the bag hanging down the back. In her first book, *Honey-Two of Lisu-Land*, Leila Cooke described the origin of the practice of wearing a Bible bag, one of the first symbols of Lisu Christianity. At that time, the Lisu catechism and Scripture portions were in short supply, and those lucky enough to possess them hated to see them get worn or dirty. One woman, the wife of Honey-Two, "made a shoulder bag of dark blue cloth and embroidered it with flowers and adorned it with beads. Then, adding love-stitch to love-stitch, she fringed it with red tassels. The other women worked with her and made similar bags, until almost everyone who had books carried them in one of these. As heathens they [the Lisu] never made book bags, so the mark of a Christian came to be one of these lovely bags. Not frontlets between the eyes or a sign upon the doorpost, but a book bag on the shoulder!"[2]

Once Barnabas's sermon was over, we sang hymn #132, "Since I Have Been Redeemed," which was followed by a benedictory prayer offered up by one of the pastors. Prayer ended with a doxology, sung in unison by the congregation:

U KW MI N∀ KW TY, SU NY..
All creatures in heaven and on earth,

A JՈ WU-S TɅ XƎ. GꞀ LɅ..
Let's altogether praise God,
Ꞁ Ꙕ XƎ, Ꙕ A JՈ GꞀ M=
Who gives all blessings.
B. B: Ꙕ TI SI-XY-M-V=
Father, Son, and Holy Spirit.

After the service, everyone filed out of the sanctuary and into the courtyard. Large speakers were moved outside from the sanctuary, and the line dancing began in a large circle around the courtyard. The entire courtyard was filled; even Ma-pa Barnabas and Ma-pa Timothy were out there with the dancers. It continued, with the same song repeated over and over so everyone could learn the moves, late into the night. I sat on a cement bench and watched, with my notebook in hand. Every face had a sheen from a thin layer of sweat, and every face was smiling. It was a joyful experience.

The 8:00 a.m. service the next day was surprisingly packed, considering the late-night dancing. As in most Lisu churches, on one side of the stage sat a dilapidated couch, empty at the start of the church service. The service leader called up several individuals who were sitting in the congregation—mostly middle-aged men who were serving as teachers or evangelists—to participate in the service in some way, one to lead the hymn singing, one to pray, another to give the benediction. These individuals sat along with the pastor on the shabby couch (see fig. 9).

This aspect of the Lisu church service used to annoy me. As I watched middle-aged men file up and take their places, I asked myself where the women were. But by this point, nearing the end of my fieldwork, my view had changed. I no longer saw the gender contest to which my Western socialization had so sensitized me. Rather, I saw a marginalized community raising up and acknowledging its own leaders, leaders from within, when so much of their daily life was structured by others from without.

The church cultivated leadership from within the community, not imposed from the outside by the state. The state school had teachers that were exogenous to the community. Likewise, the local government, while at least nominally self-governing, was heavily influenced by the Han majority, particularly in its most visible arms—military and police. Putting the men up front on the church stage, by contrast, made community leadership visible and esteemed, and that raised the whole community, both men and women.

fig. 9 The Lisu church stage for the Shee Za Village 2014 Easter festival. Photo: author.

When ethnic leadership was superseded or replaced, the results could be devastating. Many ethnic minorities in Yunnan faced problems of drug abuse, alcoholism, mental illness, suicide, and ethnic decline.[3] When a society had its own leadership, it had role models, helpers, givers of advice, and in the case of the Lisu Christians, those who would pray. All of these roles were performed within the bounds of the culture.

In the minutes before the service started, various individuals walked up front and gave the service leader a small piece of paper. Each piece of paper represented a performance that had been prepared—a line dance or a small choir act. The service leader managed the scraps of paper, announcing some acts before the sermon and the rest after.

We sang hymn #34, "Low in the Grave," and the sermon text was Mathew 26:36: "Then Jesus went with his disciples to a place called Gethsemane, and he said to them, 'Sit here while I go over there and pray.'"

After the service, groups of people sat in a circle on stools outside and ate sunflower seeds and drank tea. Children played together in the open spaces. The children of this village as well as our own Nu Ni village attended the same school near Gongshan town. They boarded at the school and returned home every two weeks for a long weekend. Happily, the long weekend happened to fall over the Easter festival, meaning that Timothy's seven-year-old daughter could attend with us, along with lots of other children.

The small group of teachers and evangelists had begun to take their meals in the kitchen building opposite where we slept, and I joined them. It was a good chance for me to talk to some old friends and to make some new ones. I first met Solomon at the Christmas festival in his home village, and I was happy to see him again. Solomon became a Christian in 1980, a common story in these parts, as that was the year the churches were allowed to reopen. He told me stories of working during the day and copying the Bible and the hymnbook by hand at night by firelight, as there was no electricity in those days.

Sitting around the midday meal, I also had my first chance to interview an elderly gentleman who became a Christian before 1958. I was eager to get Titus's story, as this period—from 1958 to 1980—had thus far proved quite opaque to me. Far from the fourth- or fifth-generation church I had expected to find, most Lisu Christians I had met thus far were first- or second-generation believers. Many came to faith in 1980 or the years immediately following. But whenever I asked about the years from 1958 to 1980, I was usually given a simple answer: "We couldn't believe then." With Ma-pa Barnabas interpreting the elderly man's Lisu into Chinese so I could understand, I asked Titus about these difficult years.

......

In 1950, after over twenty years of missionary work in the Nujiang (Salween) Valley, approximately 20 percent of the total population of 100,000 were Christian.[4] But 1950 brought the start of the Korean War, with Americans and Chinese on opposing sides. The Americans were now considered imperialists, and the Lisu Christians were pressured by the new Communist government to sever their emotional bond with their missionaries.[5] One Lisu Christian, Ti-mu-ti-wu (Timothy), defended the missionaries: "Yang Sihui [Leila Cooke] had neither rifles nor a radio receiver. The missionaries never conscripted labor or levied grain from us, but taught us to believe in God. What's wrong with that? If the missionaries in other districts are unsatisfactory, the Yang couple in our district are very satisfactory. If the imperialists treat the Han harshly, they are, however, kind to us."[6]

As a result of Communist takeover and mistreatment by cadres, the first wave of Lisu Christian refugees fled to Burma in 1950–51. Many Nujiang Lisu had already gone over the mountain passes to establish congregations on the Burmese side of the mountains.⁷ The nearness of place and the presence of kin made fleeing to Burma a viable option, which many took, although they had to leave their crops in the fields and faced famine upon their arrival.⁸

A second wave of refugees fled to Burma in 1954, facing threats of persecution, brainwashing, and death. The Burmese government, under pressure from China, refused them asylum and placed them under guard. According to Gertrude Morse, "Even the non-Christian Burmese soldiers guarding them at one place were moved to tears as they heard the almost-starving Christian refugees continually singing their hymns of hope and dependence on God."⁹ The Lisu appealed, but the appeal was denied. They were marched back under guard to the Chinese border. Upon reaching the border, however, many of the guards "looked the other way," allowing the Lisu to disappear into the jungle.¹⁰ Some of the Lisu settled in previously uninhabited jungle along the border; others went west, ending up in a finger of Indian territory that juts into Burma, now called Vijaynagar, in Arunachal Pradesh.

Despite the persecution inflicted during these first two campaigns, the number of Christians in the Nujiang Valley continued to increase between 1950 and 1957, growing even faster after the missionaries departed, according to internal government statistics for Bijiang County (one of four counties in the Nujiang Valley at that time) obtained by Tetsunao Yamamori and Kim-Kwong Chan. In those seven years the Christian population doubled, until one-third of Bijiang County's total population was Christian.¹¹

In late 1956, Chairman Mao, in what has been called the Hundred Flowers Campaign, vowed to "let a hundred flowers bloom; let a hundred schools of thought contend." But after six months, unhappy with the open and honest criticism he had encouraged, he completely reversed course. The Anti-Rightist Campaign, begun in 1957, was a crackdown aimed at eliminating the so-called rightists from the Communist Party; shortly thereafter, it became an attack on all religious elements. By 1958, the Lisu Christians in the Nujiang Valley faced their worst threat yet. In the words of the previously cited Ti-mu-ti-wu: "The Party has begun to strip its sugar coating. Many of our pastors have been arrested. They have gone mad like rabid dogs biting their own colleagues, too. So the problem facing us now is no longer how to retain our freedom of belief, but how to ensure our own safety."¹² Moreover, government attempts to collectivize agriculture led to famine in 1959. These events led to the third (and largest) wave of Lisu Christians fleeing across the border to Burma, all but decimating the

Nujiang Valley of whatever Christian population still remained. Gertrude Morse wrote that the Burmese border guards used brutal force to stop the influx, but thousands poured over the border nevertheless. Those who arrived described the conditions that caused them to flee:

> Adults who were able to work were allowed only two ounces of uncooked rice in the morning and another two ounces at night. Children and those too old to work received no allowance. There was almost no other food. About the middle of February, the Christians were forbidden to rest or gather together for worship on Sundays. Spies were sent out who reported on those who refused to obey the command. The offending leaders were severely punished. One of our beloved Lisu preachers was punished by having his ears, nose and tongue cut off. An elder was beaten before the people of his congregation until he could not stand. It was the practice to beat and torture a leader in front of his congregation as a warning. Many, many believers went through a terrible time of suffering for Christ's sake. It was reported that one of the elders was skinned alive, and others were burned alive.[13]

This wave of persecution, beginning in 1958, had a fundamentally different character than the preceding years of more random, sporadic, generalized persecution. In this wave, the churches were forcibly closed and all religious activities were suppressed. Pastors, evangelists, and church leaders were specifically targeted. Unlike the previous years of persecution, which saw an increase in the number of Christians, the third wave saw the reverse. The number of Christians in Bijiang County was 10,169 (of a total population of around 30,000) in 1957, but precipitously dropped to 1,529 by 1958.[14]

Most of the decrease can be accounted for by the thousands who fled to Burma. But not all. Many remained behind, and what became of them during the Quiet Years is a complicated picture.

Although the Anti-Rightist campaign began to die out by 1960, the churches remained closed. This campaign was followed shortly thereafter by the Cultural Revolution (1966–76), which, in addition to its other excesses, attacked religion. Mao Zedong died in 1976, and by 1978 Deng Xiaoping had consolidated power and begun to initiate policies that are now called "Reform and Opening Up." By 1980, Reform and Opening Up extended to religious activities as well, and the churches in the Nujiang Valley were allowed to open once again.

The Quiet Years

These years, from 1958 to 1980, are the Quiet Years. They are not merely the closed years; closed is an inadequate moniker, for it refers primarily to external government policies and actions. By contrast, quiet refers to the state of Lisu Christianity during these years. Lisu Christianity, by its nature, is out loud; it is expressive; it is heard. These years, however, were quiet.

Information on the Quiet Years is scant. As the missionaries either left voluntarily or were forcibly removed, there is a dearth of missionary narratives. The last CIM missionaries to the Lisu in China, John Kuhn and Charles Peterson, left in 1950.[15] The China Inland Mission withdrew from China completely in 1953, refocused on Southeast Asia, and renamed itself Overseas Missionary Fellowship. Yamamori and Chan's statistics for Bijiang County of the Nujiang Valley are absent for the years 1966 to 1979. As yet, I had found no information on the years 1958 to 1980—until I arrived at the Easter festival.

......

When I met Titus at the Easter Festival, he was ninety-four years old. He told me that when the Morse family came to Gongshan in 1936, his parents accepted the Gospel and joined the church. Although he was just sixteen years old at the time, he had a devout faith and joined the church as well.

In his early twenties, his church recommended him for a month-long Bible training course. Upon his return, his involvement in church work increased, and he began teaching hymns and leading worship. By the year 1958, he was a church administrator. This public position made him vulnerable to the government campaigns at the time. Titus was initially sent to Lanping County to repair highways. Upon his return, he was arrested, charged with being an "agent of American imperialism," and sent to a prison labor camp in Lijiang. "That time was very difficult (*jianku*)," he told me. "Every day we were given only six potatoes and some bran to eat."

Titus was released in October 1950 and was permitted to return home to Gongshan County. "Those were the closed years," he said. "The churches were closed. We had no Bibles or hymnbooks, because they had all been burned. We could not be Christians at that time."

"Did you drink and smoke?" I asked.

"We drank. We smoked. Yes, we did those things. All expressions (*biaoxian*) of faith were no more."

"Did you sing?" I asked. "No, we did not sing," he replied.

"Did you pray?" I asked. "No, we did not pray. We did not even pray."

In the Lisu conception, belief and practice are tied up together. They cannot be separated; one cannot exist without the other. Being a Christian means leading a Christian life, and if one is forbidden to be a Christian, then all expressions of faith fall away as well.

In 1980, when the churches reopened, Titus resumed his Christian life. Since 1980 he has attended more than ten short-term Bible training schools up and down the Nujiang Valley, and he has continued preaching in his church.

After the interview, Barnabas and I stayed and chatted around the fire for some time. Barnabas said that every day there were more and more believers in Gongshan County. But his fear was that their faith was not very firm (*jiangu*). "That's what I preached about this morning," he told me. "My sermon title was: Who has faith that will comfort the Lord? (*Shei lai anwei Zhu de xin?*)." Barnabas's mission as a Ma-pa, as he described it to me, was to help strengthen their inner faith.

Christianity was still a work in progress in Gongshan County. Pastors like Barnabas did not have an established church mentality; rather, they saw their church as still in the building stage and were motivated to help it grow, develop, and deepen. The shutdown of all churches between 1958 and 1980, the persecution and prison terms, and the ensuing out-migration to Burma had decimated the number of Christians in Gongshan County. Since 1980, the Lisu church has struggled to regain its foothold and restore its faith—training pastors, running Bible training centers, evangelizing the surroundings, and building churches. Yet today's numbers—about six thousand believers, or 20 percent of the population—still barely approach the 1949 figures.

On Easter morning I had an opportunity to interview an elderly woman whose faith predated the church shutdown of 1958. As it was Sunday, the noon service took place at its usual Sunday time, and attendance was much higher than normal, as many community members who were not attending the festival arrived. Since it was so crowded, I sat on a shady bench along the courtyard wall. Many others had the same idea. On my left sat a woman from the Dulong minority. Her ethnicity was apparent by her colorful, pin-striped apron. On my right sat an elderly Lisu woman wearing a black turban. I had seen old black-and-white photographs of Lisu wearing black turbans, but these days the women in Gongshan preferred billowy military-style caps, while the women of Fugong wore brightly colored plaid scarves. This was the first time I had seen an old woman wearing a turban.

This woman, whose name was Koh La Bo, took an interest in me. Pulling out her hymnbook, she instructed me to repeat after her. First, we read the title of the hymnbook: SI.. d: TⱯ DO, MU, DU MU: GW:. In English, this is usually translated simply as *Hymns of Praise*. To express a phrase in the Lisu language requires roughly double the number of syllables as in English. The term *cross*, an important word sung often at the Easter festival, required four syllables to express in Lisu: LⱯ BO T˥. DU.[16] The woman then opened the hymnbook to hymn #1, "To God Be the Glory," and read the first verse. I repeated after her. I had been studying Lisu for the past few weeks with Ma-pa Timothy, and I felt my work was paying off. The turban-wearing woman smiled and nodded, giving me her approval.

Koh La Bo said she thought she was around eighty years old, but she was not sure. She became a believer when the Morse family was working in Gongshan. Her whole family, including her grandparents and parents, believed at that time. As their village did not have a church building, the church met in her family's home. She spoke especially fondly of the Morse's oldest son, Eugene.

In 1958 the government told her she was no longer allowed to believe, so she stopped.

When, in 1980, belief was allowed once again, she resumed her faith.

I was confused by my two interviews with these elderly Christians, so I sought out Ma-pa Barnabas between services. "How could these Christians just lose belief from 1958 to 1980? Isn't belief something internal? Something no one can take away?" I asked him.

"It's not that they didn't believe," Barnabas told me. "It's just that their belief could have no *biaoxian*, no expression. They could never speak of it. *Wu banfa*. No possibility."

According to my interviews, Bibles, hymnbooks, and other Christian materials were gathered up and burned. Churches were closed or razed to the ground. In some villages, believers might meet secretly to pray for one another, one night in someone's home, another night in a different home. In other villages individual believers prayed or recited Bible verses late at night.

But these activities were not widespread. For most of the Nujiang Valley, Christian activity came to a standstill. Hymns were not sung. Prayers were not prayed. Bibles were not read. The Gospel was not spread, even from parents to children. There did not exist any kind of underground church or secret movement. Christian activity simply ceased.

Though common Christian wisdom suggests that the "blood of the martyrs is the seed of the church,"[17] this did not prove to be true in the Lisu case.[18] Lisu Christianity was stagnant and nearly died. Had the churches remained closed for another generation, it might have died entirely.

The causes of such inertia and inactivity are complex. One explanation is the character of the Cultural Revolution itself, described by Andrew Walder as "an unprecedented wave of state-instigated persecution, torture, gang warfare, and mindless violence."[19] The Lisu church, since its inception, had been an evangelistic church focused outward on spreading the Gospel. But the upheaval of the Cultural Revolution—a time when children were encouraged to report on their parents and students were encouraged to testify against their teachers—meant that parents did not even pass the faith on to their own children.

Yet the Cultural Revolution affected all of China, and in many areas, churches continued to grow underground.[20] Why did this not happen in the Lisu case? There are two factors that made the Lisu Church in the Nujiang Valley particularly vulnerable to government persecution: out-migration and internal structure.

Since the border with Burma runs parallel with the entire Nujiang Valley just a mountain range away, migration out of China was a viable option for many Lisu Christian families during the Quiet Years, as has been previously mentioned.[21] In Gongshan County waves of Lisu Christians fled west to Burma. Because of interpersonal networks and the presence of beloved missionaries, fleeing to Burma held a lot of appeal for Gongshan Lisu Christians in particular. The Gongshan Lisu had cultivated strong ties with the Burmese Lisu before 1949, and the Morse family—to whom the Gongshan Christians had strong personal affinity—had relocated there as well. According to Eugene Morse, nearly all of the Gongshan Christians went along with them to Burma.[22]

In all three counties of the Nujiang Valley, those who migrated out tended to be those who expected to be targeted: pastors, church leaders, and deeply committed believers. Forty-five Christian leaders from the Bijiang/Fugong area were sent to labor camps, at least two of whom died. The number of pastors in Bijiang County went from 283 in 1957 to 150 in 1958, dropping even further to 75 by 1959.[23] The net effect was to leave the remaining Christians deprived of pastoral leadership and guidance.

The final reason for the near death of the Lisu faith, and the one I focus on here, is the very structure of Lisu Christianity. Lisu Christianity is a communal faith; as such, its external expressions—singing, praying out loud, not drinking, and not smoking—are central to the faith. It is this aspect—togetherness—that has been the strength, but also the vulnerability, of Lisu Christianity.

......

I took a walk around the village and came upon a group of young people practicing a line dance to perform at the church. As the festival went on, the number of performances in each service increased. Most of the performers wore their traditional Lisu dress, their long pleated skirts swaying back and forth in unison, their long hair pulled back and adorned with beaded headdresses.

Before the 7:00 p.m. service started I found Koh La Bo, the turban-wearing elderly woman, and showed her a picture I had on my phone of the then ninety-two-year-old Eugene Morse, whom I had had the opportunity to interview in Chiang Mai four months previously. She was happy to see the picture, and she sat chatting about it for some time with the other elderly women.

The Ma-pas had asked if we could contribute a performance for the 7:00 p.m. evening service, so Katherine sang in the early part of the service and then returned to our room afterward. During the sermon, I went back down to our room to chat with her, knowing the service was going to be very long. I could hear Barnabas preaching over the loudspeaker, so I was able to keep track of what was going on in the service.

But then I heard hymn singing coming from a different place. Flashlight and hymnbook in hand, I went out, searching for the source of the singing. I found the kitchen staff, finished with the massive task of slaughtering pigs (more than ten during the festival, they told me), steaming huge vats of rice, and cutting and washing the vegetables needed to feed the more than four hundred festival attendees at least twice a day. They were all sitting on stools, singing. I loitered for a few seconds, listening at the door. Then two people came down the steps from the church, opened the door, and invited me in.

We sang two hymns together. After the second hymn, they all looked at each other. "It's good," they said, nodding. They were satisfied. Then they looked at me. "Please come with us," they said. They had been practicing for their performance at the festival. After the sermon was finished, we walked up to the church. We were the second act after the sermon. I filed in with them and we sang the two hymns, one of them being hymn #34, "Low in the Grave."

That last evening service lasted for four hours, not finishing until 11:00 p.m. Given the late hour, I was sure the courtyard line dancing would be cancelled. I was wrong. I could hear the music coming from the courtyard until past midnight.

The next morning was Monday, the last day of the festival, the day everyone would go home. There would be no 8:00 a.m. church service, just a final midmorning gathering. We could linger over breakfast much longer than we were used to and enjoy Lisu *ba-ba*, dough fried in oil over the fire.

While we were still chatting, Koh La Bo came in and asked Ma-pa Barnabas to pray for her. She knelt on the floor and he stood over her, hands raised, and prayed. A few moments later another elderly gentleman arrived for prayer. This time all the assembled Ma-pas stood over him in a circle, each of them praying out loud, at once.

Finally, the woman whose room we had lived in during the festival, together with her husband and granddaughter, came and asked for prayer. Barnabas asked me if I would also join the circle of prayer, and I accepted. The couple stated their prayer requests, and Barnabas translated their Lisu into Chinese for me. The first request was for their two sons, who were not believers. Their eldest son's wife had left, leaving the granddaughter behind. Finally, they had concerns over their responsibilities to care and manage the church along with the work in the fields needing to be done. We all prayed out loud for several minutes, then Barnabas closed the prayer time. The couple came around and shook all of our hands. The language barrier had prevented me from sharing more than a few words with this woman and her granddaughter, who slept in the same room with my daughter and me. Now I had insight into the serious expression she always seemed to carry.

There was one last closing service, around 9:00 a.m. It had no sermon: just a few hymns, speeches by those involved in the festival (including the man of the family just prayed for), and prayers. Finally, we sang hymn #217, "Christian Fellowship Song." This song was not a translated hymn but was of Lisu origin. The first few lines went like this:

> JI-SU RO: A. YI; TⱯ NO: ꓕ_ M Pꓶ DU-.
> Because Jesus is our older brother, we are connected,
> RO ꓕI RO ꓛO: ꓕI RO ꓕI GO Dꓱ dYꓱ; L.,O=
> One person with another, becoming one body.
> NI, Nꓵ SI J., LⱯ ꓤO=
> We have love, fellowship.

I stopped at this word, *fellowship*, and stared at the Lisu words on the page of the hymnbook: J., LⱯ ꓤO. I remembered reading in one of Isobel

Kuhn's books: "When we first said '*ja-la-ko*' no one . . . knew what we were saying; we had to explain not only that *ja-la-ko* meant fellowship, but what 'fellowship' really is."[24] After four days with the Lisu Christians over Easter—praying together, singing together, eating together, dancing together, attending church together—I was sure they had a far deeper understanding of Christian fellowship than I had ever experienced.

After singing the "Christian Fellowship Song," those standing in the back organized a handshake line, which I joined, and all the others filed out of the church, shaking hands and giving the Christian greeting, "Hwa Hwa." The festival was over.

Voice

Timothy (Gongshan County)

In 2003 we received a letter, written in Lisu, from my uncle in India. Before that, I didn't even know that I had an uncle in India.

My grandparents were Christians, living in a village about a half-hour's climb from here. In 1958, when the persecution in China started, my grandfather decided to go to Burma. My grandparents had five kids, but two had already died. His plan was to find some land, build a house, and then return to pick up my grandmother. That was his *plan*.

But his plan didn't work out. He wasn't able to get back into China. My father was seven or eight years old when his father left, and he never saw him or heard from him again. We never knew what happened to him, until we received the letter.

At that time, you weren't allowed to be a Christian in China. You could only have your faith in your heart, but never show it to the outside. Also, we did not yet have the Bible, or the hymnbook. They only had a simple catechism with some questions and answers about basic doctrines of the Christian faith. During the day, Christians would never meet. But at night, they would meet together to pray. For example, tonight at one house, tomorrow night at another house, the next night at still another house.

It wasn't until we received the letter from my uncle, who I still have never met, that we found out what happened. Because he couldn't get back

Compiled from interviews on April 4 and April 14, 2014, with Timothy, and on April 14, 2014, with Timothy's wife.

to my grandmother, my grandfather married another woman. They had at least two sons, one of which is the one who wrote the letter. My grandfather may have also had some daughters, but if so, they were not mentioned in the letter. My grandfather stayed in Burma for three or four years, but came under pressure from the Burmese government because he was a refugee from China. So he just kept on going. That's how he ended up in India. My uncle is now a head pastor of the church there. When my grandfather died, my uncle wrote to us and told us what happened.

My grandmother died in 1994. She never saw the letter, and never knew what had become of her husband. She had renounced all faith in Jesus, because she felt that it was faith in Jesus that caused her husband to leave. Even after 1980, when belief was permitted, still, she did not believe. She died with bitterness, but with no belief.

My father was born in 1950, a very unlucky year to be born because the Communists had just taken over the previous year. Unlike my father, I was born at a very lucky time. I was born in 1981. Just as the churches were reopening, I was born!

My father believed in Jesus in 1987. My mother also believed at the same time. I was about six years old at the time, and I can remember when it happened. My father used to drink and smoke, before he believed.

A few years ago our entire family believed: my parents, my two brothers, their wives, and my family. But Third Brother and his wife have been married for more than six years, and still they have no child. They stopped going to church. And now Oldest Brother no longer believes. His wife still does, but he now drinks. When we all go to church, he goes and drinks with the non-Christians in the village. A few years ago all three of my parents' sons believed. Now it's only me.

Chapter 6

"LET'S PRAY FOR EACH OTHER"

> Blest be the tie that binds
> Our hearts in Christian love;
> The fellowship of kindred minds
> Is like to that above.
>
> Before our Father's throne,
> We pour our ardent prayers;
> Our fears, our hopes, our aims are one,
> Our comforts, and our cares.

I had two evening language lessons at the Lisu Church of Chiang Mai, Thailand. For the second evening's class, my teacher had prepared several categories of phrases.

He taught me words having to do with the kitchen, such as oil, rice cooker, matches, and firewood. He taught me words about food, such as mutton, beef, chicken, fish, noodles, corn, beans, and popcorn. He taught me how to say "Never mind" and "Me too."

At the end of the lesson, he taught me to say several goodbyes. In addition to "Hwa Hwa," which could be used both as a hello and a goodbye, he

---

Epigraph from "Blest Be the Tie That Binds," lyrics by John Fawcett, 1782, hymn #215 in the 2013 Yunnan Lisu hymnbook.

taught me "See you later," "May I go now," "Goodbye everybody," and "Let's pray for each other."

At this last one I stopped, because it did not seem to fit into the "goodbye" category.

But it did, my teacher explained. This phrase was commonly used when one was taking leave.

To say "Let's pray for each other" meant that prayer was not just useful for individuals to articulate their own needs to God. Rather, prayer was used in a communal sense, to bind members of the community together, because praying for someone unites you with that person. It was saying that we are still connected even though we are parting; we will still see each other in prayer.

In this chapter I will consider how the communal nature of Lisu society affects their practice of Christianity. I examine how the strong social value of communalism has led to an important foundation for most Lisu Christian practices: togetherness. I will also examine the tension between the believer and the body in Lisu Christianity. In an imbalanced state, this tension can cause a crippled Christianity, but at its point of balance, it leads to the Lisu Christian ideal: a faith that is both outward directed and togetherness focused.

Christian practices have thrived in the soil of Lisu culture. One element of this soil is orality, which I explored in chapter 2. In this chapter I consider a second key component in Lisu culture, a culture in which a practice-oriented Christian faith has thrived: communal social structure. The Lisu are a communal people, and communal societies practice religion in ways different from Western individualistic societies.

The chasm between the missionaries, who were steeped in Western, individual practices of Christianity, and the Lisu was already evident in the 1920s and 1930s. It was a chasm that at times created tension, most clearly articulated in the term *legalism*, an expression often used by the missionaries to express some of their frustration with the Lisu Christian converts.

But this individualism/communalism chasm also led to creative adaptation on both sides. The missionaries embraced and defended the people movement, despite its criticism from folks back home. They adjusted their methods to allow Lisu social structure to remain intact. And the Lisu accepted the forms of many of the Christian practices introduced by the missionaries, although they transformed their meanings to reflect their communal society. Handshakes, prayers, festivals, and hymn singing all became communal expressions of faith for Lisu society.

Understanding Communal Societies

Before examining Christianity in a communal context, it is necessary to understand communal societies. French anthropologist Louis Dumont defines a communal society as a society in which the community, not the individual, is the holder of paramount value.[1] He further states, "Society imposes upon every person a tight interdependence which substitutes constraining relationships for the individual as we know him."[2]

Communal societies[3] are associated with more traditional, non-Western societies where there is common ancestry, a defined boundary, close affinity, common interest, and social control.[4] Communal societies are those in which communication is face-to-face and high-context, rather than the more fractured communication and low-context systems found in Western societies.[5] Community members often see each other over the course of their day-to-day activities. Relationships are close and lasting, and one's place is based on who one is, not what one has done. In communal societies, persons are born into a social order. Primacy is given to the social whole. As Dumont puts it, "Society with its institutions, values, concepts, language is sociologically prior to its particular members, the latter becoming human beings only through education into and modeling by a given society."[6]

Even in today's globalized world, communal societies still exist, most notably in the developing countries of Africa, Asia, and the Pacific but also in Latin America, particularly its remote and indigenous communities. In addition to the Lisu, the Karo of Indonesia;[7] Mulia Dani of West Papua, Indonesia;[8] Fijians;[9] Solomon Islanders;[10] and the Maasai[11] and Akan[12] peoples of Africa are all examples of authentic communal societies.

In a communal society, as John Mbiti elegantly states, "Whatever happens to the individual happens to the whole group, and whatever happens to the whole group happens to the individual. The individual can only say: 'I am, because we are; and since we are, therefore I am.'"[13] Those in Western societies might mistakenly believe that the individual is lost completely in a communal society. Members of communal societies emphasize that this is not the case. In fact, the emphasis on consensual decision-making, as opposed to the majority rule favored in most Western societies, elevates the position of the individual. As African theologian Samuel Kunhiyop states, "The individual is free to act, but actions are not done without regard to their effect on the community."[14]

In both communal and individualistic societies, individuals are important and valued; the key difference between these societies is in how each individual finds meaning. According to Kofi Asare Opoku, "Being human is understood in terms of a relationship with others—past, present and future—and one's full humanity is not realized unless one is in community."[15] According to Alan Tippett, being an individual within a communal society is not a place of diminution or loss. Rather, it is a place of belonging and satisfaction: "one of the greatest cultural feelings of satisfaction is the idea of belonging, of having a place of your own in the group, and being able to play your own specific role in the group life."[16] In a communal society, individuals find their meaning not through their own accomplishments but through their relationships and their community, of which they are an integral part.

Communal societies are unique from a religious standpoint because religion is one of the cohesive forces that bind a community together. Religion may not be a matter of personal choice; like most other matters, it may be a community decision. Moreover, religious leadership is often not separate from communal leadership. Communal leadership is usually both temporal and spiritual.[17]

The Believer and the Body: A Theological Tension

Christianity requires an interdependence between believer and the body, between individual agency and communal structures, which does not allow it to so easily fit within either a communal or an individualistic social structure. Rather, there is an inherent theological tension between individual and community that can cause stress on all social structures.

Jesus Christ was born into the communal society that was Jewish culture. Many of his teachings reflect communal concerns. Jesus tells his disciples that it is good to pray together, even stating, "where two or three gather in my name, there am I with them" (Matt. 18:20). Jesus states that loving your neighbor as yourself was a great commandment, second only to loving the Lord (Mark 12:29–31). In his final prayer before his arrest, Jesus prays for all believers, "that all of them may be one" (John 17:21a).

Paul further elucidates the teachings of Jesus. In 1 Corinthians 12, Paul explains the gifts of the Spirit in communal terms: individual believers are gifted, but the purpose of the gift is for the body of Christ as a whole. Below, I have placed together two quotations, the first from Andrew Moemeka, a secular academic and writer of the scholarly article "Communalism as a Fundamental Dimension of Culture," and the second from 1 Corinthians 12:

> Nothing done, no matter how important and useful it is to the individual, is considered good unless it has relevance for the community. No misfortune, no matter how distinctly personal, is left for the individual to bear alone.[18]
>
> If one part suffers, every part suffers with it; if one part is honored, every part rejoices with it. (1 Cor. 12:26)

Such a parallel reading demonstrates that the Pauline concept of the body of Christ is a natural fit for a communal society. Just as a communal society is not composed of a mass but rather of multi-individuals, so each believer in the body of Christ is not gifted identically but brings diversity into the unity of the body.[19]

However, Jesus often juxtaposes private religious practices against the external practices advocated by the Pharisees. Jesus urges his disciples, "But when you pray, go into your room, close the door and pray to your Father, who is unseen" (Matt. 6:6). He criticizes external faith: "You Pharisees clean the outside of the cup and dish, but inside you are full of greed and wickedness" (Luke 11:39–41). He emphasizes the heart (Luke 6:43–45). In other cases, as in those of the centurion (Matt. 8:5–13) or the sick woman who touches his robe (Mark 5:25–34), Jesus praises genuine, individual faith.

Postbiblical Christian writers further develop the significance of the individual. Augustine of Hippo (354–430), writing toward the end of the Roman Empire and within the new structure of Christendom, wrote what has been called the first autobiography. Augustine's *Confessions* declares that philosophy or reason could begin, and for Augustine did begin, with personal experience. It is perhaps with Augustine's writings that the idea of the individual who is still part of society begins to emerge.[20]

Secular achievements—the Renaissance and the Enlightenment—strengthen the influence of individualism. But on the sacred side, what begins with Augustine is nearly sealed with Luther's Reformation and Calvin's *Institutes*. Now even salvation itself, which previously could only be achieved within the bounds of the church, is given over to the individual.

As individualism gains traction in Western society, religious experience becomes more inward-focused. Theresa of Avila wrote a work called *Interior Castle*, and the second book of Thomas à Kempis's *The Imitation of Christ* is entitled "Admonitions Concerning the Inner Life."[21] The inner life of individual spirituality becomes the growing focus of Western religious experience.

Moreover, the Scriptures—previously the purview of learned priests who interpreted for the populace—are not only translated into the vernacular, but with the advent of the printing press, find their way into the hands of individuals. Religion becomes no longer the realm of the state, or even the church; rather, "the core of religion became enshrined in the conscience of each and every individual Christian."[22] The individual had emerged: the person as an autonomous being, independent of any social or political attachment.

Thus, Christianity is a communal faith that addresses the internal state of the individual heart. And Christianity is an individual faith that is best practiced within the bounds of community. Herein lies the tension. Social structures tend to be weighted heavily toward one pole or the other along the communal-individualistic axis. But since Christianity has both individualistic and communal features and requirements, some features will be a natural fit within a given social structure, while others will pull the social structure out of its equilibrium and toward the opposite pole.

This tension between the role of the individual and the primacy of the community comes fully into play in the realm of practice. Christian practices that are more common in individualistic societies, such as questioning, individual Bible study and interpretation, and personal prayer, are somewhat problematic in communal societies. Moreover, Protestant doctrines, such as the priesthood of every believer, the equality of believers before Christ, and the freedom that every believer possesses, create tension in communal societies that are characterized by community decision, obedience to authoritative structures, and tightly bound relationships. Even such religiously charged words as doubt, belief, and understanding refer to a post-Enlightenment, Western, private, internal, individualized faith.[23]

Balancing Structure and Agency: Toward a Framework

Whether one comes to faith as an individual or as part of a multi-individual people movement, the Christian life will continue to exhibit a tension between the believer and the body. While both communal and individualistic social organizations require balance between religious structure and individual agency, the point of balance for each social structure is not the same.

For a communal society, the point of balance is achieved when the religious structure of external belief is filled in with internal belief. For an individualistic society, the point of balance is when the individual believer is connected with and participating in a local Christian body. In each case, not only is structure-agency balance achieved, but it is achieved in a way that is appropriate to the social organization. To give some life to this rather theoretical explanation, I will give two examples, one from Africa and one from Fiji, that show how communal Christians have managed to achieve structure-agency balance—how they have succeeded in expressing their individual faith communally.

In the communal context of Africa, some Christian communities understand the sacrament of the Eucharist as a communal meal. For Africans, "eating a meal together is the most basic way of sharing common life; it restores what has been lost and gives strength for what lies ahead."[24] In some parts of Africa—where, as of 2016, Christians numbered 48.6 percent of the population of the continent[25]—Christians have infused the Eucharist with their cultural norm of eating together. The Eucharist in such parts of Africa does not consist of token bits of bread and miniature cups of wine. Rather, it is a feast. Food for the meal is provided by all the participants, brought in a spirit of worship and dancing. The notion that no one should go away hungry is pervasive. Nigerian theologian Izunna Okonkwo states that the Eucharist reinforces African communal values of solidarity and sharing, for to break bread and share the cup is a means of bonding.[26]

Okonkwo goes further. He states that each sacrament has vertical and horizontal dimensions. The vertical dimension is concerned with theology, having to do with sacrament as relationship and devotion to God. But there is also a horizontal dimension to sacrament, an anthropological focus, having to do with Christian life conducted as a community.[27] This communal view, as opposed to an individualistic view, of the sacraments and other markers of Christian practice and meaning can be found in table 2.

In Fiji, the focus on Christian life conducted as a community has led to the Christian practice of *bulubulu*. Bulubulu, as Joseph Bush describes, is a communal rite of confession and pardon through which to seek and receive forgiveness. Since sin is viewed as broken relationship, it is appropriate that such a rite be performed in the context of the entire community. The party seeking forgiveness, as part of its petition, presents a *tabua*, or whale's tooth—the most valuable of Fijian traditional wealth-objects—to the offended party. Acceptance of the tabua symbolizes that forgiveness has been granted.[28]

Bush emphasizes, however, that what appears to be a group rite is actually personally meaningful for all the individuals involved. The preparation period

table 2 Differences in Christian meaning and practice in individualistic and communal societies

Indicator	Individualistic societies	Communal societies
Reason for conversion	Personal conviction	Social identity/affiliation
Means of conversion	Individual decision	Community decision
Markers of faith	Internal	External
Goal of faith	Personal salvation	Put community under the dominion of Christ; communal redemption
Practice	Personal Bible study Solitary prayer	Church attendance Religious festivals
Authority	Individual is accountable to God	Individual is accountable to the community
Truth	Understood abstractly	Understood practically and in the context of relationship
Sin	Personal failing	Broken relationship
Confession	Person to God	Person to community (and therefore to God)
Sacraments	Sign of individual devotion to God	Sign of vertical devotion to God, which also reinforces communal values of solidarity and sharing
Place of religion in society	Dichotomy between sacred and secular, between church and state	Pervades all aspects of society

for a bulubulu can last six months or more. In addition to nightly community teaching, it also consists of pastoral counseling and home visitations as well as individual confessions for every person involved. According to Fijian communal Christianity, "Sin will always be manifest in broken relationship, and salvation will always find expression through well-being in community."[29]

The above two examples show balanced expressions of Christianity in a communal context. Because there is a balance between the religious structure and individual agency, faith is vibrant. Because the faith is expressed communally as appropriate to the social structure, faith is authentic.

However, because Christian practice is quite naturally imbued with the cultural norms emanating from our social organization, we are predisposed to elevate one—individual or community—over the other. In such cases, the Christian faith becomes imbalanced. In individualistic Christianity, the structure is often not attended to. A social organization that gives primacy to the individual leaves little room for the sharing and accountability of a genuine community. In communal Christian practice, the external structure can become the predominant object in Christian practice, putting individual faith aside. The church slips into nominalism. All of these problems can be thought of as problems of imbalance.

When a communal society practices faith that favors individual agency over the communal religious structure, as has often happened when the society is evangelized by Western missionaries, individuals could exhibit social dislocation, the church could lack indigeneity, and communal authority could be undermined. Often in the mission encounter, individualistic Western-style Christianity was overlaid atop communal societies. On the island of Sumba in Indonesia, one-by-one conversions, as conducted by Dutch Calvinists, have caused social dislocation.[30] Wholesale adoption of Christian ethics, with no filter through indigenous values, has created moral torment for the Urapmin of Papua New Guinea.[31] The setup of parallel religious and social structures has led to a sense of loss for Methodists in Fiji,[32] and the undermining of chiefly authority has had far-reaching consequences for the Tswana of South Africa.[33]

In other parts of Africa, new Christians were physically removed from their communities by missionaries so as to avoid their contamination by the unconverted.[34] In Oaxaca, Mexico, one-by-one Protestant conversions have led to a loss of community ethos as the Protestants switched to more individual religious practices.[35] And although mission efforts are considered successful in Korea—arguably Asia's most Christian country—Heup Young Kim contends that the individualistic version of Christianity presented by missionaries and adopted by Koreans means that Christianity is still foreign and Western, not rooted in Korean soil: "The individualistic soteriology and missiology of amnesia dissociates people from their own past and communities to impede Koreanization of the Christian faith."[36]

When a communal Christian society loses balance in the opposite direction—adopting Christianity in external structure, or even in self-identity, but never filling it in with interior faith—nominalism or syncretism usually ensue. Some communal Christian churches that could fall into this category are found in the Solomon Islands,[37] North Sulawesi in Indonesia,[38] Vanuatu,[39] and India,[40] as well as in portions of Catholic Latin America and Orthodox Russia.

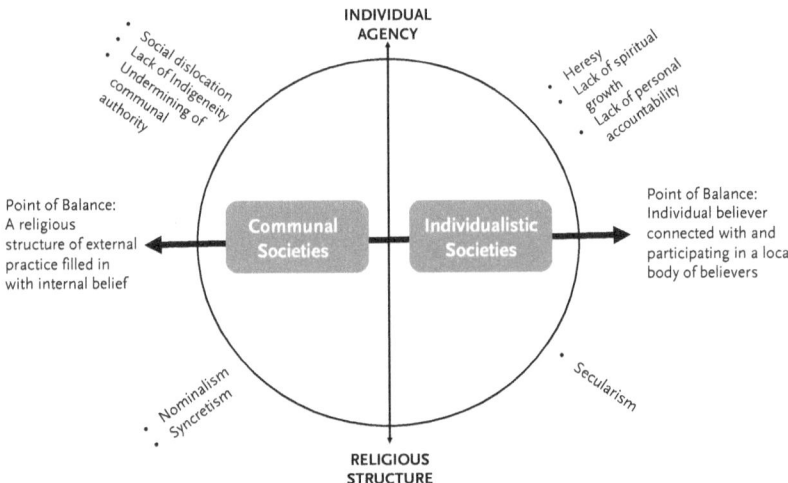

fig. 10 Model of structure-agency balance and imbalance for communal and individualistic societies. Drawn by the author.

Christians from individualistic societies face different pitfalls, but pitfalls all the same. When individual agency is overly stressed, Christians withdraw from their local bodies and practice an individual spirituality. Such interior spirituality without the bounds or structure of the church is often heretical; further, spiritual growth is often stunted. Conversely, an individualistic society in which religious structures are overly stressed moves into secularism, as can be seen in much of present-day continental Europe.

Christian practice in communal societies and in individualistic societies is not—and should not be—the same. Rather, people convert within their social structure, and they live lives of faith appropriate to that social structure.

Conversion as Switching Groups

I frequently asked the students at the Gongshan Bible training center how they became Christians. Always, the story was one of individual conversion, and this moment was expressed in terms of belief (*xinyang*). Lisu no longer came to faith as families, groups, or villages, as they did during missionary times. The people movement was a historic event whose time had passed. Now, individual conversion was the norm and individual belief was expected.

However, once that belief was expressed, faith was then practiced within a strongly group-oriented Christian society. In effect, when an individual converted, that individual joined a new group. Or to put it in less sociological and more theological terms, to be a Christian was to be incorporated into the body of the church. This body was defined by the music it sang (Christian hymns), by the behaviors it shunned (smoking and drinking), by its literacy (written Lisu is generally used for religious purposes only), by its fashion accessories (embroidered Bible bags), by its handshake (signifying Christian fellowship), and even by the language it used (such as the special goodbye). And in a group-oriented society, changing one's group, or joining a new body, is a significant change indeed.

But when conversion meant changing one's group, individual conversion could be a painful experience of separation and estrangement from family. The story of A-cha illustrates this.

I met thirty-three-year-old A-cha during a class break. She asked me if I could understand Lisu, as it was the language of instruction in the Bible training center. This was the first month of my fieldwork so I told her honestly that for the most part, I could not.

"But I know a lot of the songs you sing," I said to her in Chinese. Then I sang the first few lines of "Jesus Loves Me" in English. The Bible training center had sung that particular hymn (with great gusto, I might add) at the start of the last class hour. "I've known that song since I was a small child," I added.

"When I was a child I didn't know Jesus," A-cha said quietly.

She told me that she had not been raised in a Christian family; in fact, her parents were still not Christians. A-cha converted in her twenties, and she now attended services several times a week at her village church, along with her husband and two sons. A-cha had recently sent her older son (aged thirteen) to a three-day Bible camp organized by the Gongshan Zion Church.

Later she lamented to me: "Why must I be the only Christian in my family?!"

"But you told me your husband and your children are also Christians," I said.

"Yes, they are. But my parents. My sisters. My husband's parents. None of them are."

In a group-oriented society that now experienced conversion at the level of the individual, there was pain and rupture when family members did not follow the Christian convert. They were left in different groups. A-cha's very name meant "third sister" in the Nujiang Valley dialect; Lisu names reflected their position in the family. It was thus painful that A-cha, the third sister, had joined the Christian group while her first and second sisters remained outside.

Lisu Christian conversion began with an interior change, but external manifestations were required, from clothing to behavior to manner of speaking. Conversion began with belief, but it did not end there. The process of living life as a Christian was one of internal commitment and external participation in practices—of togetherness.

Togetherness

Isobel Kuhn mentioned the difficult environment of the Nujiang Valley as a reason for the communal structure of the Lisu: "The magnificently beautiful mountain giants are cold and indifferent to the human speck who tries to live along their sides, so the human specks, recognizing a common struggle for existence, are banded together in necessary loyalty."[41] In another book Kuhn wrote, "To the Lisu mind, to be left alone is an affliction!"[42]

Throughout my fieldwork, I made the same observation: Lisu were rarely alone. They were socially embedded. Lisu will easily have not one minute to themselves at any time of day or night. Days are filled with preparing meals, eating together, washing clothes, attending churches, intercessory prayer meetings, listening to the radio, line dancing, sitting around the fire drinking tea, and gathering firewood, leaves, and grasses. Lisu society—from the interior arrangement of homes to the clustering together of huts on the canyon walls to form villages, the organization of the Bible training center, and the group-rally farming method—is based on the principle of togetherness.

During key moments in the agricultural cycle, such as planting and harvest, the villagers had to work together to accomplish immense tasks. One particular Monday was the designated day to rally and help Ma-pa Timothy's family plant corn in their upper fields. The first sound I heard upon awaking that morning was squealing, the very long, very panicked squealing that I could by that time recognize quite clearly: a pig being led to slaughter. About seven or eight people were expected to show up and help plant the upper fields, and they would all need to be fed.

The farmhouse compound was a bustle of activity. Pig parts were being washed. Peas were being shucked. Dishes were being washed. Fires were being stoked. Corn seed was being prepared. Baskets were being donned. After breakfast, everyone, each with a hoe, together with the donkey, headed up the hill to the fields. Together, they planted corn all day. In the evening they all returned, ate together, and sang into the night. Such agricultural events showed the strong cord of togetherness that bound Lisu society together. There was no reason to expect their practice of Christianity to be any different.

Togetherness, for the Lisu, did not just mean that mutual support was necessary to survive. Togetherness meant that wholeness and joy were best found in being together with others. A Lisu who, due to death or difficulty, was left with few family relations was declared pitiful (*kelian*). Every activity of the day—cooking breakfast over the morning fire, gathering weeds for pig slop, assembling with other villagers to help plant a field, sitting around the evening fire drinking tea—happened together. Individual activities were hard to comprehend in the lively and bustling context of a Lisu village. From a Christian standpoint, the strongest practices were those that could be done together, that expressed the communal life of the Body of Christ: gathering together to practice line dancing, attending church, singing in four-part harmony, and participating in intercessory prayer meetings.

I observed Lisu engaged in individual prayer at times, particularly upon entering church. But Lisu prayer was much more than a silent dialogue between the individual and God. The most authentic Lisu prayer was said out loud and together with others—a binding practice, stitching the community together. Lisu intercessory prayer was a physiologically active event. After hymn singing and discussion and sharing of burdens, those who would pray stood up and encircled the fellow believer, who knelt in the midst of the circle. Everyone prayed at once, each prayer "borne heavenward on the wave of the surrounding prayers."[43] The prayers offered were loud, filling all the space in the tiny huts.

Lisu Christians prayed often, for it was usually their only recourse, their only power. They prayed for each other, for it bound them together into the Body of Christ. They sought out the pastor after the sermon and requested prayer on their behalf. They invited fellow villagers over, fed them a meal, shared their burdens, and knelt before their prayers. They traveled long distances and traversed great altitudes, staying two or three nights, just to be together with other believers in prayer. They prayed before every meal, sometimes singing their prayers. They prayed sometimes in rhyming patterns, balancing and counterbalancing their thoughts and emotions. They prayed for the foreigner, that she might have a safe journey back down the mountain.

While communal Christian practices were strong for the Lisu, individual Christian practices were generally much more subdued. Individual Bible reading was a particularly infrequent practice. This was certainly in part due to low levels of literacy, but Bible reading is also a painfully solitary practice, requiring quiet and solitude, both of which were scarce in Lisu culture.

"How does their faith then grow," I asked Ma-pa Timothy, "if they don't read the Bible?"

"By prayer. By attending church. By being together (*yiqi*) with other Christians," he replied.

Timothy said that if people did not go to church, and were not together with other Christians, gradually their faith would begin to disappear. As shown in the previous chapter, when the Chinese government closed the churches and prevented meeting together, Lisu Christianity nearly did die out. The Lisu could not practice their faith if they were not together.

Reconciling Belief and Behavior

The Easter festival was over and I returned with Ma-pa Timothy and his family to Nu Ni village as my fieldwork was nearing completion. I was still struggling to comprehend my interviews with the two elderly Lisu who had converted, with their families, in the 1940s and 1950s, and their "no belief" period from 1958 to 1980. During the Sunday evening service, Ma-pa Timothy introduced me to another nonagenarian, whom I interviewed after church. He had essentially the same story.

Wang Jian told me that he was ninety-four years old, born in 1921. When I expressed surprise at his age, he told me he seemed younger because he used to hunt high up in the mountains and eat a lot of wild animals when he was young, such as tiger, bison, and monkey.

Wang Jian became a Christian as a small child. When the Morse family was working in Gongshan, his parents and the rest of his family believed. But in 1954 he was drafted into the army. "I could no longer believe," Wang Jian said. "Then I joined the Communist Party, so I still could not believe.

During that time, I drank and I smoked. Did I pray? If there were some difficulties, I would pray, secretly. But otherwise, not."

"In 2004," Wang Jian continued, "I withdrew from the party. So in 2004, after fifty years, I could openly (*guang ming zheng da*) believe. My wife has passed away now, but she was a good Christian. My children are all Christians as well."

I struggled to understand the nature of this no-belief period. I could not comprehend how, if these elderly Lisu Christians were truly converted, they could simply stop believing, even if it was on account of severe government persecution. I thought perhaps they might have hidden their faith, practiced in secret, or simply prayed silently. But they did not mention these things. Rather, in their own words, they did not *believe* during those years.

As I climbed back up the mountain after church to Ma-pa Timothy's home, I continued to mull over these stories. I could not reconcile these aspects—belief, yet its renunciation—into one acceptable narrative. The sun was setting early, as it did in the valley, and the air was beginning to assume its evening chill. Ma-pa Timothy walked outside, and I raised my concerns.

"How could they believe, and then not believe?" I asked. "Isn't belief something internal, something inside your heart? Something the government has no control over?"

"If you have belief, it has to show itself," Timothy told me. "*Ruguo meiyou biaoxian, meiyou xin.*" If there's no expression, there's no belief. He repeatedly used the Chinese term *biaoxian*, which could be translated as show, display, manifestation, expression, or behavior. All of these meanings are characterized by their exterior nature.

The Lisu do not have a strong divide between the inner and the outer self as Westerners do. They do not live comfortably with a great divide between spirit and body. Arriving for church one Sunday, our group—carrying Bible bags and wearing Lisu dress—walked through another group sitting around smoking and drinking. It was quite obvious that one group was Christian and the other group was not.

"You can easily tell who the Christians are," Ma-pa Barnabas once told me. Even backsliders (to use the term in the missionary narratives) were obvious: they worked in the fields on Sundays, and not only did they start drinking but a mound of beer cans started piling up in the yard. There seemed to be no such thing as keeping up appearances. There was little disconnect between their internal self and their external self.

Timothy's older brother, raised in a Christian family, stopped going to church. When I asked others if he was still a Christian, the reply I received was: "*Ta bu xin. Ta he jiu*" (He doesn't believe. He drinks beer).

These sentences were stated as equivalent terms, for in Lisu Christianity, they were. Even the failure of belief had external markings.

Continuing our conversation, I then asked Timothy, "Can you have the outer manifestations (*biaoxian*), but have no inner belief (*xinli de xin*)?"

"*Bu xing*," he replied. Not possible.

He pulled the Lisu Bible out of my Bible bag and turned to James 2:14: "What good is it, my brothers and sisters, if someone claims to have faith but has no deeds? Can such a faith save them?"

"Do you understand now?" he asked. He turned to another passage, Matthew 6:2: "So when you give to the needy, do not announce it with trumpets, as the hypocrites do in the synagogues and on the streets, to be honored by others. Truly I tell you, they have received their reward in full."

Timothy then showed me James 2:17: "In the same way, faith by itself, if it is not accompanied by action, is dead."

He set the Bible down, looked straight at me, and summarized the matter: "*Biaoxian, hen zhongyao*" (Behavior is very important). "*Xinxin, ye hen zhongyao*" (Belief is also very important). In using *xinxin* (in which the second *xin* attached the meaning "heart" to the initial *xin*, which means "belief" or "faith"), instead of the more common singular *xin* or *xinyang* to denote faith, Timothy was emphasizing the interior nature of faith that he was describing. Interior faith was still necessary; it was not just about external appearances.

"*Tamen yiqi zuo de*," he concluded. They—behavior and belief—go together.

Then he pointed to his two legs. "You need two legs to walk. If you try to walk on just one leg"—he hobbled around a bit—"it doesn't work. You need both, working together. *Liang ge shi yiqi de.*" The two must go together.

It is not surprising that in outlining his Two Legs Theology Timothy drew from the letter of James, for James is an epistle about praxis. In the faith and works debate, James is often placed dialogically opposite Paul and his doctrine of justification *sola fide*, likely the reason Martin Luther famously called the letter of James an "epistle of straw," going so far as to question its very placement in the New Testament canon.

The Lisu practical expression finds more kinship with James, while the missionaries of the first half of the twentieth century related more to the writings of Paul. Latina theologian Elsa Tamez believes that Paul is more attractive in Western societies because abstract thought is given privileged place: "That is, ethics, behavior, deeds are considered of secondary importance in logocentric societies. Thus a letter like that of James, which focuses its attention on the daily practice of Christian life, is easily marginalized, while the 'theological' letters of Paul are highly esteemed."[44]

In drawing on James to outline his Two Legs Theology, Timothy was speaking from his canyon context to one of the longest-standing theological issues of Christianity. Two Legs Theology is an elegant claim not just for the equality of faith and works, or even for the necessity of both. Two Legs Theology places faith and works in mutual reciprocity. They need each other. One cannot walk the Christian life without both—an instinctive understanding in an oral, agricultural culture but perhaps more difficult to grasp in cultures shaped by post-Enlightenment rationalism that have elevated reason above practical action.

Imbalanced Lisu Christianity: Not Nominal, but Crippled

To return to the theoretical discussion, the Lisu were a strongly communal people who, initially, adopted the Christian faith as a people movement. The people movement has ended, and Lisu today are expected to convert as individuals. At its point of balance, Lisu Christians experienced a wholeness of the external and the internal, of outward expressions of faith and interior belief. They lived comfortably within an essential unity of soul and body, of belief and behavior.

The great rupture of the years 1958 to 1980 pushed Lisu Christianity out of balance, because external manifestations of belief were banned. In fact, the Chinese state had found that the strength of Lisu Christianity—togetherness—was also its vulnerability. Shutting down the churches was devastating to a group-oriented society such as the Lisu, even more devastating than forbidding Bibles. How could you sing if you were not together? How could you practice faith as a group when there was no group? Could individual belief be maintained when the group was gone? While a more inward and individual faith might have been better able to withstand government persecution, the external and group orientation of Lisu Christianity struggled to maintain belief when external expression was forbidden.

When the Lisu Christians were banned from meeting together, banned from expressing their faith in a palpable, external way, Christianity nearly died out. The Lisu Christians could not survive on interior faith (*xinxin*) alone. They could not walk with one leg only, and thus they were crippled. Belief, even interior belief, declined nearly to extinction. Belief (internal) and behavior (external) were so tied up together in Lisu Christianity, so inseparable, that when certain behaviors were forbidden by the state, in the Lisu mind, they were left hobbling around, and their faith could not move forward at all. They essentially had no faith.

The Western tradition has long been comfortable with a dualism between the inner and the outer. This Christian dualism is a Western phenomenon, foreign to the Lisu conception of self.[45] Lisu thought did not pass through Greek philosophy or the Enlightenment. Ideas about inwardness and individuality were not part of its expression of Christian faith. According to the philosopher Charles Taylor, "Our modern notions of inner and outer are indeed strange and without precedent in other cultures and times."[46] And theologian Owen Thomas writes, "Here we come on one of the great paradoxes of Christian history. On the one hand, the biblical tradition seems to emphasize the primacy of the outer—the body, speech, and action—while, on the other hand, the Christian tradition under the influence of Stoicism and Neoplatonism via Augustine and Dionysius, among others, tends to emphasize the inner."[47] Moreover, given this dualism, primacy has been given to the inner.

Thomas, while not dismissing the idea of dualism as others do, rather, advocates that the outer, the exterior, the external, should in fact be given primacy.[48] "From the call of Abraham and Moses to the Decalogue of the Sinai covenant, the covenant with David, the preaching of the eighth-century prophets, and Jesus' teaching about the reign of God, the biblical emphasis is on the outer: faith manifest and visible in obedience, sacrifice, and just action; repentance shown in the rending of garments and weeping; thanksgiving seen in dancing, singing, and feasting; and the reign of God perceived in preaching and healing and compared to buying a pearl, sowing seed, and holding a feast."[49] Thomas further points out that when John the Baptist's disciples come to Jesus and ask if he is the expected one or if they should wait for another, Jesus responds, "The blind receive sight, the lame walk, those who have leprosy are cleansed, the deaf hear, the dead are raised, and the good news is proclaimed to the poor" (Matt. 11:5). What is notable is Jesus's failure to report on inner states, on spiritual growth, or even on that evangelical—and most highly individualistic—catchphrase, "a personal relationship with Jesus Christ." Rather, Jesus cites external evidences of his Messiahship.[50]

Outward-Directed, Togetherness-Focused

To return to the Lisu, they had a conception of self that acknowledged an inner and an outer self, but they saw these two as integrated, as in a state of essential unity. They did not denigrate that which was external as a deceptive covering over the inner self, which contained one's true nature. Rather, they viewed external manifestations as authentically showing the nature of one's interior soul. For this reason, outward displays—attending church, wearing ethnic costume, not drinking, not smoking—were essential elements of faith. Further, this Christian faith was expressed outward toward God and toward those one is in relationship with, expressed in communal fashion, by singing together, praying together, planting in the fields together: outward-directed, togetherness-focused.

Chapter 7

COPYING THE BIBLE BY TORCHLIGHT

> To God be the glory, great things He hath done,
> So loved He the world that He gave us His Son,
> Who yielded His life an atonement for sin,
> And opened the life-gate that all may go in.
>
> Praise the Lord, praise the Lord,
> Let the earth hear His voice;
> Praise the Lord, praise the Lord,
> Let the people rejoice;
> Oh, come to the Father, through Jesus the Son,
> And give Him the glory; great things He hath done.

On New Year's Eve morning, the mountain air in Tso Lo hamlet was brisk and cool. The morning sun pierced the woven bamboo wall with pinprick shafts of light. Naomi's father sat by the fire, reading a book of Bible stories with black-and-white pencil drawings. Her mother roasted pounded rice cakes over the embers of the fire. Right after breakfast, the village children clambered up the hill to continue practicing their line dance, performing the same song from the previous night.

Epigraph from "To God Be the Glory," lyrics by Fanny J. Crosby, 1875, hymn #1 in the 2013 Yunnan Lisu hymnbook.

New Year's cleaning had begun. Second Brother's wife swept the hard-packed dirt under the house where the animals lived. Naomi wiped down the woven bamboo floors and walls. Outside the house across the way, a young mother gave her baby a bath in a basin. Children swept the path leading up to the storage room chapel, sending dust flying everywhere.

Two of the older teenage boys of the village, both wearing their Bible bags and with hymnbooks in hand, gathered up the younger children together on the high ground above Naomi's house and taught them a hymn. Naomi's father and a few of the other hamlet elders walked past them, heading down to the patchwork mountain church to pray. When Naomi came back around 4:00 p.m. with several village children, all with baskets filled with leaves and grasses to be mulched and fed to the animals, the hamlet, tucked inside the mountain, was entirely shrouded in shade, as was usual for this time of day.

After dinner, the village children gathered for more line dancing at the hut up the hill, with Naomi leading them. I went with them and watched. Afterward, I went inside and drank tea with the family. This family was smaller than Naomi's, with four sons and two daughters, the youngest of whom was eleven years old. She was one of few in the village who could speak Chinese to me, even though she had only completed first grade. One of the older sons was married with a small child, a daughter. I talked with his wife for a while, as we all sat around the fire eating roasted rice cakes and drinking tea.

She was nineteen years old and also from a big family. But unlike her in-laws, her natal family did not come from Myanmar, "just from down below," she told me. She had given birth to her daughter up here in the hamlet. She told me, "When people down below get sick, they go to the hospital; when we get sick, we pray."

Around 10:00 p.m. it seemed that everyone was getting ready for bed. Naomi's mother lay in her bunk near the fire. Naomi's sister-in-law was washing her sons' feet in preparation for bedtime. I climbed in bed myself, assuming that there would be no further New Year's activities.

At the stroke of midnight, I was jolted awake. A village choir had gathered outside our hut, just on the other side of the woven bamboo wall from my bed, and sang two songs. The first song was a chorus written just for this occasion: New Year's 2014. It was a simple composition: no four-part harmony, just a line of melody. The church on the patchwork mountain down below had been teaching it to all the villagers in the weeks preceding. It was unique for this time and this locality.

The second was a Happy New Year's chorus to the same tune as "Happy Birthday to You." Right after the song ended, Third Oldest Brother rushed out and gave them a rice cake. The village choir tore down the faded Christian poster that had been pasted to the doorway and put up a fresh new one (see fig. 5).

As the singing stopped and quiet descended upon the house, voices of prayer began to rise: first Naomi's mother, then her father, and finally a village elder. All three praised God for the events of the past year and petitioned him for the needs of the household for the year to come. Quiet once again fell in our bamboo home, and I closed my eyes. A few minutes later I heard the same song again, a little farther away, as the village choir repeated these events at every other house in the hamlet.

Unlike the three big Lisu Christian festivals—Easter, Thanksgiving, and Christmas—which are large church gatherings focused on Christian fellowship, the New Year's celebration was about family. At church festivals, the wider Christian community was given precedence over the family unit. Sleeping arrangements split husbands and wives, and folks tended to congregate with their own age/gender cohort. New Year's was decidedly different. It was much more about family reunion, about sitting around the fire with one's own family. Rather than traveling to a larger church for the festival, everyone who was away, such as Naomi, traveled back to their own home.

New Year's has long been a Lisu cultural festival, but with no particular religious meaning attached. Naomi's father said that when he and his wife left for Burma in 1958, the New Year's festival was still just a cultural festival. But when they returned in the 1980s, it had gradually begun to turn into a Christian festival. This desecularization occurred alongside the growth and development of the Nujiang Lisu Christian church as the Lisu reclaimed their Christian faith once the churches reopened.

Reclaiming the Faith

After Mao Zedong died in 1976, Deng Xiaoping initiated the Reform and Opening Up policies. By 1980, Reform and Opening Up extended to religious activities, and the churches in the Nujiang Valley were allowed to open once again.

Once the churches reopened and religious activities were allowed once more, the old Christians still remaining began to tell their family members and their friends to go up into the hills to find the Bibles and hymnbooks they had hidden. In addition, Nujiang Lisu who had fled into Burma came for short visits to visit the family members they had been unable to see for decades, bringing the Gospel with them from Burma back into China. Several members of the current leadership of the church, Pastor Jesse among them, converted in the early 1980s when an elderly person in their village told them about the Gospel. This was the first stage in reclaiming of the faith.

This was not a great evangelistic wave; it was the spreading of Christianity to close friends and family, but not beyond. Villages with no remaining Christian presence remained without belief. Church growth remained hampered on many fronts. Not only was the number of Christians down to less than one-tenth of previous levels, but pastors and leaders were nearly nonexistent. Xuejun Han reported the following in 1986: "The minority churches are encountering an acute shortage of preachers. From the very beginning, the pillars of the Christian mission in Yunnan were sustained by a group of zealous indigenous preachers and pastors nurtured by foreign missionaries in their simple seminaries and rainy-season Bible schools. During the past twenty-five trying years, those who had been the core of the churches were decimated by flight, superannuation, and their natural as well as atrocious deaths, with no recruitment of replacements."[1] Han also stated that in 1984, along the entire length of the Nujiang Valley, there was only one remaining pastor from the old days.[2] Most church leaders had fled or died, with no training of replacements during that time. It takes years to grow a new Christian into a trained pastor; this lack of trained pastors and teachers was an obstacle the Lisu church has only in recent years begun to overcome.

Moreover, not only were Bibles and hymnbooks scarce, but the few Bibles that were available were still incomplete. In 1954, the revised New Testament plus the Psalms had been printed in Lisu.[3] This was the version of the Bible that, in copies of ones and twos, had sustained the remnant of Christian faith in the Nujiang Valley, and this was the version of the Bible that was taken out of the hidden places and read and copied in the early 1980s. During the Quiet Years, the Bible translation effort had continued at first in Burma and then in Thailand, where many Lisu Christians had resettled in response to government repression in Burma. The Old Testament translation was completed in 1968; however, it was 1986 before the Nujiang Lisu finally received the Bible in its entirety.[4]

Bibles and hymnbooks remained scarce in the early 1980s, requiring the initial cohort of young believers—the first generation of post-1980s Christians—who worked in the fields during the day to copy (*chao*) Bibles and hymnbooks at night. Each village usually had one or at best two copies, each of which was passed around from house to house to be copied by hand. There was no electricity; new Christians would gather around a torch and copy by hand into the night. According to Solomon, one of this first generation, some Lisu Bibles were printed in Kunming in 1982, and some Lisu Christians from Gongshan travelled there and picked up about twenty copies. But the Bible cost 50 Chinese yuan, and the hymnbook, 30 yuan. Few had that kind of money.

In the 1990s, the reclaiming of Lisu Christianity reached its second stage, characterized by a resumption of the evangelistic spirit that had long distinguished the Lisu. Christianity in the Nujiang Valley began to spread beyond the initial friends-and-family networks of its first post-1980 phase. The Gospel spread from village to village, even to new ethnic groups. "But this was really a work of the Holy Spirit," Pastor Jesse told me.

The third stage in reclaiming the faith was marked by the building of infrastructure, both physical and pedagogical. Most of the pre-1958 churches had been razed, converted to other uses—such as rice barns—or had simply decayed from the harsh, rainy climate. Nearly all had to be rebuilt, a project that took great amounts of time and resources throughout the 1990s and beyond. The church in Nilada village, just across the Nujiang from Gongshan town, was built in 1995. The Zion Church of Gongshan town was not built until the year 2000. The erection of physical church structures made a symbolic, and public, allegiance claim on the part of the Christians. They also manifested and enriched the communal nature of Lisu Christianity. With their attached courtyards—one of the few public spaces in a Lisu village—the churches provided a place for meeting together, practicing hymns, hosting group suppers, or just hanging around and talking. But the physical structures had to be manned with teachers, evangelists, and pastors.

Bible Training Centers

This need for trained personnel was met by the resumption of Lisu Bible schools. Short-term Bible schools were a staple of Lisu Christian life during missionary days, but shut down completely during the Quiet Years. In 1988, the first short-term Bible training centers—around fifteen days long—began. In 1995, the first long-term Bible training center began in Liuku, holding classes for a few months each year. The teachers were the first generation of post-1980 Christians, who by that time had been believers for a decade or more. The Gongshan Bible training center started in 2000. At first the course lasted for three months per year; in 2005, it became five months per year. In 2014 they started a Chinese-language class in addition to the Lisu-language class.

Restarting Bible training centers allowed for local training of Lisu Christian pastors and teachers. As most Bible school graduates return to their home villages, it created a pipeline of Christians trained in literacy, homiletics, hymn singing, and the Bible to teach those in village churches up and down the valley.

In August 2013 I stayed at the Gongshan Bible training center for one month, and in May 2014, I stayed at the Liuku Bible training center for a week. To live at the Liuku Bible training center was to enter into a particular soundscape. The training center consisted of a courtyard surrounded on all four sides by classrooms, dormitories, and the chapel. Sounds echoed from one end of the courtyard to the other, completely filling the space.

School bells punctuated the day, beginning with the 6:30 a.m. wake-up bell, calling students to morning chapel. There were bells at the top of every hour to signal the beginning of class, and bells at forty minutes past the hour to announce break time. In the evening, there were bells to announce that it was time for the 7:00 p.m. CCTV national news broadcast, 8:00 p.m. evening chapel, and 10:30 p.m. lights out.

Then there was the singing. Hymns were sung in morning and evening chapels. Hymns were also sung to begin, and sometimes end, most class hours. At 10:00 a.m., Lisu or Chinese Christian popular music was piped over the loudspeakers for morning exercises. "HA-LI-LU-Y" sounded from the courtyard as students moved in choreographed steps and sang along. Students or teachers broke out in song as they were walking across the courtyard during their afternoon rest period or hanging their laundry on the lines strung on the flat roofs. Or students might grab one of the beat-up guitars lying around and sing their own prayer of individual devotion. On Friday evenings, as students prepared to go, three by three, to the neighboring villages for the weekend to lend preaching and teaching assistance, the trios gathered in classrooms, in dorm rooms, in the cafeteria, in the sanctuary, and in the courtyard to practice the hymns they would use in leading worship.

Various classes, in two-hour instructional blocks, spanned the week: Old Testament Survey, Geography of the Bible, History of the Hebrew People, Revelation, and New Testament Survey. The previous semester had classes in Acts and the Life of Jesus. According to the posted schedule, most classes met three times per week, and some only two. Every day at 5:00 p.m., just before dinner, was the only class that met daily, the only class where the students from the Lisu- and Chinese-language classes were combined: Sacred Music. This class met in the sanctuary, and each day the class was led by a different Ma-pa. Singing was an integral part of Lisu theological education. Every Ma-pa was considered capable of singing and teaching music. This was simply part of the job description, as essential as praying or giving sermons.

Unlike the Gongshan Bible training center in the northern end of the valley, where students sat in the cement-floored church sanctuary at long planks that had been nailed atop the pews to form desks, the Liuku Bible training center had actual classrooms. The larger classroom was used for the Lisu-language class, which had about sixty students. The smaller classroom was reserved for the Chinese-language class, with only twelve students. The majority of both classes were Lisu, though a few other ethnic minorities attended as well—Dulong, Nu, and Bai.

The classrooms were basic: shabby desks piled high with Bibles and hymnbooks and notebooks, straight-backed chairs or stools, blackboard and chalk. Most students had a modicum of Chinese writing ability from their years in state education but could read and write Lisu quite poorly when they arrived at the training center. Whenever I asked students to write this or that for me in Lisu, they usually demurred and directed me to one of their instructors. Following most lectures, the teacher or one of the students wrote the teacher's notes on the blackboard for everyone to copy. This practice not only reinforced the instructional material but also helped students in their writing ability.

The instructional model was quite similar to the Chinese instructional model, which was no surprise, as it was the only model with which the teachers and students were familiar. Students were lectured to and they read aloud in unison. Teachers asked questions sometimes as a pedagogical device, and the students were expected to return the correct answer. Students rarely raised their hands to ask a question, nor did the teachers give space for such an activity. There was no discussion between the teacher and the students or among the students themselves. There was also no essay writing or any other writing, other than copying what was written on the blackboard or taking notes from the class. In other words, personal interpretation or application was not required or expected.

"Most of the students seem to come from villages," I said to Ma-pa Cornelius, one of the teachers.

"*All* of the students come from villages," he replied.

A Lisu raised in one of the county towns—Liuku, Fugong, or Gongshan—was likely to have received several more years of state education in

Chinese, have a shot at passing the *gaokao*—the college entrance examination—and attending university, particularly with the preferences given to minority students. But a village-raised student would have no such opportunities. Raised in small villages at high altitudes, Lisu children learned non-standard Chinese. Their home linguistic environment was entirely Lisu. Most had graduated from primary school, and a few from middle school, but that was the end of their formal education. These were the students in the classes at the various Bible training centers in the Nujiang Valley: students whose formal education was low but whose spiritual fortitude, toughened by a life of subsistence farming on the geographic, political, and social margins of Chinese society, was high.

"Town churches are growing smaller," Ma-pa Cornelius said. "The other church in Liuku used to have a hundred members, and they got the government to give them money to build a new church. But now they are down to twenty or thirty people. They learned their faith as youngsters growing up in the village, but as they grew older China has developed. In the towns, there are now many enticements (*youhuo*), and slowly, many of them have lost their faith."

"But up in the villages," he added, "the faith remains firm (*wengu*)."

China's development had largely escaped the Lisu villages that clung to the mountainsides, where homes were still made of woven bamboo and animals still lived under the floor, where days and seasons were structured by the agricultural calendar and the church calendar, by planting and harvesting, by Easter and Christmas. It was from these villages that the Bible training center students came.

The Bible training centers were very important (*feichang zhongyao*), emphasized Ma-pa Jesse. Because of the oral nature of Lisu culture, Lisu Christian education was essential for cementing the textual elements of Christian faith and practice. In Jesse's estimation, about 10 percent of Lisu Christians in Gongshan County attended the two-year course of study (five months each year) offered by the church. The long commitment prevented many from attending, though some would attend short-term courses (ten days or a few weeks). About one-fifth of the students were women. The Bible training centers aimed to improve Bible literacy and give deeper teaching about the faith. Graduation did not mean attainment of a ministry credential; rather, the purpose of the Bible training centers was to build up the personal faith of the students, to firmly establish them in their Christian belief. However, most pastors and teachers had attended at least one session.

While the Fraser Script was quite simple and easy to learn—one could figure it out by singing hymns and reading Scripture references in church—attending the Bible training center interiorized Lisu writing in the mind, cementing it. It produced a class of higher-level readers and sent them back to their village churches.

The impact of the Bible training centers extended far beyond the 10 percent who had an opportunity to attend the two-year course. Most of the younger generation of Lisu would participate for a number of years in state education, attending schools where the medium of instruction is Chinese. As the schools were centrally located, students in higher altitude villages had to board at their school, usually beginning in the third grade. According to Hongcheng Shen and Minhui Qian, "School education, as a symbol of state power, always endeavors to transform internal Others into modern citizens. It devises a closed venue and separates students from everyday life situations to place them in a system of abstract knowledge. In local culture, however, students form practical knowledge in the course of enculturation. Due to the sustained expansion of modernity, an unequal power relationship is formed between abstract knowledge and practical knowledge."[5]

In school, Lisu children learned abstract knowledge taught in Chinese. But this was not all they learned. Schools were also "symbols and manifestations of the state will" that "constantly transmit ideology, mainstream culture, and modern knowledge systems to the local people, even in ethnic minority districts in the most remote and distant border regions."[6] When Lisu students attended school, they shifted from one cultural system to another, from the more practical, experiential knowledge learned at home or in the fields in their mother tongue to the abstract knowledge gained in the Chinese language at school. But as Shen and Qian emphasized, these two knowledge systems were in an unequal power relationship.

The Lisu Bible training centers were a means of balancing this power gap. First, the Lisu Bible training centers promoted literacy in the Lisu language. Only the Tibetans and the Uighurs had bilingual education provided by the state; the Lisu did not have this, so it was only in church—singing songs and reading the Bible—that most Lisu read their own language. The Bible training centers reinforced Lisu literacy, cementing and interiorizing the language in students and sending them back to their villages.

For an ethnic minority, language is symbolic of ethnic identity, and its loss is tantamount to ethnic extinction. Ma-pa Jesse was very aware of this potential danger. "Look at the Mongolians," he told me. "Such an important ethnic group in Chinese history. They went all the way to Europe! But now so much of their culture is lost. And look at the Manchu people. Another important minority people in Chinese history. But now they have been all but absorbed into the Han majority, and can no longer even read or write their own language. Here in Gongshan," Jesse continued, "the other minorities have learned to speak and even read Lisu." The Lisu possession of a written language gave them an elevated cultural position with other area minorities.

Second, the Bible training centers raised Lisu cultural knowledge. State school was a place where emphasis was laid upon learning Chinese characters, speaking standard Mandarin dialect, and mastering the subjects of mathematics, science, and politics, all with the underlying message that these subjects, none of which had any place in Lisu culture, were the legitimate and important sources of knowledge. Abstract, national knowledge was affirmed; local, experiential knowledge, while not explicitly rejected, was useless.

The Lisu Bible training centers, however, presented Lisu knowledge in a school environment, thus legitimizing Lisu knowledge on the Chinese educational playing field. By transmitting Lisu religious and cultural knowledge using the Lisu written and spoken language in a formal educational environment with desks, teachers, blackboards, exams, and books, Lisu culture was elevated.

Schools formalize the cultural system to pass on knowledge that is outside of (though not in opposition to) the home. Even for those who will never attend them, the very existence of schools means that their culture is worthy and valuable. Few of Yunnan Province's twenty-six ethnic minorities operated their own schools; most suffered from the power inequality of state schools that sought to raise them out of their perceived cultural backwardness.

Third, the Bible training centers provided for the societal role of teachers within Lisu culture. There are informal and formal teachers. Informal teachers usually operate within the home and within the community. They socialize the young into the norms of culture, with teaching done experientially in the home or in the fields. As long as there are parents or older people, there will be informal teachers.

In addition to informal teachers, which are present in every culture, Christianity has given the Lisu formal teachers: of the Bible, of Lisu reading and writing, of Lisu Christian hymns. Teachers are respected within Chinese mainstream culture and within Lisu ethnic culture. Thus, a Lisu teacher achieves recognition within and outside his ethnic group, in Lisu culture and in Chinese society. Moreover, the existence of Lisu teachers elevates Lisu culture in the eyes of the majority Chinese. Teachers provide role models within Lisu culture. When an ethnic minority has formal teachers, the young can strive for an educational goal that is still within the bounds of their own language and culture. A minority culture that no longer has a place for teachers is in danger of cultural decay.

Finally, the Bible training centers reclaimed power and agency by presenting an alternative curriculum to the state education project. Michael W. Apple, who calls schools "institutions of cultural preservation and distribution,"[7] states, "The issues surrounding the knowledge that is actually taught in schools, surrounding what is considered to be socially legitimate knowledge, are of no small moment in becoming aware of the school's cultural, economic, and political position.... Questions about the selective tradition such as the following need to be taken quite seriously. Whose knowledge is it? Who selected it? Why is it organized and taught in this way?"[8]

Lisu Bible training centers presented Lisu knowledge, language, and culture and thus declared that this knowledge was legitimate. Bible training centers were places where Lisu Christianity, language, special history, and music were affirmed, rather than ignored, as was done in the state school system. The Bible training centers declared that there was an alternative path, an alternative education, and an alternative knowledge base to that offered by the Chinese state. As independent schools, the Lisu Bible training centers presented a curriculum and a knowledge base that represented the local church.

Several gifted Lisu Bible scholars I met were on an academic path that would be nonexistent without the church. For example, Jesse, of the Gongshan Bible school, was writing, organizing, and compiling a Lisu study Bible. The bilingual Cornelius, of the Liuku Bible school, was preaching in Chinese at the 8:00 a.m. Sunday service and in Lisu at the noon service as well as teaching New Testament Survey twice weekly to both the Lisu-language-track and the Chinese-language-track students. Moreover, these scholars were able to take their education and return to the Lisu people as teachers within their own culture, staying close to their mountain village roots. By their presence at the podium and in the classroom, they were personifications of the inherent worth of Lisu language, culture, and religion.

Lisu Bible scholars did not travel the educational path laid out by the Chinese government: attendance at elementary and middle school, a passing score on the college entrance exam, and finally attendance at university—likely one of the universities that focused on ethnic minorities, such as Yunnan Nationalities University. This educational path most often led out of the Nujiang Valley and away from the Christian faith.

Rather, Lisu Bible scholars were likely not to have completed their secondary schooling but to have risen to their current status as teachers through attendance at Lisu Bible training centers and other Chinese-language Bible schools for minorities scattered throughout Yunnan Province. They had been validated in their calling as teachers not through formal credential or government approval but through the affirmation of their own communities.

To be socialized into the Chinese state education project was to believe that education was the means for a brighter future, the path of upward mobility. Yet this model of education took place outside of the ethnic culture, and the brighter future envisioned nearly always necessitated leaving the local communities for a big city, for a wage-earning job, for a profession other than farming. Lisu Bible education offered the opposite; it trained teachers and leaders whose knowledge was only useful in the small churches of the hamlets and villages of the canyon walls. The Lisu Bible training centers were not just spiritual centers but also a means to cultural empowerment.

Reclaiming Factors

The reclaiming and revival of Christianity among the Lisu in the Nujiang Valley of Yunnan Province was not assured. Christianity in the valley had reached its nadir by 1980. Yet it did recover. Red crosses atop village churches now dotted the rugged landscape up and down the entire valley. Bible schools, one in each county, trained pastors and teachers. Evangelists were sent out into Tibet and other neighboring areas. The Fraser Script had been retrieved and relearned. The old hymns were remembered and sung a cappella in four-part harmony once again. Several factors allowed the Nujiang Valley Christians to reclaim their Christian faith.

The first factor is the faithful remnant who retained a seed of belief throughout the Quiet Years: those such as Jesse's grandfather, who continued to pray and believe, and those such as Titus, who shelved their belief and practice during the difficult years of persecution but who quickly took it up again once the doors were opened. These Christians, who by 1980 were few in number and quite elderly, were the one single strand of continuity in this great rupture. They began the initial reevangelization of their friends and family, spreading the Gospel through their kinship networks, building the foundation of believers that allowed the faith in subsequent years to spread rapidly.

A second factor is the expansion and development of the Burmese (and later Thai) Lisu church, with a full Bible translation (completed in 1986), Bible training schools, pastors, radio stations, and evangelists. While Christianity was being snuffed out in China, it was growing and expanding just across the border in Burma. Once China reopened, the Nujiang Lisu, connected by culture, language, and kinship, had these resources at their disposal. They did not have to start over.

Most of the Lisu who fled to north Burma did not return to China, although a few did. Those who did return are essentially stateless, denied the full rights of citizenship in either country and without facility in either national language. They live in small, scattered hamlets high above the Nujiang. Tso Lo hamlet is one of those hamlets, a place with a vibrant and pervasive faith as the villagers had little recourse to secular solutions and thus relied completely on God. Other Burmese Lisu came back to the Nujiang initially to visit family members and spread the Gospel through kinship networks, and later, to offer short-term Bible schools. Many Nujiang Lisu also went over to Burma for Bible training, a trend that continued during my fieldwork.

The presence of Burma just across the Gaoligong Mountains was critical for the reclaiming of Nujiang Christianity. Initially, Burma provided a place to which to escape. Then the Lisu church had time to incubate in north Burma, to grow there unhindered, to be preserved until it could be exported back into its original home. Together with the faithful remnant, the Burmese Lisu provided institutional memory, which does much to explain why, despite such a great rupture, Nujiang Christianity today has remained traditional, close to its missionary roots.

The third factor explaining the reclaiming of Nujiang Lisu Christianity is the suitability of Christianity to Lisu culture. This fit, consciously worked at since missionary times, made it easy for Lisu to believe and practice once the churches reopened, even if it was their first time hearing. It was not a completely fresh start. Christianity was embraced quickly, because what was brought back was not foreign. The Gospel message that was spread by the old, faithful remnant, or that came back over the Gaoligong Mountains from Burma, was easily accepted; it required no cultural dislocation. The Christian practices of a cappella hymn singing, gathering together for intercessory prayer out loud, and abstaining from smoking and drinking fit well with Nujiang Lisu culture, for they had in fact originated there. They had been born and forged around the fires and in the villages with their great-grandparents. Bible schools, embroidered Bible bags, evangelism, singing hymns, attending church, praying together—none of these were new. The Old Story and the Christian practices were reinhabited and reclaimed.

The final factor is the deep and thorough spiritual grounding of the first generation of post-1980 believers. While literacy for most Lisu Christians is just a thin veneer, this first generation was truly literate, their literacy earned through arduous copying of the Bible and hymnbook by firelight. During my fieldwork, these were the older generation of Christian leaders. According to Jesse, a member of this generation, these believers know the Bible very well; it is completely in their head; they do not need to look things up. Also, they can write the Lisu language beautifully. The younger ones, who became Christians after 1995 and obtained a Lisu Bible through the mere act of purchasing it, do not have that same ability. The first generation of post-1980 believers experienced childhood and adolescence during the privations of the Cultural Revolution. Their young adult years were spent in reclaiming the Bible, handwritten letter by handwritten letter. Their passion and knowledge are unmatched.

None of these factors was decisive in and of itself to account for the rebirth of Nujiang Christianity. But together, they were enough to bring the Christian faith to the tipping point where momentum could build. Today, estimates are that of more than six hundred thousand Chinese Lisu,[9] at least half are Christian.[10]

Although Lisu Christianity has stayed very close to its roots and its historic traditions, all of this had to be consciously and intentionally resurrected after 1980. The Lisu church can be considered a missionary church, true to the roots planted by J. O. Fraser, the Cookes, the Kuhns, the Morse family, and the many other Lisu church elders and deacons. But at the same time, it is a post-1980 church, restarted by the elderly Christians who retained a seed of belief, as well as by Pastor Jesse and the first generation of post-1980 believers, a process that still continues. The initial evangelization of the Lisu happened at the missionaries' behest and initiative.[11] But the revitalization of Lisu Christianity, after more than two decades of dormancy, was an almost entirely Lisu project.

A New Year

We woke up on New Year's Day to a few bags of candy and two bottles of Sprite, a very special treat. Our big event of the day was the 1:30 p.m. church service down at Patchwork Village, the church atop the patchwork mountain. Midmorning, Naomi gathered up the hamlet children for one last dance practice, as they would be performing for the church. The song Naomi had chosen was not Lisu Christian pop but a Chinese song, based on Psalm 119:11–12. She stopped the children, pulled out her Lisu Bible, and read the verses:

> I have hidden your word in my heart
> that I might not sin against you.
> Praise be to you, Lord;
> teach me your decrees.

After giving them a short teaching, she ran them through the dance a few more times until she determined they were ready to perform.

We departed single file down the trail for the church down below. Lisu from all the neighboring villages and hamlets congregated for church, the various narrow trails converging into an anthill of beaded headdresses, long pleated skirts, purple and black velvet vests with embroidered trim, and Bible bags with brightly colored tassels.

Inside the packed church, the song leader asked us to sing hymn #288, "Gloria, from Twelfth Mass," one of the long oratorios from the back of the hymnbook. Though these oratorios were translated, their source is now unknown. They have been lost to their original Western context and are only maintained in the Lisu hymnbook. Such oratorios are not usually sung on an ordinary Sunday morning, but they often made an appearance at festivals, and they were taught at the Bible training centers. The oratorios were through-composed—that is, they were not broken up into stanzas but contained one line of continuous melody. This oratorio was particularly difficult. It contained long rests in which the entire congregation had to count the beats, without the aid of any musical accompaniment, and then sing exactly in unison on the proper beat. Any miscounting would mean coming in with great gusto in an unexpected and unwanted solo.

The fifth line had a particularly troublesome spot, and the first time through, unpracticed as this congregation was, the oratorio fell apart. Undaunted, the song leader had us try again, only for the congregation to falter once more when it hit that fifth line. After the two false starts, the third time we pressed on and were able to make it past the troublesome spot, if not confidently, at least with the ability to carry the music forward.

Naomi brought up her group of twelve children from Tso Lo hamlet for the performance part of the service. She had all the kids recite Psalm

119:11–12 in Lisu before they performed the dance, as the lyrics were in Chinese and not understandable to the congregation.

For the evening service, we returned to the storage room chapel above Tso Lo village. The first hymn we sang was hymn #1, "To God Be the Glory," written by Fanny J. Crosby (1820–1915). Crosby, blinded in childhood, wrote thousands of hymn texts over the course of her life, several of which were contained in the Lisu hymnbook. "To God Be the Glory" was published in 1875 by Ira Sankey in various British hymnals, but it did not become popular in the United States until it was used in a Billy Graham Crusade in 1954.[12] "To God Be the Glory" was a personal favorite of mine. Judging from the loudness and enthusiasm with which the Tso Lo villagers sang it, it was a favorite of theirs as well. Having spent so many months with the Lisu, I was still struck by how loudly they sang. In that small square storeroom, four parts thundered across the room and back again, particularly when they sang the familiar chorus. As I sang with them, I noticed the translation was not quite exact. In English, the line "Praise the Lord" is repeated; in Lisu, there is no repetition:

>   Praise the Lord!   SI.. d T∀
>   Praise the Lord!   DO, MU, L∀=

What in English could be said in three syllables required six syllables in Lisu. The Lisu version literally could be read "To the Lord, let us praise." These two lines of translation demonstrated just some of the challenges that faced the translators of the hymnbook, where the musical requirements of meter and cadence were much more exacting than with the translation of the Bible.

But something else could be seen in these two lines of translation. The Lisu version contained a communal element that was absent in the original English. The particle L∀, meaning let's, often followed a verb, giving such common everyday expressions as JI L∀, "Let's go," or Z L∀, "Let's eat." In this case, the L∀ particle followed DO, MU, meaning praise. The nature of the Lisu language and the requirements of its grammar worked together to insert the idea of togetherness, an idea completely at one with Lisu culture, into this American hymn.

Voice

Jesse (Gongshan County)

I always thought my grandfather was strange.

I used to hear him chanting scriptures, at midnight or one in the morning. (Of course he never did this during the day). I knew it was the Lisu language but still I couldn't understand it. Actually I thought he was a bit crazy.

My grandfather had become a Christian when the Morse family brought the Gospel to Gongshan around 1936. Here in Gongshan, we were the last of the Lisu to receive the Gospel. When the Communists razed his church, my grandfather climbed up into the mountains, carved a hole in the trunk of a tree, and hid his Bible.

Everyone in our village had wooden houses with thin walls, so they all knew about the prayers. But my grandfather had "a strong character and a long knife," so cadres left him alone.

In 1980 the churches were allowed to reopen. A group of old people like my grandfather began meeting in our home, singing and praying. Very soon my parents and I believed as well. I was sixteen years old.

Some of the old people, like my grandfather, had copies of the New Testament plus Psalms that they had hidden away in the mountains. There were perhaps one or two copies of a partial Bible and one hymnbook per village. The old people taught us how to read and write Lisu in the evenings.

Compiled from interviews on August 3 and 26, 2013, December 24, 2013, and April 16, 2014, as well as from Graham-Harrison, "Christians in China Border Valley."

The one or two Bibles were passed around from house to house every night, and we would take turns copying. We didn't have electricity then, so everything was done by torchlight.

Those of us who became Christians between about 1980 and 1995 can write beautiful Lisu letters, because we spent so much time copying the Bible and copying the hymnbook. We know the Bible so well, we don't even need to look verses up! The Bible is in our minds and in our hearts. Today's young Christians don't have that ability. They can't write Lisu very well. They grew up having their own Bible, and never had to copy to get one. They have cell phones and computers, and never had to write like we, the first generation of new believers, had to write.

Chapter 8

HYMNS OF THE EVERLASTING HILLS

> Jesus! what a Friend for sinners!
> Jesus! Lover of my soul;
> Friends may fail me, foes assail me,
> He, my Savior, makes me whole.
>
> Hallelujah! what a Savior!
> Hallelujah! what a Friend!
> Saving, helping, keeping, loving,
> He is with me to the end.

"We Lisu people have three treasures: *chiben*, knife, and crossbow," says Ah-Cheng in the opening scene of the documentary film *Treasure of the Lisu: Ah-Cheng and His Music*. "Among them, the *chiben* is the dearest to our heart, because it brings us laughter and joy."[1] The remainder of the film shows Ah-Cheng, a Nujiang Valley Lisu Christian, as he works to maintain the traditions of his forefathers by keeping the music of the chiben, a four-stringed lute, alive.

In reading the rather voluminous missionary literature on the early evangelization period of the Lisu, the crossbow and the knife are mentioned

---

Epigraph from "Our Great Savior," lyrics by J. Wilbur Chapman, 1910, hymn #69 in the 2013 Yunnan Lisu hymnbook.

often, but the chiben, not at all. And during my time in the Nujiang Valley, I never saw a chiben, either inside the church or out.

The loss of the chiben remained a mystery until I uncovered two sources in the literature. First, ethnomusicologist Hans Peter Larsen, in describing the music of non-Christian Lisu of northern Thailand, notes, "There exist two distinct categories in Lisu musical culture—instrumental music and songs. Only men play instruments, although both sexes may sing. *Instruments and songs are never used in combination*, and instrumental music is mainly used for dancing, which is not the case for the dominating song styles" (emphasis mine).[2] Thus, one could argue that the a cappella nature of Lisu hymn singing accords with their pre-Christian musical culture. Yet this did not explain the abandonment of the chiben. Here, an excerpt from Leila Cooke's missionary narrative proved explanatory. She described the Christian conversion of a Lisu village: "So they went from house to house, tearing down the altars. They built a big bonfire in each home and many hands piled incense, altar shelves, lucky paper and all in the cleansing flame, until every bit of heathen paraphernalia in the whole village was consumed. *They even did away with the musical instruments used at their dances*" (emphasis mine).[3] As can be seen from the above example, the Lisu choice of a seemingly nonindigenous form of worship—a cappella singing of translated Victorian-era Western hymns—cannot be explained so simply. While the translated Western hymns certainly reflected the influence of the missionaries upon Lisu culture, it could also be argued that a cappella singing was itself an indigenous form, and that the loss of the chiben was a local choice. Regardless, the forces of missionization and indigenization are not linear; rather, they reflect a complex interplay of Westerner and native, of new belief and old culture, before a new cultural form—in this case, the Lisu Christian hymns—settles in.

In this chapter I will take an in-depth look at the Lisu Christian practice of singing translated Western hymns a cappella in four-part harmony. Hymn singing is a special category of practice, for unlike most practices, where teasing out theology can be a difficult enterprise, in the hymns, fragments of doctrine, belief, and creed are embedded within the bodily practice itself.

The Creation of the Lisu Hymnody

As mentioned in chapter 1, J. O. Fraser used hymns as part of his initial evangelization effort with the Lisu. Before there were any printed books,

Gospel portions, or even a catechism, he would teach each family who had turned Christian a simple prayer and a hymn.[4] But as the Lisu church grew and developed, Fraser, as the CIM superintendent for Yunnan Province, found himself more in the background of the Lisu work. The day-to-day work of teaching Bible school, translating the Lisu New Testament, and developing the hymnbook fell to other missionary couples—most notably, Allyn and Leila Cooke.

Fraser called Allyn and Leila Cooke "our missionary-musicians" and credited them with teaching the Lisu to sing in parts.[5] Both Allyn and Leila were exemplary classically trained musicians, Allyn on the violin and Leila at the piano. Rev. Raymond Buker, a missionary one mountain range over, recalled seeing Leila Cooke sit down at the piano for the first time in ten years and play Beethoven's *Moonlight Sonata* without a note of music.[6]

In the first Bible school event of the newly emerging Lisu church, the Cookes taught classes in Bible, writing, and four-part singing.[7] In teaching hymns to the new church, the Cookes were following long-established missionary practice.[8] According to James Krabill, "Translating hymn texts has been a common practice throughout much of the missionary era and is generally as helpful to new converts as it is satisfying to the missionaries themselves."[9]

Within China, there had long been debates about the use of translated Western hymns. These debates played out on the pages of the *Chinese Recorder*, a widely read publication in the missions community, which from the 1870s on contained numerous articles, editorials, and letters surrounding the translation of hymns into Chinese.[10] Missionaries in China were frustrated on several accounts. First, the Chinese were used to a pentatonic scale and found the heptatonic arrangements of Western hymns unfamiliar and difficult to learn. In an article in *The Chinese Recorder* entitled "Chinese Music and Its Relation to Our Native Services" (1890), W. E. Soothill, a music scholar and sinologist who later taught at Oxford University, wrote, "Here let me lay down *an axiom for universal guidance* in choosing tunes that are suited to the native voice; if you don't want good tunes spoiling never choose one that cannot be played entirely on the black keys of the piano, or one that at least has no sustained notes on any of the white keys. The Chinese cannot, except after long and careful training . . . sing a tune in which the major fourth or seventh appears, especially if it be a sustained note."[11]

Further, the Chinese were not used to singing in groups and found it distressing to listen to harmonies. Bliss Wiant, a pioneer in the development of an indigenous Chinese hymnody, offers that the Chinese ear did not enjoy the simultaneous singing of different pitches.[12] In his book *The Music of China*, he describes one Chinese Christian who, upon hearing singing in harmony for the first time, "was so emotionally stirred with horror that it seemed as if his hair stood straight on end."[13] Another problem lay in the linguistic difficulty of translating the poetic forms of the lyrics from English into Chinese. Many felt that literary quality was lost in translation, and the results lacked sophistication and sounded like low-level gibberish to the Chinese.[14] One anonymous contributor to the *Chinese Recorder*, writing in 1887, summarizes the frustrations the missionaries felt: "It is only with the greatest difficulty that the average Chinaman can learn even one of our tunes."[15]

More from the seemingly inherent difficulties and transitions than from any firm belief in the merits of indigenization of aesthetic forms, there was an early movement toward indigenization of Chinese hymns. Soothill captures the emotion of these early missionaries: "Oh, for the day when the native poets of China shall arise in their strength to purge our hymn books of the watery stuff they contain and give us soul-inspiring hymns to rouse the church into a blaze of enthusiasm for Christ."[16]

A few indigenous hymn writers did emerge. The most notable was Pastor Hsi (Xi Shengmo), a Confucian scholar and former opium addict affiliated with the CIM, who became known in the West through a sympathetic biography written by Hudson Taylor's daughter-in-law Geraldine Taylor.[17] More recently, Alvyn Austin describes Pastor Hsi's hymns as "glorying in the value of being poor and persecuted and small because 'Jesus loves me.'"[18] Another Chinese hymn writer, T. C. Chao, dean of the School of Religion at Yenching University, aimed to write hymns that would express the religious feeling of ordinary Chinese. According to Bliss Wiant, "He deliberately chose [Chinese] characters of simple construction and meaning, carefully and prayerfully fitting them into the rhythm and nuance of the Chinese tunes."[19] The fine efforts of these Chinese hymn writers notwithstanding, for the most part, today's Chinese hymnody reflects Western origins.[20]

Yet, where translating hymns brought difficulty and frustration in greater China, the opposite happened in Lisuland. While the Chinese were not used to singing in groups, choral singing was part of Lisu culture, used in courting, marriage, and religious rituals as well as during the New Year's festival.[21] The Lisu took to the hymns immediately; they particularly enjoyed singing in four-part harmony. Isobel Kuhn recounted, "And the Lisu with a little training could sing in parts! Oh, how my soul had been galled by the monotone singing of the Chinese peasant! This glorious love of music and keen aptitude for it was a luxury."[22] Hymn singing became an essential element at the Rainy Season Bible School, and translation of a Lisu hymnbook proceeded apace with the Lisu New Testament. In the Village of Olives in the Nujiang Valley, the Christians took to sitting according to their choral parts during all chapel services.[23]

Despite their obvious love and affinity for Western hymns sung in four-part harmony, the Cookes still made an effort at indigenizing the Lisu hymnody. As mentioned above, in greater China missions the debate over the indigenization of the Christian hymnody had been going on since before the Lisu field even opened. The 1934 version of the China Inland Mission hymnal contained twenty-eight hymns (out of a total of four hundred) written by Pastor Hsi or other Chinese Christians.[24] Fraser taught one of Pastor Hsi's hymns to members of the Tsai family of Six Family Hollow, some of his first converts,[25] and published his thoughts regarding the superiority of setting Christian music to indigenous tunes.[26]

Allyn and Leila Cooke, together with Fish Four (Moses) and his family, moved to the Nujiang Valley—what Leila Cooke called "the largest and most densely populated Lisu field in the world"[27]—so they could provide teaching to the new Lisu converts but also be in a purer Lisu linguistic environment. The Lisu in Muchengpo and Gospel Mountain, living closer to Chinese civilization, had more Chinese words in their vocabulary. The Lisu of the Nujiang Valley were more remote and isolated, and thus their language had remained more thoroughly Lisu. It was there, in the Nujiang Valley, that the Lisu New Testament and the Lisu hymnbook were completed. Leila Cooke reported that, in addition to helping with the New Testament, Fish Four (Moses) was very involved in the translation, correction, and production of the Lisu hymns.[28]

Leila Cooke sought out some Lisu poetesses to gain a greater understanding of the language for the purposes of Bible translation. In addition to incorporating words (such as four-word couplets learned from Lisu poetic chants), the missionaries translated many hymns using Lisu poetic structure. As Leila Cooke described it, "Lisu poetry is very similar in style to that of the precious Psalms of David. Each thought is repeated with the same number of words, and companion phrases to express it."[29]

Upon discovery of the Lisu poetic forms, the missionaries sought to use this language in the translation of the Bible and the hymnbook. As Leila Cooke recalled, "The result was that hymns soon began to appear in Lisu poetry. Fish Four's mind took to it like a duck to water. But the deacons came with grave faces and protested that the new hymns had a heathen flavor. For once the missionary won out, however, and the hymns were later included in their hymnbook."[30] The incorporation of Lisu poetic forms into the translation of Christian hymnody is an enduring legacy of the missionary work in the Nujiang Valley, allowing translated Western hymns to root themselves deeply into the steep Lisu mountainsides.

Evangelist Moses (Fish Four) had come with the Cookes to the Nujiang Valley to continue serving as their translator-helper. One day, he was carrying a load of bamboo to make a chicken coop, and he fell. His fall likely resulted in an internal hemorrhage, as he continued to spit up blood for some time.[31] Moses was never the same, though it took several months for his condition to become grave. As he lay dying, he heard the Lisu singing a new hymn that Allyn Cooke had just translated: "Our Great Savior" Moses loved the hymn, asked to see it, then insisted on making a few corrections.[32] The next day, he died.

Leila had this to say in her next circular letter: "His lips are silent now, but the Lisu translation of the New Testament is largely his gift to God's work, for he has labored on it for years. And he also continues to speak to us through the many hymns he has translated."[33]

A month or two before he passed away, Moses composed this hymn in the Lisu poetic style. This hymn is #140 in the Lisu hymnbook, and is still sung today.

> Lord Jesus, Thou art my road!
> Lord Christ, Thou art my way!
> Oh, what joy when my journey's done!
> Oh, what happiness when I've arrived!
>
> My hope is up above.
> My trusting-place is up yonder.
> Because of that my joy is full.
> For that reason my joy is complete.
>
> When this house of flesh falls over.
> When this tabernacle falls down.
> I hope for the Great House,
> I think of the Great Home.
>
> My trusting-place is secure.
> My hope also is sound.
> May God's will be done.
> May the Lord's wish be accomplished.[34]

140 SI.. ꝺ YE-S ʌW J GU
Lord Jesus, My Road

```
ᑊB 4/4 — — 4                                                                    (LI ɜ,)
  | 3, 5,  | 1 —.  5,  | 5̄,  4̄,  3̄,  5̄, | 6, — —  5. —  | 1 —       | 7 —.  6,     5, —  6, —  | 5, —    —    3, —
  | 3, —   | 3, —.  3.  | 3̄,  2̄,  1̄,  3̄, | 4, — — 3. —   | 5, —      | 4, —.  4,    4. —   4, —  | 3̄,  —  4̄,  2̄,  3̄, —
  (1) SI..    ꝺ    YE- SU AW    J       GU=  SI..     ꝺ      JI- SU AW    JE           dE;=
  (2) AW      LO.  T    GU NYɜ KW       ʌO=  Dn       J      T   GU NYɜ  KW            ʌO=
  (3) AW      VI   Bɜ.. Bɜ: Kꝺ.. BY     ꓕY=  AW       Ɔ..    KU. ME, JE  BY            ꓕY=
  (4) AW      V    Lɜ   GU  ꓕꞀ.. M      ʌO=  AW       AO     LO. GU  ꓧE.. M           ʌO=
  | 1' —    | 5 —.  5     | 5 —   5 —    | 1' — — 1' —   | 3' —      | 2' —.  2'  7 — 2 —     | 1' — — 1' —
  | 1 —     | 1 —.  1     | 1 —   1 —    | 4 — — 1' —    | 1' —      | 5 —.  5  5 — 5 —      | 1̄' — 5̄ — 1' —

  | 3, 5,   | 1 —.  5,   | 5̄, 4̄, 3̄, 5̄,   | 6, — —  5. —  | 1 —      | 7 —.  7,    7̄, 6̄, 5, — | 6̄, — 7̄, — 1 —
  | 3, —    | 3, —.  3.  | 3̄, 2̄, 1̄, 3̄,   | 4, — — 3. —   | 3, —     | 4, —.  4,    4. —  4, —  | 4, —  —   3, —
  (1) Xɜ:     LO   YE NY AW            K,      Ɔ I=    JE     GU  LE   NY  AW   NI,           dU=
  (2) GO      M    KW BE AW            K,      Ɔ I=    GO     M   PꞀ   DU  AW   NI,           dU=
  (3) VI      D:   M  TV AO            LO.     TY= KW  D:     M   TV   Dn   J                 TY=
  (4) WU-     S    NI, LꞀ dYɜ;         L       FI=     SI..   ꝺ   Nn.. M   dYɜ; L             FI=
  | 1' —    | 5 —.  5      5 — 1' —    | 1' — — 1' —    1' —       | 5 —.  5    2' —   7 —   | 1̄' — 2̄ — 1' —
  | 1 —     | 1 —.  1      1 —   1 —   | 4̄ — 6̄ — 1' — 1' —         | 5 —.  5   5 — 5 —       | 5 — —  1 —
```

fig. 11 "Lord Jesus, My Road" by Pastor Moses. Photo: author.

Each line is repeated with a companion phrase that restates, or even expounds upon, the meaning of the first line, a style known as synonymous parallelism that is common to and resonant with oral cultures.

The Cookes did not just encourage the Lisu to write hymns according to their own poetic style; they also translated about thirty Western hymns in the Lisu poetic style, using synonymous parallelism. One of those is the well-known Easter hymn "When I Survey the Wondrous Cross," written by Isaac Watts. The Lisu version, along with a retranslation back into English, is below:

ꓭO CE; SU ʌW W TI. D: M-.	Creator of man, my great sovereign king;
W: C; SU ʌW SI.. ꝺ D: M-.	Creator of all, my Lord and master.
ꓕI: HO: NU TV NI, ZO SI NYI-.	One group hated you;
ꓕI Bɜ NU TV NI. VꞀ., SI NYI-.	The other half was angry with you.
NU TV ꓫꞀ., NYI VI C ꓭO, SI-.	They slandered you and tied you with a rope
NU TV Jꓵ.. NYI SI, D., DꞀ SI-.	They prosecuted you and hit you with a rod.
ƆU: N: VO, FU. SI W: Xɜ.,_ LO=	They put a crown of thorns on your head and mocked you;
Bꓵ ꓒꞀ NI.. GꞀ SI X. CI._ LO=	They divided your clothes and ridiculed you.

HO., ƆU: ⊥∀; NYI XՈ: DO L SI-.	They hammered you with nails, you bled;
A. ⊥: K. NYI XՈ: YI L SI.	They pierced your side, blood and water flowed.
NU ⊥∀; SE; DU KW NI, X._ LO=	When they killed you, you were distressed;
LA; BO T⊓. DU KW NY X._ LO=	When you were on the cross, you were worried.
NI, J: MY KO.. SU CYU SI d-.	Dearly beloved, our Savior;
XU: ⋊O; NI, ΛO.. SU XU, SI.. d-.	Through Your blood, our Redeemer,
ΛW N., BƎ ⊓ NY NU N.,_ LO=	You suffered when I should have suffered;
ΛW XU., BƎ ⊓ NY NU XՈ_ LO=	You died when I should have died.
SI.. d NU ⊥Ǝ ⋊⊓ X. JՈ_ NYI-.	Lord, you suffered for us.
JI- SU NU ⊥Ǝ ⋊⊓ XƎ. ᴙ_ NYI-.	Christ, you paid for us.
dU JO., NU T∀ LI. GꞀ M: LO;=	Money cannot cancel our debt;
XՈ. JO., NU T∀ CƎ, GꞀ M: LO;=	Gold cannot pay what we owe.
ΛW S∀; SƆ. NI, ⊥I NI, M LƎ.;-.	My strength, my knowledge, my whole heart,
ƆI d∀, L∀ d∀, ⊥I GO DƎ; LƎ.;-.	My hands, my feet, my whole body,
NU T∀ TI GꞀ DU dYE; L FI=	To you I offer as my sacrifice,
NU T∀ SƎ GꞀ DU dYE; L FI=	To you I give as my praise.

While the melody line is intact, the translation completely transformed this old and familiar hymn. The synonymous parallelism obliged the Lisu version to extend for six verses, while the original English contained only four. The key word *cross*, in the first line of the English version, is pushed back to verse three in the Lisu version. The end result was a cadence and rhyming, a balance and counterbalance of phrases and thoughts that flowed quite naturally with the poetic sensibilities of the Lisu mind.

But in addition to changes in format required by the Lisu poetic structure, there were other changes as well. The language of the English version, rather abstract and distant words such as *gain*, *loss*, *contempt*, and *pride*, was replaced with concrete imagery in the Lisu version. Poetic allusion in the English version—for example, "See from his head, His hands, His feet, /

Sorrow and love flow mingled down!"—was replaced with stark reality in the Lisu translation: "They hammered you with nails, you bled; / They pierced your side, blood and water flowed." Moreover, such imagery used everyday, common Lisu words. The poetic structure and the concrete imagery combined to make this hymn "very meaningful."[35] When I asked Ma-pa Timothy to help me learn an Easter hymn ahead of the upcoming Easter festival, "When I Survey" was the hymn he chose to teach me. Mere translation does not aptly describe the Lisu version; this hymn has been utterly transformed.

The Meaning of Hymns for Lisu Christianity in the Mission Period

The missionary narratives are replete with mentions of the Christian hymns and their role in the teaching of the church. In this section I will quote extensively from these narratives to recapture the meaning the hymns had during this time.

Fraser, now superintendent in Yunnan province and visiting the Lisu areas, wrote to his mother:

> I would love you to hear our Lisu singing in this district. Mr. and Mrs. Cooke, our missionary-musicians, have always taught them to sing in parts, and they do—with no organ either. It is <u>really inspiring</u>, and has often brought tears to my eyes. I do not know any other place in China where I have heard congregational part-singing.... I have heard very few congregations at home, either in England or America, whose singing is so inspiring. They themselves love it— how you would like to go to bed on Sunday night to the strains of some sweet hymn-tune which they are still singing in one of their homes in the village—and in parts?... Oh, how I love to hear them sing—"When my lifework is ended and I cross the swelling tide...!" But I must not seem to boast—I know one poor missionary heart that has swelled with emotion and praise, listening to the hearty and tuneful singing of these aborigines of the Burma-China border.[36]

Crossman describes another time Fraser walked up on a Lisu village: "Suddenly, out of the darkness came the sound of singing. They [Fraser and his companion] stopped in their tracks to listen. Slowly it dawned on them that somewhere in the forest Lisu were singing hymns. They followed the sound and came upon a newly-built chapel at Water Bowl that James [Fraser] had never seen. The meeting was being held in total darkness because the Christians could not afford oil for their tiny lamps."[37]

Isobel Kuhn described her husband, John, visiting a Lisu village in Burma for the first time:

> His party arrived on a Saturday after dark, and the villagers were all at chapel. Of course the visit was unannounced and unexpected, but as the weary band climbed the mountainside (at the end of seven days' travelling) grateful that the long, hard trek was nearly over, through the dark there came a sound of singing, and as they listened, they heard these words floating down the trail to greet them, like a heavenly welcome:
>
> Have you been to Jesus for the cleansing power?
> Are you washed in the Blood of the Lamb?
> Are you fully trusting in His grace each hour?
> Are you washed in the Blood of the Lamb?
>
> "Before we saw their faces, we heard their testimony!" said John, touched to the heart.[38]

And Isobel described the immersive experience of Lisu hymn singing felt by those present and experiencing it: "As the song gathered volume the room seemed flowing with waves of wonderful melody until we were bathed, drowned, in the beauty of it. Tenor, bass, alto, soprano flowed together into one exquisite harmony, and sung from hearts that believed and loved Him wholly."[39]

Hymns were not just sung as part of chapel services. They were part of the rhythm of life for the Lisu Christians, sung while hoeing in the fields,[40] at picnics,[41] to comfort the dying,[42] while traveling along the road,[43] and at times of personal grief.[44]

Hymns also became the centerpiece at the Christmas festivals held throughout Lisuland. Isobel Kuhn mentioned that more than a thousand guests were usually expected at the Christmas festivals. For one festival, "They had asked Ma-ma [Isobel Kuhn] to translate a new Christmas song which only they would know, and now they must practice it in four parts so as to be able to surprise the guests."[45] Also key to the Christmas festival was a welcoming hymn:

"One-three-five (doh-me-soh)," sings out the leader of the reception committee. "Let it come!" And voices in four parts rise up from behind the flowers.

> Christmas guests are at the door!
> Let them in.
> It is duty to receive them,
> Let them in.
> That of Jesus we may think,
> His Great Day that we may keep;
> Praise to God, we come to greet.
> Let them in!

Then through the arch they come, shaking hands with each of the long line of singers.[46]

Singing, as mentioned, was taught from the earliest days of the first Bible schools. It continued to play a prominent role when John and Isobel Kuhn started the Rainy Season Bible School in the Nujiang Valley in 1938. When the Bible School for Girls was started in 1942, the Kuhns always tried to have new hymns translated so that the girls would have a contribution to bring back to their village chapels.[47] Closing day ceremonies for the Bible schools always involved hymns, even the Hallelujah Chorus (#286 in the 2013 Yunnan Lisu hymnbook):

> The Rainy Season Bible School for boys asked for the *Hallelujah Chorus* again this year, so they are practicing it these evenings. Much of the success of this noble oratorio depends on alert and instant obedience to the leader. If this is missing you will find yourself singing, "Ha . . . " with lusty enthusiasm all alone while your neighbors bury their noses in their sleeves and snicker; and you have a miserable feeling that public prominence is not what you covet after all. For who could sing the *Hallelujah Chorus* without enthusiasm? "*The kingdoms of this world are become the kingdoms of our Lord and of his Christ . . . King of kings and Lord of Lords—Hallelujah!*"[48]

The ability to sing hymns fused quickly with Christian identity. Isobel Kuhn related this humorous exchange when two Lisu evangelists, Born-on-the-road and A-che, were seeking shelter at a Lisu home during a time when people were nervous because of a spate of brigandry and robbery.

The head of the home they had approached threatened to shoot them with poisoned arrows unless they could prove their identity. Here is the exchange:

> "I am Born-on-the-Road all the same, and my pal is A-che from Luda and we are on our way to preach."
> "Hm. If you are ma-pa-ra [evangelists] then you can sing. Tune up a hymn and perhaps we will believe you." So out in the dark, hungry and weary, our two lads sang *The Holy Spirit is with me*.[49]

Some indigenous Lisu hymns developed to mark ritual events, such as weddings, deaths, and the welcoming of visitors. In many cases the hymn singing was a functional substitute for a pre-Christian custom. Kuhn narrated the death of Me-do-me-pa, a church deacon and her neighbor: "It was eight the next morning when we heard a soft sound of weeping, up the hill. Before I could get galoshes on to go, the voices of Job, Luke, and others started to sing the Lisu funeral hymn, 'Sleep On, Beloved,' and I knew that the dear suffering one was with the Lord."[50]

In another funeral context from the same book, Kuhn provided the words to the Lisu funeral hymn:

> Although we Christians die,
> There will be an awaking from sleep:
> Because the Savior died for our sins,
> When Jesus returns we shall meet again.[51]

One cannot read about Lisu missionary work without reading about Lisu hymn singing. And one cannot encounter Lisu Christianity even today without experiencing hymn singing. Despite the great rupture from 1958 to 1980, hymn singing in the Nujiang Valley is just as important today as it was during missionary times.

Lisu Hymn Singing as Christian Practice

The Christian practice of hymn singing most fully embodies the expression of Lisu Christianity. It appeals to the inmost recesses of the oral aesthetic, for it is an entity of sound, one closely tied to emotions and memory. And hymn singing is the most shared of activities. Hymn singing as a practice touches upon the deepest stores of who the Lisu are as a people.

The Lisu practice of singing hymns cuts across various layers of meaning for Lisu Christians. At the levels of individual, church, and ethnicity, the hymns have affected Lisu Christian practice in many ways: as spiritual handbook, guard against heresy, link to personal and collective stories, literacy primer, personal devotional, embodiment of togetherness, and provider of stability. Ultimately, the Lisu Christians hymns have served as mediator of theology.

Spiritual Handbook

The Bible and the hymnbook form an "inseparable pair."[52] They were translated together during the missionary period. The Bible and the hymnbook were copied in longhand together by torchlight in the early 1980s as Lisu Christianity revived. And today, the Bible and the hymnbook are carried together in their distinctive woven bags. Hymnbooks are not left in church buildings for public use; rather, all Lisu Christians have their own, which accompanies them from home to church and back again.

While Lisu Christians regard the Bible as the authoritative source of truth, they have seldom read it outside of a ritualistic context. In contrast, the hymnbook, as a companion text, has been used as a ready reference handbook on the Christian life. This practical aspect is not surprising, for many of the hymns were associated with the revival movements of Dwight Moody and the theology of the Keswick Conventions that focused on holiness and sanctification, on living a victorious Christian life. Of the 319 hymns in the Yunnan Province Lisu hymnbook, published in 2013, the selection features hymns by Fanny Crosby (14), Philip Bliss (13), Charles Wesley (7), Isaac Watts (5), Frances Havergal (3), and other writers and arrangers. Seventeen hymns are of Lisu origin, with five of those attributed to Pastor Moses (Fish Four).

The hymnbook is divided into sections—God the Father, the Lord Jesus Christ, the Holy Spirit, Easter Hymns, the Bible, Prayer, Eternal Life, and so on—making it easy to reference. In my early days of studying the Lisu language, when I asked a young Lisu Christian the Lisu term for Holy Spirit, he quickly told me. Then he reached over to his end table, where he had stacked the Lisu Bible, the Chinese Bible, and the Lisu hymnbook. Pulling out the hymnbook and turning to the Holy Spirit section, he showed me how the term *Holy Spirit* was expressed in Lisu writing.

It is the hymnbook that had the most practical applications to Lisu daily life, and it is the hymnbook they reach for should a question arise. The hymns teach how to deal with life's troubles (NI . . . X . . . MY . . . X): hymn #242, "Take

It to the Lord in Prayer." The hymns urge forward evangelism: hymn #228, "Win the One Next to You." They provide assurance: hymn #177, "I Know Whom I Have Believed." They advise reliance on Jesus: hymn #138, "Trust and Obey." They promise victory: hymn #146, "Onward Christian Soldiers." They look forward to eternal life: hymn #256, "When We All Get to Heaven." They promote a holistic Christian life: hymn #224, "Living for Jesus."

While the Bible remains somewhat out of reach for the vast majority of Lisu peasant farmers with rudimentary skills in literacy, the well-worn hymnbook is widely known, its contents easy to find, and many of its most familiar hymns memorized.

Guard Against Heresy

The hymnbook is a sung catechism, a guard against heresy. This is especially important because as a result of low education levels and a largely oral culture, Bible literacy remains low. The most common heresy (at least what most Christians would label heretical) among Chinese house churches that have spread through the countryside has been the rise of a messianic leader.[53] That is unlikely to happen in the Lisu church when believers are singing such hymns as #56, "The Church's One Foundation (Is Jesus Christ Our Lord)." The hymnbook has kept the Lisu Christians on the straight and narrow path of orthodox faith.

Link to Personal and Collective Stories

At the 10:45 break at the Gongshan Bible training center, I asked A-cha her favorite hymn. She said hymn #116, "Whosoever Will," a hymn we had sung at least twice since my arrival the previous week. A-cha said this was one of the first hymns she learned after her conversion, so, whenever she sang it, she remembered that time. "Whosoever Will" was written during the winter of 1869–70 by Philip P. Bliss after hearing Henry Moorhouse, of England, speak for a week on John 3:16. Thus it was not surprising that A-cha so closely associated the hymn with her own salvation.

In this case, there was a congruity between lyrics pertaining to salvation and her own remembrance of her initial experience of salvation. For A-cha, every time she sang this hymn she was reciting again the narrative of her own conversion, her own individual Christian story, and placing it in the context of the larger Gospel story of salvation.

In addition to personal stories, the singing of the hymns tied the Lisu Christians back to a big story: the collective narrative of their conversion as an ethnic group. The hymnbook used during my fieldwork in the Nujiang Valley is virtually unchanged from the hymnbook translated by Allyn and Leila Cooke in the 1930s and 1940s, printed in Los Angeles in 1948 with the help of Eugene and Robert Morse, and painstakingly copied by hand by the light of a torch by the first generation of post-1980 Lisu Christians. This continuity is all the more striking given the twenty-two-year rupture from 1958 to 1980, when Bibles and hymnbooks were burned. In resurrecting the hymnbook, and in singing the hymns a cappella in four-part harmony just as before, the Lisu are quite consciously reaching back to the narrative of their own conversion, the missionary days of J. O. Fraser, Allyn and Leila Cooke, and others, all of whom are revered by the today's Lisu. While the Bible is the sacred book of Christians worldwide, past and present, the hymnbook is their own.

Literacy Primer

The hymnbook, with its concrete words and musical phrases, is easier to read than the Bible. Most Lisu Christians can learn to read at a basic level simply from singing along. Phrases in the hymnbook are not mere text but text embedded in music, music-text phrases that are familiar because they have been heard many times before. Simply by singing hymns at Sunday, Wednesday, or Saturday services, Lisu Christians can obtain a basic level of familiarity with the Fraser Script and a low functional level of literacy.

For most lay Lisu Christians, this level is sufficient to sustain the rest of their Christian lives. It allows hymn singing and gives the ability to read the Bible in the read-and-repeat style favored by most churches. It gives them a foundation to go further in self-study, for those who choose to do so. It provides a base to build on for those attending a Bible training center.

Personal Devotional

I observed several instances of Lisu Christians using hymns in their personal devotional practice. On one occasion I could hear Naomi playing the guitar in her room, so I walked over and knocked on the door. On her desk the hymnbook lay open. "I was singing my prayer," she said. Another afternoon (with farmwork proscribed, as it was Sunday), Ma-pa Timothy's father sat on the porch and sang hymns quietly to himself. Every so often his wife joined him from the kitchen. And another time, as everyone was sitting in the courtyard as usual, chatting before the evening service began, I walked into the church building since the air was a bit chilly. Three of the more elderly members of the church were inside as well, sitting in pews, quietly reading. As I was not used to seeing Lisu reading, I walked past each one to see what it was they were reading. All three were reading the hymnbook.

The hymnbook, with its simple phrasing, concrete images, and theology emphasizing a victorious Christian life, has a devotional quality that allowed it not just to be sung but to be read in rare times of quiet, individual worship. But hymn singing reaches even greater heights as a communal act.

Communal Act

The Lisu hymns are what Thomas Turino calls participatory performance, defined as "a special type of artistic practice in which there are no artist-audience distinctions, only participants and potential participants performing different roles, and the primary goal is to involve the maximum number of people in some performance role."[54] Further, Turino states that "participatory music and dance is more about the social relations being realized through the performance than about producing art that can somehow be abstracted from those social relations."[55]

A successful participatory performance is measured not by technical standards of musical quality, such as form, pitch, or artistic sensitivity. Rather, a successful event engenders maximum participation from the group. Turino explains, "Participatory music making leads to a special kind of concentration on the other people one is interacting with through sound and motion and on the activity in itself and for itself. This heightened concentration on the other participants is one reason that participatory music-dance is such a strong force for social bonding."[56] Music is a shared activity, one that creates a sense of belonging.

Of the various genres of music, group singing is perhaps the most communal in nature. Deborah Van Heekeren states that "singing promotes a participatory ontology."[57] Unlike instrumental forms of music, singing involves sound that emanates from one's own body. Singing does not involve passively listening to a performance; rather, it is participating from one's own interior and blending one's voice into a communal sound.[58]

Worship, as a participatory act, shares this communal quality with music. Yet hymn singing takes this communal quality of music and extends it, for, as J. R. Watson states, "Hymns are sung by those people who share certain things: Bible-reading, doctrine, common prayer, and moral precept."[59] In the singing of the hymns, Lisu Christians are not simply making music together; they are declaring common belief, common allegiance, common lifestyle. Watson explains, "The singer becomes part of a group process, engaged, committed, the vocalized 'I' or 'we' of the hymn becoming part of the involvement with public worship."[60] In singing a hymn, the individual small story locates itself within the big story of collective faith.

The Lisu love to sing hymns because it is something that they do together. It is a shared Christian practice that represents their embodiment as a church, as a community, as people who rely and depend on each other. While one can retreat into oneself during unison singing, singing in parts requires an awareness of those singing adjacent, of those singing the same part, and of those singing complementary parts. It creates a mindfulness of all of those in church, an accentuated communal feeling when the harmony and intertwining of parts rise in majestic song that fills every space in the plain and simple church buildings.

Provider of Stability

Of added interest to the loud and meaningful singing of hymns is that the canon of hymns has remained largely unchanged for nearly eighty years, many of them Victorian-era hymns translated by Western missionaries. Less interesting than musical change (which is natural and expected) is musical continuity (which is unexpected). The enduring presence of the Lisu hymnody in their Christian worship is a question that must be addressed.

This stability, or non-change, in their Christian music is remarkable for two reasons. First, around the world, particularly in Africa, local Christians are taking charge of their musical forms and infusing them with local color.[61] In fact, many have deemed this process a necessary step in the proper indigenization of Christianity.[62]

Second, the period from the creation of the canon of hymns until today has been fraught with persecution and turmoil. After 1949, much of the traditional music of Yunnan Province was scuttled for a time. When revitalized, the form had changed, often with the religious aspects dropped.[63] The Lisu Christian hymns thus have not been simply maintained; they have been consciously revived.

The Lisu hymns are a stable connection at a time when ethnic identity is in flux, even endangered. As John Baily states, "Ideas about the special link between music and identity are frequently offered to explain why a particular social group—a community, a population, a nation—cultivates outmoded and seemingly irrelevant musical practices."[64] According to Paul Westermeyer, "Church music is a cultural matter. The music the church uses does not happen in a vacuum. It happens in a specific time and place. The time and place have a history, memory, community, and trajectory that attend them, which at times—like our time—are in various states of upheaval."[65]

Lisu Christian history has been in upheaval since its inception. The very items that constitute cultural and religious identity have been continuously threatened. Thus, it is not surprising that the Lisu have clung to their hymns and have been loath to consider experimentation. No matter one's citizenship, dialect, or level of literacy, these hymns have united Lisu Christians not only in place but also back through time, to a common collective story. They cannot be easily discarded.

Lisu Hymns as Theological Mediator

As discussed previously, translating the more abstract theological concepts of Scripture posed a great challenge for the missionary translators. They met this challenge, at least in part, by employing words found in funeral chants and other forms of Lisu oral poetry, and by coining new words according to Lisu oral poetic forms, such as four-word couplets.

Yet while such appeals to oral poetry brilliantly created words based on Lisu cultural patterns, the underlying categories were still nonexistent. The question remaining is this: How are more abstract theological concepts—such as grace, sanctification, and forgiveness—of a religion like Christianity, which highly values the written word, translated into the oral context of the Lisu?

I contend that these biblical abstractions have been mediated through the Christian practice of singing. The hymnbook is the bridge between the written Word as sacred object and the lived, spoken, and sung words of the people. If the Lisu Bible was an icon, sacred and revered, the hymnbook, the second item in this two-book set, was the religious handbook. Singing the written words of the hymns brought the two realms—oral and literate—together. The various functions of the hymns overlap and intersect at various levels of meaning and experience, which can be encapsulated into one central understanding: the Lisu hymns serve as a theological mediator for Lisu Christians, bridging the gap between the text-intensive religion that is Christianity and the oral world of Lisu culture. The very reasons that hymns are denigrated by literary critics as an art form—their simplicity and lack of sophistication, their constraint by orthodoxy, their use of common phraseology[66]—are their very strengths in the mountainous reaches of Lisuland, where reading the Bible is culturally and linguistically out of reach and where people need a concrete theology that has meaning in their own lived experience.

The Lisu hymns serve as what Eric Havelock calls a "storage language"[67]—that is, directives from a governing body (in this case, the Bible, God, or the Church) that are proverbial-type utterances distributed by being sung or chanted aloud. The hymns are Christian theology converted into concrete imagery, constantly repeated in formulaic set phrases and clichés:

"There's power in the blood."
"Wash me and I shall be whiter than snow."

Because the hymns are sung—because they are text that is not remote, but rather embedded in musical phrasing—their power is heightened. Peter Wood and Emma Wild-Wood also observe this primacy of the sung word in Africa: "'Sermons preach a little but songs preach a lot' is a frequent refrain among Christians in North-East Congo. Such a sentiment clearly prioritizes the musical word over the spoken word, suggesting that what Christians sing is also what they believe/experience."[68] Moreover, taking a cue from Walter Fisher's narrative paradigm, hymns are poetic truth, public stories, and as such they confirm communal identity.[69] By singing along, one is entering the narrative, expressing identification, and affirming community-recognized truth:

"I once was lost but now am found, was blind but now I see."
"What a friend we have in Jesus, all our sins and griefs to bear!"

They are a practical, everyday, lyrical kind of theology.

But the Lisu hymnbook is not just essential: it is loved. These translated hymns are precious (*baogui*) to the Lisu people. Hymnbooks were hidden in the mountains during the Quiet Years; they were resurrected in 1980 through laborious copying; and the songs within the hymnbooks echo today throughout the mountainous reaches of the Nujiang Valley. In the everyday arena, in the practical living out of what it means to be a Christian for a communal and still largely oral-preference people such as the

Lisu, the Lisu Christian hymns are the centerpiece of worship and devotion, of prayer and penitence.

In singing hymns that hail from their missionary period, the Lisu acknowledge and honor this special history. In singing hymns in four-part harmony, the Lisu embody the communal nature of how they most authentically practice Christianity: together, as a community. In singing hymns containing revival theology, the Lisu are signaling the use of Christianity in leading a victorious Christian life. The hymns have given Lisu Christians a narrative structure in which to place themselves, and it is perhaps this aspect that makes hymn singing the apotheosis of Lisu Christian practices.

Voice

Naomi (Fugong County)

My name is Naomi. I have four brothers and four sisters. I am the ninth. Yes, the ninth child.

Okay, let me explain about my family. My parents fled to Burma in 1958. They were Christians, so they had to flee, because you couldn't be a Christian in China at that time. While in Burma they had eight kids. By 1986 the situation in Burma had deteriorated. China was open again, so they could come back. Then I was born. I am the only one who was born in China, and I am the only one in my family with Chinese *hukou*. [Hukou refers to the household registration system in mainland China. Hukou entitles the citizen to land, public services, education, and other benefits.] Because the rest of my family doesn't have hukou, they cannot go to school, they cannot go out to work, and they don't have any land.

When my family returned from Burma our homes and land were gone. So now our village is high up above Fugong, in a place nobody else wanted. Life is difficult. We built our house completely by ourselves, the woven bamboo walls and floors, the beds, everything.

My grandfather was an evangelist. My father is an evangelist and a pastor. My oldest brother is an evangelist. Including all of the in-laws and grandkids, there are now fifty-six people in my family, and all fifty-six of us are Christians. But many of my brothers and sisters are very poor. All of us are in China now, except my oldest sister. She stayed behind in Burma.

Compiled from interviews on August 11, 19, and 22, 2013, and December 27 and 28, 2013.

My profession is Bible teacher. My mother said that I came out of her womb (and she was forty-eight when she had me) believing the Gospel and teaching the Bible. I have been attending Bible training schools since I was sixteen years old. Now I'm twenty-three. I have attended Bible training schools in Gongshan, Fugong, Liuku, Kunming, and Burma. The Bible training school in Burma was for three separate one-month periods, so I went to Burma three times. I don't need a passport; I can just cross the border because I'm a Lisu.

Now I am teaching at the Gongshan Bible training center for this month. I know I am young, but I have been teaching at my village church every Sunday and every Wednesday for years (when I'm not attending Bible school).

My favorite hymn is "Take Me as I Am," the same one I was singing as my prayer the other day. I like it because we are sinners, but Jesus takes us as we are.

I won't marry. If I married, I would have to move away from my parents and my village, and take care of my husband's parents. I will stay here, with my own parents, and continue teaching the Bible.

Chapter 9

BUILDING THE HOUSE OF PRAYER

> "Great is Thy faithfulness," O God my Father,
> There is no shadow of turning with Thee;
> Thou changest not, Thy compassions, they fail not
> As Thou hast been Thou forever wilt be.
>
> "Great is Thy faithfulness!" "Great is Thy faithfulness!"
> Morning by morning new mercies I see;
> All I have needed Thy hand hath provided—
> "Great is Thy faithfulness," Lord, unto me!

The Nu Ni village church, built of whitewashed cinderblocks and surrounded by fields of corn, sat alone on a promontory overlooking the river below. The worn-looking church had bare cement floors, wooden benches for pews, and a pulpit covered with a bright blue and white checked cloth. A large cross was cut out of the façade, doubling as a skylight.

One entered the church through the courtyard, a wide-open space covered with cracked cement, the largest flat space in the area. Between services, villagers sat on vertical cement blocks ringing the courtyard to watch the children playing. One villager, who usually wore a green Chinese

---

Epigraph from "Great Is Thy Faithfulness," lyrics by Thomas O. Chisholm, 1923, hymn #3 in the 2013 Yunnan Lisu hymnbook.

army jacket several sizes too big, often played his one-stringed lute with a bow. Elderly women, wearing their ethnic dress, found shade against the church walls. In keeping with the exterior nature of their faith, constructing church buildings has been a priority for the Lisu community throughout its century-long Christian history. The churches have been built without any foreign assistance, using local materials and in local style. During the missionary period, they had earthen floors, thatched roofs, and log benches for pews. More recently, cinder blocks and cement are the building materials of choice. Then and now, building a church meant staking their claim, stamping their presence, proclaiming a kind of architectural testimony.

In the Lisu language, church literally means "house of prayer": WA ꓨU VI. This name reflects the idea that the church is a place where the community gathers together to pray, expressing in bodily form the communal life of the body of Christ. It is also a designation with biblical resonance. According to all three Synoptic Gospels, Jesus used this term when he threw the money changers out of the temple courts, quoting its original Old Testament reference below:

> Their burnt offerings and sacrifices
>   will be accepted on my altar;
> for my house will be called
>   a house of prayer for all nations. Isaiah 56:7b

The house of prayer is a fitting metaphor for Lisu Christianity, for the starting point of Lisu theology is not a systematic category such as creation or Trinitarianism; rather, Lisu theology begins with the redemption of their community.[1] As Robert Schreiter states, "In many places in the world where community and family form the basis of identity and relation to God, ecclesiology becomes the prism through which theology is seen."[2] The house of prayer is itself a theological structure.

As a theological structure, the house of prayer is the keeper of the narrative of the community. It is a repository of stories. There are stories drawn from the Bible. On the walls of the Gongshan Zion Church were large murals of biblical characters, sketched with black chalk. There were the big stories of Lisu Christianity, stories of missionaries and evangelists, stories of hymns and Bible schools, stories of persecution and migration. These stories were strung together as vital pieces of the community narrative, a shared story that encompassed past and present, including all those who participated in the handshake. And there were the small stories, stories of fields planted, borders crossed, prayers uttered, faith gained, and faith lost.

The Lisu are a people precisely because of their shared story. When they sing their hymns, carry their Bible bags, and decline to drink or smoke, they are retelling that story. Their viability as a people depends on a church whose organization provides for the authentic retelling of these stories.[3]

It is perhaps fitting that enshrined in the name for a church is a Christian practice—prayer. Lisu houses of prayer were meant to be places of action, tabernacles to which people would muster for festivals, in which hymns would be sung and prayers would be prayed. The entire church structure is designed and intended for a Christian life that would be practiced communally.

Up and down the Nujiang Valley are small village churches, each of them following the same pattern as the Nu Ni village church. They are simple structures built of inexpensive materials. They seem simultaneously to fit in yet stand out from their surroundings. They are unified structures, made up of component parts—a courtyard, a threshold, a chancel, and a sanctuary. This built environment serves as an organizing schema for a theology of practices.

The Courtyard

The courtyard epitomizes the very exteriority of Lisu Christian practice. It is in the courtyard where folks gather, meals are eaten, and people line up to dance, reflecting the Lisu need for togetherness. No matter how small the village, I never saw a Lisu church without a courtyard. This outer court is the physical embodiment that Lisu Christianity is a communal faith. Christians gather in the courtyard to hang around and talk, to practice singing from the hymnbook, to go over church business. The church provides one of the few—if not the only—public spaces in most villages. The courtyard is where togetherness is on display.

Communal societies are known for their interdependence, enduring relationships, sense of belonging, and social control. For Lisu Christians, worth and meaning are found in belonging to the community; the Christian life is a life practiced together. Lisu Christian conversion is more than mental assent to a creed. It means accepting a lifestyle and joining a community. Christian practices resonate with the Lisu precisely because they are shared. They are done together. And in that togetherness, there is a sense of fullness and joy.

Christians around the world employ practices as an expression of faith. In Africa, according to Jehu Hanciles, the most resonant Christian practices are those that undergird the African worldview that all of life is spiritual.[4] For Korean-Americans, Christian practices give structure to the chaos of turmoil on the Korean peninsula and the resulting discontinuity of immigration to American soil.[5] In Mizoram, in northeast India, the most salient Christian practices are those that organize the ethnic self.[6] And in Lisuland, the resonating Christian practices are those that embody the value of togetherness. Just as the courtyard was designed for community, Christian practices are intended to express the communal life of the church.

Spiritual disciplines that are often private, individual activities in the Western tradition have been transformed by the Lisu into shared practices, done as a group. For example, Bible reading in the context of the Lisu church, with its out loud, responsive nature, is not an internal, meditative experience but a participatory group activity. Thanksgiving, Easter, and Christmas—holidays that are family-oriented in the United States—are church-sponsored festivals in Lisuland, times of singing and dancing and matchmaking. According to Wenger, "In the process of sustaining a practice, we become invested in what we do as well as in each other and our shared history. Our identities become anchored in each other and what we do together."[7] A solitary Lisu Christian nearly cannot not exist; faith needs community.

The Threshold

Between the exterior expanse of the courtyard and the inner space of the chapel is the threshold. The threshold is a transitional space, distinguishing that which is outside from that which is in. To step on the threshold is not just to enter the church but also to make a public self-declaration of who one is and the God that one worships. The threshold marks one's identity.

When Lisu convert, it is not simply a matter of altering belief; their entire identity is transformed. This new identity is confirmed by new practices. In the Lisu conception, humans are defined not so much by their thoughts and ideas (which is a highly individualistic concept) but rather by the group to which they belong and the practices in which they partake.

Stepping on the threshold means acceding to a life of Christian practices—practices that will form, shape, and determine one's identity.

After each church service, one steps on the threshold once again. Quite often, a handshake line forms at the threshold and extends out into the courtyard, consolidating identity as one leaves the church.

My first experience with the Lisu Christian handshake was during a preliminary trip to Gongshan. When the Wednesday night service was over, I had intended to remain in the sanctuary to take photos of some of the Christian murals on the wall. But I realized that everyone was filing out row by row, and my staying back was putting things out of order and causing consternation. I quickly assumed my place in line and filed out of the church. Once outside, I entered the handshake line.

I went down the line shaking hands and saying "Hwa Hwa" (hello) until I reached the end of the line, at which point I joined the line myself, and shook hands with everyone coming behind me. Isobel Kuhn recalled handshaking during her time with the Lisu: "Oh this handshaking in Lisuland! (It is the token of church fellowship.) Down the line you go, hot hands, cold hands, dry hands, wet hands, lean hands, fat hands, hands that grip heartily till you wince, hands that lie limply like dead fish and are worse than any other kind! Even baby strapped on mother's back must not be overlooked, and his is the only really soft hand in the line."[8] Handshaking was a last reminder before they all went their separate ways that everyone gathered was united in the body of Christ.

Handshaking was an identity marker, a sign of Christian fellowship. The Lisu adapted what in the West is a generic act of greeting and endowed it with spiritual significance. Lisu utilized the handshake when meeting other Christians for the first time, as it made an immediate declaration of their common bond. And the handshake was also used when family, friends, or villagers saw one another, a reaffirmation of their shared belief and bond. In missionary times, suspension from handshaking, an indication that one was being placed outside of the community, was even a form of church discipline—a kind of Lisu excommunication.[9]

In both the coming in and the going out, statements of Christian identity were broadcast. Nearly every Christian practice has a like effect, from wearing a Bible bag to declining to drink to attending church five times weekly. A declaration of who one is, an identity found in belonging, is built into the structures of both the house of prayer and the Christian practices that occur within and without.

The Chancel

200 Upon stepping off the threshold and entering the chapel, one's eyes are immediately drawn to the chancel. From this raised platform the service leader conducts each service with the help of others who will preach, conduct singing, and pray. Those on the chancel are recognized leaders whose leadership extends off the platform into community matters. Leaders provide discipline, serve as moral compasses, keep outliers in line, coordinate intercessory prayer, and organize group activities, such as a work day to help a church member who has been in the hospital and whose fields have yet to be planted. The church provides an authority system and a structure for the Lisu ethnicity.

Self-leadership has been built into the Lisu church structure since Fraser and his insistent focus on indigenous principles. The Lisu were on the margins then, as they still are today. Christianity has provided the Lisu with an administrative system that, shut out of mainstream Chinese politics, society, and education, they would not otherwise have. It has provided leadership roles within their own society: teacher, evangelist, song leader, pray-er. In providing a podium for leadership, the church has given Lisu society something communal to be responsible for, a place in society to aspire to, and community work to be proud of, all very important in the face of a strong state.

The chancel serves another purpose. Aesthetic culture is particularly important for minorities as a means of differentiating themselves and maintaining their identity, but as subsistence farmers, the opportunities to do so are few. The church chancel, however, doubles as a stage for expressive culture in terms of dress, performance, song, and dance. Small groups sing or perform line dancing during church services, nearly always garbed in the bright colors and tassels of their Lisu ethnic costume. The church, with its five-times-weekly services and annual festivals celebrating Easter, Christmas, and harvest, gives occasions for the wearing of ethnic costume. The Lisu turned to Christ in a people movement; redemption was seen as turning the Lisu people from their lascivious and backward past. Consequently, Lisu expressive culture—ethnic costumes and Bible bags, dancing and singing—was all put in the service of Christ, for redemption came as an ethnicity.

A chancel assumes that it will be inhabited with leaders and performers and thereby uplifts the value of being Lisu. The practices do the same. In wearing ethnic costume and in singing hymns in the Lisu language, both Christian identity and ethnic identity are strengthened.

The Sanctuary

The sanctuary is where worship happens, where the altar is approached. Worship, according to John Witvliet, "is an occasion when the instinctive beliefs, dispositions, and values of a given community are on full display."[10] Worship is a religious encounter between a finite believer and an infinite God.

Worship is a ritual of intensification. It is during worship that the Lisu open their Bibles and repeat the passages, line by line, after the service leader. It is during worship that Lisu gather together to approach an Almighty God in prayer. It is during worship that Lisu declare their allegiance as a body to the Trinitarian God of the Old Testament and the New, to the God in the stories brought to them by the missionaries, to the God in whose name they practice their daily faith.

Worship is also the arena where faith is engaged by culture. As Witvliet states, "Across the spectrum of Christian traditions, distinctive worship practices are crucial for revealing the basic impulses of faith. We simply cannot comprehend Puritans without looking at meetinghouses, Pentecostals without considering tongue-speaking, the Orthodox without icons, or Catholics without the Mass."[11] And, I would add, we cannot understand Lisu Christianity until we experience a Lisu church sanctuary completely consumed with song.

To enter the sanctuary is to participate in an immersive experience of worship. I well remember the first church service I attended in the Nujiang Valley. The congregational hymn singing in four parts utterly filled every corner and crack in the sonic space of the sanctuary. Mouths were open wide; vocal cords were pushed to their limits; voices were blended in harmony. Although my ear was untrained, I knew the singing of these hymns contained meaning. Isobel Kuhn recalled just such an experience, as noted above: "As the song gathered volume the room seemed flowing with waves of wonderful melody until we were bathed, drowned, in the beauty of it. Tenor, bass, alto, soprano flowed together into one exquisite harmony, and sung from hearts that believed and loved Him wholly."[12]

Lisu Christian practices are not confined to worship services. They are theology lived weekly, daily, moment by moment. Prayer happens before meals. Line dancing is practiced in the evenings. Christian practices are recurring and regular, cadenced to the agricultural seasons of the hills, drastically impacting quotidian timetables. There is an overflowing of the sacred into all aspects of time. Just as the sanctuary is intended for a completely immersive worship experience, life lived according to a rhythm of Christian practice is intended to fill every space and interval with the sacred, to bring every aspect of life into obedience.

Conclusion

Each Lisu house of prayer serves as a cohesive structure organizing relations between the self, the community, and God. In its standard design elements—courtyards, thresholds, chancels, and sanctuaries—community is valued, identity is accentuated, ethnicity and leadership are strengthened, and God is worshipped. The Christian practices follow this same grid. In the enactment of their practices, as in the design of their churches, the Lisu have been a community engaged in theological reflection.

Every culture must ask the question: What does it mean to be human? Western culture, the culture of the missionaries, answered that question in a particular way, based on the Bible but also on the Enlightenment, modernism, Greek philosophy, and so on. Lisu culture answers the question in quite a different way. The Lisu definition of what it means to be a disciple is also vastly different. Since mankind is viewed less in terms of cognitive complexity and more in terms of a holistic tapestry, discipleship is less about thinking and more about doing.

Rather than breaking up matters into constituent parts or dichotomies, the Lisu view most matters as integrated wholes. Minds and bodies are not distinct entities but are unified systems of knowing.[13] Time is not divided up into sacred time and secular time; rather, there is an overflowing of the sacred into all aspects of time. And belief and practice are bound fast to one another, conjoined into one indivisible whole. Beliefs without practices are unmoored. Practices without belief are vacant. The two go together, in the words of Ma-pa Timothy, like two legs. Walking cannot happen without both.

......

After my last breakfast at Tso Lo hamlet, the donkey was taken out of its stall under the house. A group of eight or nine men and boys gathered up top to watch Naomi's mother and brother load the donkey with our ridiculous amount of luggage. As the donkey set off, they lined up at the end of the path—the older teenage boys who I had watched line dancing, the young father I had prayed for during the intercessory prayer service, the village elders I had worshipped with in the storage room, Naomi's little nephews I had sat with around the fire—and all shook our hands in Christian fellowship.

We headed out of Fugong on the 9:05 bus the next morning. As we left the county town, I kept my eyes fixed on the opposite bank, looking for Patchwork Village and the mountain of terraced fields with the church atop where we had attended Sunday and New Year's services.

The perspective from below was far different than that from above. Most noticeably, the church was invisible; it could not be seen from the lowland and its world of towns and shops, cars and roads, schools and government buildings. On two recent trips into the Nujiang Valley, including this last one, I had arrived in Fugong County by bus on a Sunday. On both trips, I had seen Lisu men and women walking to church along the main road, a few here, a few there. What I had not realized, until those six days in Tso Lo hamlet, was that there was an invisible traffic of folks in the highlands. Coming out of the mountain crags, along the narrow donkey trails at high elevations, were Lisu Christians walking to church, in all their beads and pleats and velvet finery, an eruption of vivid hues. All were approaching the house of prayer.

Postscript

My last hour of fieldwork in the Nujiang Valley was spent in the evening Sacred Music class at the Liuku Bible training center. The instructor chose Hymn #289, "The Heavens Are Telling," one of the oratorios in the back of the hymnbook. Like many of the oratorios in the back, Hymn #289 is of unknown origin, one of several oratorios translated into Lisu by the Western missionaries and then lost to the Western canon.

This oratorio was one of the longest (seven pages) and most difficult. It had four separate parts; that was not unusual. But it also had sections with four different lines of lyrics, one for each part, which entered and echoed at different times. And it had long periods of rests, requiring precise mental counting to avoid entering at the wrong moment. Singing hymn #289 required utmost concentration.

As the students' confidence grew, their voices swelled. There was a joining of voices that engulfed the courtyard and its cracked cement and cheap white tiles with a sound that was nothing short of majestic. The simple sanctuary was transformed into a cathedral.

The next morning, I boarded a cramped minibus for the four-hour ride to Baoshan. That trip, which would have taken about twelve days in missionary times, had one purpose. I had to pay my respects at the grave of J. O. Fraser, missionary, linguist, translator, engineer, and musician.

James O. Fraser died on September 25, 1938, at the age of fifty-two, after a short and sudden bout of cerebral malaria. His wife, Roxie, was pregnant with their third daughter. He lived to see the New Testament completed, but he died before it was printed. Even though Fraser had passed away, his influence was still felt. The nascent church in the Nujiang Valley was built according to indigenous principles, the wisdom of which Fraser had taken great care to instill in the next generation of missionaries to the Lisu. Within the church, the rank-and-file members attended church, sang hymns, prayed for each other, evangelized their neighbors, and abstained from smoke and drink, just as Fraser had taught his first converts.

In one of his last lucid moments, wearied but not yet incapacitated by his illness, Fraser suggested that he and Roxie, together with two single women

POSTSCRIPT

missionaries who had stopped by en route to Dali, have an evening service of prayer and hymn singing. They went around the table, each choosing a hymn from the old Methodist hymnbook. When it came Fraser's turn, he chose "Man of Sorrows, What a Name," by Philip Bliss.

> Man of sorrows, what a name
> for the Son of God, who came
> ruined sinners to reclaim:
> Hallelujah, what a Savior!
>
> Bearing shame and scoffing rude,
> in my place condemned he stood,
> sealed my pardon with his blood:
> Hallelujah, what a Savior!
>
> Guilty, helpless, lost were we;
> blameless Lamb of God was he,
> sacrificed to set us free:
> Hallelujah, what a Savior!
>
> He was lifted up to die;
> "It is finished" was his cry;
> now in heaven exalted high:
> Hallelujah, what a Savior!
>
> When he comes, our glorious King,
> all his ransomed home to bring,
> then anew this song we'll sing:
> Hallelujah, what a Savior!

As the group prayed together, Fraser fell asleep with his head in his hands. Roxie had to wake him once the meeting was over. That was Tuesday evening. He died on Sunday.[1]

Fraser was buried on a hillside outside of Baoshan. His gravestone displays the words of Jesus—"I am the Resurrection and the Life"—in Chinese, Lisu, and English.

Notes

Introduction

1. Berger, *Sacred Canopy*.
2. *Breakthrough: The Story of James O. Fraser and the Lisu People* (Overseas Missionary Fellowship International, 2008), DVD.
3. I. Kuhn, *Nests Above the Abyss*, 20.
4. Ibid., 54.
5. Ibid., 106.
6. "Geographic Distribution of Minorities," *China Statistical Yearbook 2010*, http://www.stats.gov.cn/tjsj/ndsj/2010/indexeh.htm.
7. Covell, "To Every Tribe."
8. According to Giersch, there were "almost no demarcated borders between Yunnan and Southeast Asian states until the 1890s"; see Giersch, *Asian Borderlands*, 13.
9. Bradley, "Language Endangerment and Resilience Linguistics"; Shi, *Lisu-zu de gen yu yuan*.
10. I. Kuhn, *Nests Above the Abyss*.
11. J. O. Fraser, *Handbook of the Lisu (Yawyin) Language*, iii.
12. Mullaney, *Coming to Terms with the Nation*.
13. Bays, *New History of Christianity in China*.
14. Yamamori and Chan, "Missiological Ramifications." See also Huang and Liu, "Faith as Lived."
15. Graham-Harrison, "Christians in China Border Valley."
16. Such research situations are detailed in Heimer and Thøgersen, *Doing Fieldwork in China*, and Mueggler, *Age of Wild Ghosts*.
17. The *lianghui*, literally "two organizations," refers to two organizations within the government-sanctioned Protestant church, the Three-Self Patriotic Movement and the China Christian Council. Because the relationship between them is so close, these two organizations are usually referred to by the single term *lianghui*.
18. Wenger, *Communities of Practice*, 47.
19. See, for example, Maffly-Kipp, Schmidt, and Valeri, *Practicing Protestants*.
20. MacIntyre, *After Virtue*, 208.
21. Wenger, *Communities of Practice*, 52.
22. Smith, "Reading Practices and Christian Pedagogy," 53.
23. Hauerwas and Willimon, "Embarrassed by the Church." Further, Hauerwas and Willimon state that "liturgically, the Scripture functions not as a text to be dissected but a canon to be lived" (119).
24. Schreiter, *Constructing Local Theologies*, 42.
25. Ibid., 103. According to Schreiter, the "sure knowledge" form of theology had several implications. Theological reflection became the province of full-time professionals. Training in theology emphasized intellectual discipline over spiritual wisdom. Finally, theology came to be thought of as a school enterprise, with vocabulary and categories designed primarily for professors and students, and only secondarily for the illumination of the experience of the Christian community.
26. McGrath, *Justification by Faith*, 54.
27. My discussion of the Pauline explication of the biblical and theological idea of justification is collapsing into one paragraph what has been a theological debate for centuries, what several eminent theologians have written volumes on even in recent years, and what has become a focal issue regarding the so-called New Perspective on Paul. For a more comprehensive treatment of justification, Alister McGrath provides a good historical overview in *Iustitia Dei*. Michael Horton wrote a two-volume study of justification, appropriately titled *Justification*; volume 1 details the approaches of the patristic fathers, while volume 2 details present-day discussions.

John Piper's book *The Future of Justification* takes issue with the New Perspective on Paul, as espoused by N. T. Wright. Wright responded with his own book, entitled *Justification: God's Plan and Paul's Vision*, which argues that justification cannot be understood apart from God's covenant faithfulness.

28. Martin, *James*, 79; Moo, *Epistle of James*, 99.

29. Irvin, "What Is World Christianity?," 4.

30. Irvin, "World Christianity."

31. Cabrita and Maxwell, introduction to *Relocating World Christianity*, 2.

32. The term is associated with Klaus Koschorke and the "Munich School" of World Christianity. See *Journal of World Christianity* 6, no. 1 (2016), a special issue dedicated to the Munich School.

33. Farhadian, introduction to *Introducing World Christianity*.

34. Mills, *Sociological Imagination*, 6.

35. Mannon, *City of Flowers*, 13.

36. Wolcott, *Ethnography*.

37. Scharen and Vigen, "What Is Ethnography?," 16.

38. Fackre, "Narrative Theology," 345.

Chapter 1

1. Conversation with Mr. Fraser, December 21, 1934. Box 11, Papers of FHT, CIM Archive, SOAS Archives, University of London.

2. As cited in Crossman, *Mountain Rain*, 4.

3. Fraser applied to the CIM three separate times, getting turned down the first two times because of an issue with one of his ears. "When he wrote offering the third time he added that whether he was accepted or not he would be going because God had told him to": Mrs. J. O. Fraser, *Fraser and Prayer*, 8.

4. Mrs. H. Taylor, *Behind the Ranges*, 17.

5. Roxie [Mrs. J. O.] Fraser, Letter to Mrs. Howard Taylor, 6. Box 11, Papers of FHT, CIM Archive, SOAS Archives, University of London.

6. Mrs. J. O. Fraser, *Fraser and Prayer*, 4.

7. Cable, "Book Review," 43.

8. Mrs. J. O. Fraser, *Fraser and Prayer*, 9.

9. *China and the Gospel*, 67.

10. Conversation with Mr. Fraser, December 21, 1934, 2.

11. Ibid., 3.

12. J. O. Fraser, *Handbook of the Lisu (Yawyin) Language*, iii.

13. Hu, preface to Shi, *Lisu-zu de gen yu yuan*, 1.

14. J. O. Fraser, "Work Among Aborigines," 128.

15. Litton, *Report on a Journey*, 24.

16. T'ien, *Peaks of Faith*.

17. Conversation with Mr. Fraser, December 21, 1934, 3.

18. As cited in Crossman, *Mountain Rain*, 27.

19. Ibid.

20. As cited in Mrs. H. Taylor, *Behind the Ranges*, 34.

21. The Lisu Language—Mr. Fraser, 5. Box 11, Papers of FHT, CIM Archive, SOAS Archives, University of London.

22. J. O. Fraser, "Work Among Aborigines," 128.

23. Crossman, *Mountain Rain*, 30.

24. Conversation with Mr. Fraser, December 21, 1934, 3.

25. Crossman, *Mountain Rain*.

26. Mrs. H. Taylor, *Behind the Ranges*, 59–60.

27. Conversation with Mr. Fraser, December 21, 1934, 4.

28. J. O. Fraser, "Work Among Aborigines," 128.

29. Conversation with Mr. Fraser, December 21, 1934, 4.

30. Letter from J. O. Fraser, as cited in Mrs. Howard Taylor, *Behind the Ranges*, 67.

31. J. O. Fraser, "Work Among Aborigines," 129.

32. Conversation with Mr. Fraser, December 21, 1934, 5–7.

33. Ibid., 8.

34. Ibid., 10.

35. Crossman, *Mountain Rain*; Mrs. H. Taylor, *Behind the Ranges*.

36. As cited in Mrs. H. Taylor, *Behind the Ranges*, 91.

37. J. O. Fraser, "Fruitfulness of Prayer," 53.

38. Conversation with Mr. Fraser, December 26, 1934, 3.

39. The Lisu Language—Mr. Fraser, 1.

40. Bradley, "Language Endangerment and Resilience Linguistics." Fraser said this:

"When I taught my youngest sister to read [English], I taught her by sounds, initials and finals. I thought I would teach the Lisu—as we spell combining letters. B. A. = Ba; M. O. = Mo. Found they could not analyse sounds—could not put them together. So we gave all our consonants the sound of A (ah). This they took to at once!" The Lisu Language—Mr. Fraser, 1.

41. I. Kuhn, *Nests Above the Abyss*, 51.
42. McConnell, "J. O. Fraser and Church Growth."
43. Mrs. H. Taylor, *Behind the Ranges*.
44. Conversation with Mr. Fraser, December 26, 1934, 4.
45. Ibid.
46. Crossman, *Mountain Rain*; Mrs. H. Taylor, *Behind the Ranges*.
47. Conversation with Mr. Fraser, December 26, 1934, 4.
48. Memoirs of J. O. Fraser by John B. Kuhn, 9. Collection 215, Records of OMF, Box 4, Folder 55, BGC Archives, Wheaton, Ill.
49. Cable, "Book Review."
50. Cooke, *Fish Four*, 18–19.
51. Roberts, *No Solitary Effort*.
52. I. Kuhn, *Nests Above the Abyss*, 134–35.
53. J. O. Fraser, "Review of the Lisu Work," 70–71.
54. Jennie K. Fitzwilliam, interview by Paul Ericksen, June 13, 1984, transcript of recorded interview, Archives of the Billy Graham Center, Wheaton, Ill.
55. Fitzwilliam, interview, June 13, 1984.
56. I. Kuhn, *Nests Above the Abyss*.
57. As cited in Crossman, *Mountain Rain*, 186–87.
58. Letter from John Kuhn to Arnold Lea, February 9, 1953, as cited in Roberts, *No Solitary Effort*, 103.
59. According to Jennie Fitzwilliam, who with her husband, Francis "Fitz" Fitzwilliam, worked side by side with Fraser in the Lisu work, Fraser was considered for the directorship of the CIM, but his commitment to indigenous principles stood in the way. In an interview recorded in 1984, she stated,

> He wasn't a difficult person, but he had his convictions and he stood up for them. He made some very . . . not . . . unhappy people, I should say maybe, in the CIM because his . . . because of his strong stand on the indigenous churches and the way a missionary should live and that sort of thing. Not everybody went along with his it [sic] at that time. I think it's the understood policy of missions these days but in Mr. Fraser's day, that wasn't accepted by everybody. The old style missionaries did things differently.

Further, "As I understood . . . Mr. Hoste who was the . . . general director at that time, wanted Mr. Fraser to succeed him but Mr. Fraser felt that there were so many . . . in the mission that didn't agree with his strong stand on . . . the indigenous policies of church planting that it just wouldn't work. So he wouldn't consider it. And shortly after that the Lord took him home." Jennie K. Fitzwilliam, interview by Paul Ericksen, July 12, 1984, transcript of recorded interview, Archives of the Billy Graham Center, Wheaton, Ill.

60. As cited in Crossman, *Mountain Rain*, 76.
61. J. O. Fraser, "Aborigines of the Burma Border," 225.
62. For further discussion, see Maggay, *Gospel in Culture*; Chan, *Grassroots Asian Theology*.
63. Letter from J. O. Fraser to his mother, as cited in Mrs. H. Taylor, *Behind the Ranges*, 143.
64. As cited in Mrs. H. Taylor, *Behind the Ranges*, 150.
65. Crossman, *Mountain Rain*.
66. This focus on faith as "allegiance" is receiving new attention. See Bates, *Salvation by Allegiance Alone*.
67. As cited in Crossman, *Mountain Rain*, 130.
68. Roxie [Mrs. J. O.] Fraser, Letter to Mrs. Howard Taylor, 5.
69. The Lisu Language—Mr. Fraser, 7.
70. Ibid., 2.
71. As cited in Mrs. H. Taylor, *Behind the Ranges*, 165.
72. Miroslav Volf argues that "in most cases, Christian practices come first and Christian beliefs follow—or rather, beliefs are already entailed in practices, so that their explicit espousing becomes a matter of

bringing to consciousness what is implicit in the engagement of the practices themselves." Volf, "Theology for a Way of Life," 256.

73. Leila R. Cooke, handwritten note. Collection 215, Records of OMF, Box 4, Folder 8, BGC Archives, Wheaton, Ill.

74. The Lisu Language—Mr. Fraser, 2.

75. From a letter from Fraser (n.d.) cited in Mrs. H. Taylor, *Behind the Ranges*, 166.

76. Mrs. J. O. Fraser, *Fraser and Prayer*, 11; conversation with Mr. Fraser, December 26, 1934, 2.

77. Mrs. H. Taylor, *Behind the Ranges*, 183–84.

78. The Lisu Language—Mr. Fraser, 3–4.

79. Crossman, *Mountain Rain*; Mrs. H. Taylor, *Behind the Ranges*.

80. Mrs. J. O. Fraser, *Fraser and Prayer*, 11.

81. As cited in Mrs. H. Taylor, *Behind the Ranges*, 197.

82. The Lisu Language—Mr. Fraser, 7.

83. Conversation with Mr. Fraser, January 2, 1935, 2. Box 11, Papers of FHT, CIM Archive, SOAS Archives, University of London.

84. Mrs. H. Taylor, *Behind the Ranges*, 236.

85. Mrs. J. O. Fraser, *Fraser and Prayer*, 7.

Chapter 2

1. Allen, *Educational Principles and Missionary Methods*, 67.

2. I. Kuhn, *Nests Above the Abyss*. Just because a term does not exist in a language does not mean that the concept does not exist or that the speakers of the language do not have the ability to comprehend the concept. Fellowship is a good example here. The Lisu, as a communal people, would have had an intrinsic understanding of fellowship. Likely the concept was so assumed in Lisu culture it never needed its own term (though understanding fellowship in its religious dimensions would have been a new take).

3. Ong, *Orality and Literacy*, 150.

4. See Juzwik, "American Evangelical Biblicism."

5. I. Kuhn, *Stones of Fire*, 102.

6. Ong, *Orality and Literacy*, 73.

7. Ibid., 31.

8. Ibid., 39.

9. D'Andrade, *Development of Cognitive Anthropology*.

10. Ong, *Orality and Literacy*, 65.

11. Scott, *Art of Not Being Governed*, 230.

12. Ong, *Orality and Literacy*.

13. J. O. Fraser, *Handbook of the Lisu (Yawyin) Language*, 58.

14. L. R. Cooke, *Fish Four*, 30.

15. Mrs. A. B. Cooke, *Honey Two of Lisu-Land*, 78.

16. L. R. Cooke, *Fish Four*, 30.

17. Ong, *Orality and Literacy*, 32.

18. David Morse, personal communication, March 14, 2013.

19. Ong, *Orality and Literacy*, 42, 49.

20. Ibid., 72.

21. Ibid., 46.

22. Ibid., 67.

23. Havelock, *Muse Learns to Write*.

24. Ong, *Orality and Literacy*, 41.

25. Niditch, *Oral World and Written Word*, 45.

26. Ibid.

27. Ibid., 57.

28. Ibid., 77.

29. Ong, *Orality and Literacy*, 176.

30. I. Kuhn, *Stones of Fire*.

31. I. Kuhn, *In the Arena*, 51.

32. Bradley, "Language Endangerment and Resilience Linguistics."

33. Crossman, *Mountain Rain*.

34. Yang, "Mainstreaming, Popularising, and Packaging."

35. Cooke, *Honey Two*, 15, 23–24.

36. Isobel Kuhn, Circular Letter, February 1940, 3. Records of OMF, Box 4, Folder 36. BGC Archives, Wheaton, Ill.

37. Jin, "Jidujiao Chuanbo dui Lisu-zu Yuyan."

38. Ibid., 133–34.

39. L. R. Cooke, *Fish Four*, 29–30.

40. Jin, "Jidujiao Chuanbo dui Lisu-zu Yuyan," 145.

41. In the 1970s, as the Bible was revised, this term was changed to ꓶ; DO: Xꓱ, DO: in which the DO: means *news* (ibid., 147). The Lisu Christians used the new term during my fieldwork.

42. Jin, "Jidujiao Chuanbo dui Lisu-zu Yuyan," 147.

43. Ibid., 150; Jin, personal communication, April 22, 2014.

44. This couplet could also be translated "I will do as I please" (Jie Jin, personal communication, April, 22, 2014), or "My . . . control . . . My . . . decision" (David Morse, personal communication, September 17, 2014).

45. Jie Jin, personal communication, March 26, 2014.

46. Bradley, "Language Endangerment," 135.

47. According to Jie Jin, successive Bible translations have tried to incorporate more elements from the northern dialect (personal communication, March 26, 2014). Examples of this are the birth order terms, such as A. ꓒU meaning *oldest son*, A-Dꓶ. meaning *second son*, and A. ꓵE meaning *third son*, which are a particularity of northern Lisu (Bradley, "Birth-Order Terms in Lisu," 55). For example, in the 1986 version of the Bible, 1 Samuel 17:13b reads: "A. ꓒU NY E-LI-BꓛO -. A-Dꓶ. NY ꓱ-BI-N-D-. A. ꓵE NY XY-MꓒO-H ꓥ L O=" (The firstborn was Eliab; the second, Abinadab; and the third, Shammah).

48. Bradley, "Language Endangerment."

49. Soukup, "Orality and Literacy," 51.

50. The Lisu linguistic situation is further complicated by the presence of the Yunnan dialect. In Yunnan Province the Mandarin dialect (based on the Beijing dialect) is used in all schools and the media. However, the daily spoken dialect is usually the Yunnan dialect. The Yunnan dialect is unique among Chinese dialects. While most dialects change from region to region or even village to village, the Yunnan dialect is the same across the entire province, likely stemming from the settlement of Chinese soldiers in Yunnan during the Yuan, Ming, and Qing dynasties.

51. Bradshaw and Melloh, *Foundations in Ritual Studies*.

52. Niditch, *Oral World and Written Word*, 40.

Chapter 3

1. Leila R. Cooke, Letter to J. O. Fraser, August 3, 1925. Collection 215, Records of OMF, Box 4, Folder 1. BGC Archives, Wheaton, Ill.

2. Bartlo, "Biola's *The Fundamentals* Still Relevant Today."

3. For an excellent summary of the role of premillennial eschatology in missions, see Pocock, "Influence of Premillennial Eschatology."

4. Allyn B. Cooke, Circular Letter, October 7, 1926, 3. Collection 215, Records of OMF, Box 4, Folder 1. BGC Archives, Wheaton, Ill.

5. Leila R. Cooke, Letter to parents, August 25, 1924, 3. Collection 215, Records of OMF, Box 4, Folder 1. BGC Archives, Wheaton, Ill.

6. Leila R. Cooke, Letter to parents, August 3, 1924. Collection 215, Records of OMF, Box 4, Folder 1. BGC Archives, Wheaton, Ill.

7. Leila R. Cooke, Letter to parents, August 25, 1924, 3.

8. L. R. Cooke, *Fish Four*, 7.

9. Ibid.

10. Mrs. A. B. Cooke, "Fish Four," 212–13. "Thou Didst Leave Thy Throne" is #19 in the 2013 Yunnan Lisu hymnbook.

11. Gowman, "On the Burmese Border," 154.

12. Ibid.

13. L. R. Cooke, *Fish Four*, 18; Conversation with Mr. Fraser, December 21, 1934, 1. Box 11, Papers of FHT, CIM Archive, SOAS Archives, University of London.

14. A. B. Cooke, Circular Letter, October 7, 1926.

15. L. R. Cooke, *Fish Four*, 22.

16. Leila R. Cooke, Circular Letter, October 22, 1937. Collection 215, Records of OMF, Box 4, Folder 6. BGC Archives, Wheaton, Ill.

17. Allyn B. and Leila R. Cooke, Circular Letter, May 25, 1927, 1. Collection 215, Records of OMF, Box 4, Folder 1. BGC Archives, Wheaton, Ill.

18. Isobel Kuhn, unpublished manuscript. The Records of OMF. Collection 215, Box 4, Folder 40. BGC Archives, Wheaton, Ill.

19. Leila R. Cooke, Circular Letter, February 12, 1926. Collection 215, Records of OMF, Box 4, Folder 1. BGC Archives, Wheaton, Ill.

20. L. R. Cooke, *Fish Four*, p. 25.

21. Allyn B. Cooke, Circular Letter, June 3, 1926. Collection 215, Records of OMF, Box 4, Folder 1. BGC Archives, Wheaton, Ill.
22. Ibid.
23. L. R. Cooke, *Fish Four*, 25.
24. Leila R. Cooke, Circular Letter, December 30, 1925, 2. Collection 215, Records of OMF, Box 4, Folder 1. BGC Archives, Wheaton, Ill.
25. L. R. Cooke, Letter to J. O. Fraser, 3 August 1925.
26. Leila R. Cooke, Letter to her parents, 20 October 1924. Collection 215, Records of OMF, Box 4, Folder 1. BGC Archives, Wheaton, Ill.
27. J. O. Fraser, Letter to Mrs. Howard Taylor, 31 October 1933, 1–2. Box 11, Papers of FHT, CIM Archive, SOAS Archives, University of London.
28. Conversation with Mr. Fraser, January 2, 1935, 2. Box 11, Papers of FHT, CIM Archive, SOAS Archives, University of London.
29. A. B. Cooke, Circular Letter, October 7, 1926.
30. Allyn B. Cooke, Circular Letter, April 27, 1929, 1. Collection 215, Records of OMF, Box 4, Folder 1. BGC Archives, Wheaton, Ill.
31. Conversation with Mr. Fraser, January 4, 1935, 4. Box 11, Papers of FHT, CIM Archive, SOAS Archives, University of London.
32. L. R. Cooke, *Fish Four*.
33. Leila R. Cooke, Circular Letter, March 26, 1931. Collection 215, Records of OMF, Box 4, Folder 1. BGC Archives, Wheaton, Ill.
34. L. R. Cooke, *Fish Four*.
35. Leila R. Cooke, Circular Letter, July 29, 1929. Collection 215, Records of OMF, Box 4, Folder 1. BGC Archives, Wheaton, Ill.
36. The letter in the archives was written in Lisu with English translation. Collection 215, Records of OMF, Box 4, Folder 1. BGC Archives, Wheaton, Ill.
37. Rose, "Chinese Frontiers of India," 202. British botanist and explorer George Forrest, in a trip to the Upper Salween in 1905 accompanying Consul Litton, stated that "the people are all Lissoo [sic], but with a strong admixture of Chinese blood. The men dress in Chinese fashion, but the women, while adopting the Chinese cotton cloth, retain the petticoat and profuse decoration of head, bracelets, necklaces, and armlets, which is so characteristic of the true Lissoo garb. Few of them can speak any Chinese except the chiefs and their families. The people hardly go beyond their own villages, and seem to live quiet happy lives, only disturbed by the occasional difficulty of getting food, and by the trouble and petty exactions which attend the work of collecting the chief's tribute, or house-tax of half a tael per year. The usually peaceable condition of this portion of the valley is no doubt partly due to the general absence of interference by the Chinese mandarins, which is owing to the fact that the country is too poor to be worth squeezing. The chiefs have none of the machinery, and exercise none of the functions, of a regular government, except collecting their dues, in which they are assisted by a Chinese clerk. Each village seems to regulate its own affairs through its headman" (Forrest, "Journey on Upper Salwin," 244).
38. I. Kuhn, *Nests Above the Abyss*, 19.
39. Leila R. Cooke, Circular Letter, September 6, 1941. Collection 215, Records of OMF, Box 4, Folder 10. BGC Archives, Wheaton, Ill.
40. I. Kuhn, *Nests Above the Abyss*, 20.
41. Payne, "Undermanned Field," 6.
42. I. Kuhn, *Nests Above the Abyss*, 23–24.
43. L. R. Cooke, *Fish Four*, 19.
44. Ibid., 28.
45. Talks with Charles Peterson, June 1939, 1. Box 11, Papers of FHT, CIM Archive, SOAS Archives, University of London.
46. L. R. Cooke, *Fish Four*, 20.
47. Ibid., 19–20.
48. Ibid., 62.
49. Talks with Charles Peterson, June 1939, 1.
50. Isobel Kuhn, Prayer Trust, 1 May 1938, 2. Box 11, Papers of FHT, CIM Archive, SOAS Archives, University of London.
51. Leila R. Cooke, Circular Letter, July 17, 1933. Collection 215, Records of OMF, Box 4, Folder 2. BGC Archives, Wheaton, Ill.
52. Leila R. Cooke, Circular Letter, April 6, 1934. Collection 215, Records of OMF, Box 4, Folder 3. BGC Archives, Wheaton, Ill.

53. Leila R. Cooke, Circular Letter, October 5, 1934, 2. Collection 215, Records of OMF, Box 4, Folder 3. BGC Archives, Wheaton, Ill.
54. Lin, *Fuyingu*.
55. L. R. Cooke, *Fish Four*, 61.
56. Isobel Kuhn, Circular Letter, June 3, 1935. Collection 215, Records of OMF, Box 4, Folder 32. BGC Archives, Wheaton, Ill.
57. L. R. Cooke, *Fish Four*.
58. Isobel Kuhn, Circular Letter, September 29, 1941. Collection 215, Records of OMF, Box 4, Folder 37. BGC Archives, Wheaton, Ill.
59. Lin, *Fuyingu*, 109–10.
60. Paul was a Muchengpo Christian who was ordained at Gospel Mountain in 1930 by Fraser, Allyn Cooke, Carl Gowman, and Mr. Casto. "We now regard Paul as having equal authority with ourselves in the Gospel Mountain Lisu work," said Fraser. J. O. Fraser, Circular Letter, July 18, 1930. Reels 7 and 8, Yale Divinity School Archives, New Haven, Conn.
61. Leila R. Cooke, Circular Letter, October 22, 1937.
62. As cited in L. R. Cooke, "Missionary Mother Takes Furlough," 59.
63. Isobel Kuhn, Circular Letter, February 7, 1939, 5. Records of OMF, Box 4, Folder 35. BGC Archives, Wheaton, Ill.
64. Isobel Kuhn, Circular Letter, February 1940, 3. Records of OMF, Box 4, Folder 36. BGC Archives, Wheaton, Ill.
65. Isobel Kuhn, Circular Letter, June 1939. Records of OMF, Box 4, Folder 35. BGC Archives, Wheaton, Ill.
66. Leila R. Cooke, Circular Letter, September 6, 1941, 2.
67. Eddy, Beilby, and Enderlein, "Justification in Historical Perspective."
68. Categories are from Carl Gowman's personal copy of the catechism. Unprocessed Accession 14-01. BGC Archives, Wheaton, Ill.
69. "Civilizing mission" usually refers to the efforts of colonial powers, but as missionaries often worked closely with colonial administrators, or at least under their umbrella, they were often active participants in the civilizing mission. See Kalusa, "Elders, Young Men"; Ranger, "Godly Medicine"; Selwyn, *Paradise Inhabited by Devils*.
70. I. Kuhn, *Nests Above the Abyss*, 106.
71. Peterson, "Shepherding the Flock," 166–67.
72. I. Kuhn, *Nests Above the Abyss*, 138–39.
73. Ibid., 143.
74. Isobel Kuhn, Circular Letter, May 27, 1941, 3. Records of OMF, Box 4, Folder 37. BGC Archives, Wheaton, Ill.
75. Leila R. Cooke, Circular Letter, September 4, 1935. Collection 215, Records of OMF, Box 4, Folder 4. BGC Archives, Wheaton, Ill.
76. L. R. Cooke, *Fish Four*.
77. I. Kuhn, *In the Arena*.
78. Isobel Kuhn, Circular Letter, May 1939, 3. Records of OMF, Box 4, Folder 35. BGC Archives, Wheaton, Ill.
79. Mrs. J. B. Kuhn, "Rainy Season Bible Classes," 167.
80. Isobel Kuhn, Circular Letter, August 2, 1941. Collection 215, Records of OMF, Box 4, Folder 37. BGC Archives, Wheaton, Ill.
81. I. Kuhn, *Nests Above the Abyss*.
82. Isobel Kuhn, Circular Letter, February 27, 1943. Collection 215, Records of OMF, Box 4, Folder 39. BGC Archives, Wheaton, Ill.
83. I. Kuhn, *Nests Above the Abyss*, 113.
84. Isobel Kuhn, Circular Letter, January 1940. Collection 215, Records of OMF, Box 4, Folder 36. BGC Archives, Wheaton, Ill.
85. L. R. Cooke, *Fish Four*.
86. Gertrude Morse, *The Dogs May Bark but the Caravan Moves On* (Joplin, Mo.: North Burma Christian Mission, 1998), 142–43.
87. Ibid., 156.
88. Ibid., 164.
89. Personal communication, January 12, 2014.
90. Morse, *Dogs May Bark*, 343.
91. Personal communication, January 21, 2014.
92. Ibid.
93. Morse, *Dogs May Bark*, 197.
94. Ibid., 204.
95. Ibid., 212–13.
96. Ibid., 214–15.
97. Eugene Morse, personal communication, January 21, 2014.
98. Morse, *Dogs May Bark*, 239.
99. Ibid., 249.

100. Personal communication, January 21, 2014.
101. Morse, *Dogs May Bark*, 249–50.
102. Ibid.
103. Mrs. F. L. Canfield, "In Memoriam," 109.
104. Crossman, *Mountain Rain*.
105. Personal communication, January 21, 2014.
106. David Morse, personal communication, September 1, 2014.

Chapter 4

1. Douglas, *Purity and Danger*, 2.
2. Ibid.
3. Sanders, *Paul, the Law, and the Jewish People*, 102.
4. Edersheim, *Life and Times of Jesus*, 3.
5. Wright, *Jesus and the Victory of God*, 379.
6. Neyrey, "Idea of Purity in Mark's Gospel."
7. Ibid.
8. DeSilva, *Honor, Patronage, Kinship, and Purity*.
9. Sanders, *Paul*, 6.
10. Douglas, *Purity and Danger*, 35.
11. Ibid., 41.
12. Douglas, *Natural Symbols*.
13. Wu, *Saving God's Face*.
14. Douglas, *Natural Symbols*, 62.
15. Neyrey, "Body Language in 1 Corinthians," 134.
16. Levine, *JPS Torah Commentary: Leviticus*, 256.
17. Ibid.
18. DeSilva, *Honor, Patronage, Kinship, and Purity*, 270.
19. Ibid.
20. Yamamori and Chan, "Missiological Ramifications."
21. L. R. Cooke, *Fish Four*, 28–29.
22. I. Kuhn, *Nests Above the Abyss*, 47.
23. As cited in Crossman, *Mountain Rain*, 141.
24. Francis Khek Gee Lim argues that Christianity "can itself be a kind of ethnicity, and . . . can act as a crucial principle upon which new boundaries can be drawn to form social groups that display many features of ethnicity." In describing such, Lim flips the oft-used term "ethno-religion," which describes religion that is closely related to ethnicity, and proposes that religions such as Lisu Christianity be termed "religio-ethnicity," since it is religion, in this case Christianity, that forms the primary boundary marker, not ethnicity. Lim, "'To the Peoples,'" 108.
25. Douglas, *Purity and Danger*, 115.
26. Ibid., 124.
27. Douglas, *Natural Symbols*, 78.
28. Neyrey, "Body Language in 1 Corinthians."
29. DeSilva, *Honor, Patronage, Kinship, and Purity*.
30. Ibid., 243.
31. Ma, *Lahu Minority in Southwest China*, 205.
32. DeSilva, *Honor, Patronage, Kinship, and Purity*, 262 n. 38.

Chapter 5

1. Personal communication, July 5, 2014. See also Diao, "Mediating Gospel Singing."
2. Mrs. A. B. Cooke, *Honey Two of Lisu-Land*, 34–35.
3. For examples, see Luo et al., "Alcohol Use and Subsequent Sex"; Ma, *Lahu Minority in Southwest China*; Mueggler, *Age of Wild Ghosts*.
4. Yamamori and Chan, "Missiological Ramifications," 404.
5. T'ien, *Peaks of Faith*, 71.
6. Archives of the Yunnan Academy of Social Sciences, vol. 340, sec. 9, as cited in ibid., 72.
7. Morse, *Dogs May Bark*, 271.
8. Ibid., 278.
9. Ibid., 327.
10. Ibid.
11. Yamamori and Chan, "Missiological Ramifications," 405.
12. Archives of the Yunnan Academy of Social Sciences, vol. 331, sec. 11, as cited in T'ien, *Peaks of Faith*, 102–3.
13. Morse, *Dogs May Bark*, 368.
14. Yamamori and Chan, "Missiological Ramifications," 405.
15. Crossman, *Mountain Rain*, 238.

16. L∀ BO ᅚ. DU, meaning "cross" in English, literally means "a place to stretch the arms across" in Lisu. David Morse, personal communication, September 17, 2014.

17. This quote is widely attributed to Tertullian, who made the statement after observing church growth in Carthage, in North Africa, during Roman persecution.

18. Nor in many other cases, such as the Nestorian church or the Jacobite Syrian Church in much of the Middle East. See Jenkins, *Lost History of Christianity*, and Lee, "Sorry, Tertullian," 18.

19. Walder, "Cultural Revolution Radicalism," 42.

20. Daniel Bays suggests that "the turmoil of the Cultural Revolution . . . gave Christianity an opening, an opportunity to grow. . . . All churches during these years were by definition house churches, and some proved very adept at adjusting to the new situation. Talented and charismatic leaders emerged among the believers, and proved to be effective evangelists, recruiting many new converts. Despite the almost total lack of empirical evidence, my guess is that Protestants increased their numbers by a factor of five or six during the 12 years from 1966 to 1978, when churches reopened" (Bays, *New History of Christianity in China*, 186).

21. Various governments of China have long been concerned that its southwest border is inhabited by many minority groups and that these groups may not be loyal to the Chinese state. While the Christian faith has usually been added to the list of reasons for disloyalty, Diana Junio records that this was not always the case. In 1939, the Nationalist government in Chongqing and the Church of Christ in China, the largest Protestant church in Republican China, formed a cooperative venture—called the Border Service Department—with the aim of providing educational and medical services to "border peoples" and the political goal of wooing them to the Chinese state. See Junio, *Patriotic Cooperation*.

22. Personal communication, January 21, 2014.

23. Yamamori and Chan, "Missiological Ramifications," 405.

24. I. Kuhn, *Nests Above the Abyss*, 203.

Chapter 6

1. Dumont does not use the term *communal* but rather *holistic*. Since Dumont's time, *communal* has become more widely used. See Dumont, *Essays on Individualism*.

2. Ibid., 25.

3. In using the term *communal* I am choosing not to use another widely used term: *collectivist*. There has been much research conducted on collectivist societies by such esteemed researchers as Harry C. Triandis and Geert Hofstede. While some of the features they describe in collectivist societies also apply to communal societies, there is not an exact match. The primary difference is that collectivist societies are based on groups that have voluntarily joined together for mutual benefit, while communal societies are usually based upon common ancestry, culture, and affinity. In making this distinction I am drawing from the work of Andrew Moemeka, who states that the individualism-collectivism dichotomy should be replaced by individualism-collectivism-communalism. Because the bonds of community are so strong, communalism is actually much more to the opposite pole than is collectivism. Further, in describing the nature of their own Christian communities, theologians from Africa and Oceania have used the term *communal*, not *collectivist*.

4. Moemeka, "Communalism as a Fundamental Dimension of Culture," 121.

5. "A high-context (HC) communication or message is one in which most of the information is either in the physical context or internalized in the person, while very little is in the coded, explicit, transmitted part of the message. A low-context (LC) communication is just the opposite: i.e., the mass of the information is vested in the implicit code" (Hall, *Beyond Culture*, 91).

6. Dumont, *Essays on Individualism*, 74.

7. Kipp, "Conversion by Affiliation."

8. Hayward, *Vernacular Christianity*.

9. Bush, "Land and Communal Faith," and Tomlinson, *In God's Image*.
10. Boseto, "Gift of Community."
11. Donovan, *Christianity Rediscovered*.
12. Opoku, "Communalism and Community."
13. Mbiti, *African Religions and Philosophy*, 106.
14. Kunhiyop, "Towards a Christian Communal Ethics," 14.
15. Opoku, "Communalism and Community," 492.
16. Tippett, *Introduction to Missiology*, 78.
17. Moemeka, "Communalism," 129.
18. Ibid., 124.
19. McGavran, *Understanding Church Growth*, 228.
20. Dumont, *Essays on Individualism*.
21. Thomas, "Interiority and Christian Spirituality."
22. Dumont, *Essays on Individualism*, 71.
23. Bialecki, Haynes, and Robbins, "Anthropology of Christianity."
24. Kustenbauder, "Rediscovering the Eucharist as Communal Meal."
25. Johnson, Zurlo, and Crossing, "Religions by Continent," 84.
26. Okonkwo, "Sacrament of the Eucharist."
27. Ibid.
28. Bush, "Land and Communal Faith."
29. Ibid., 33.
30. Keane, *Christian Moderns*.
31. Robbins, *Becoming Sinners*.
32. Tomlinson, *In God's Image*.
33. Comaroff and Comaroff, "Christianity and Colonialism in South Africa."
34. Opoku, "Communalism and Community."
35. Gross, "Incompatible Worlds."
36. Kim, "Asian Journey Seeking Christian Wholeness."
37. Tippett, *Solomon Islands Christianity*.
38. De Jonge, "How Christianity Obtained a Central Position."
39. Nehrbass, *Christianity and Animism in Melanesia*.
40. Pickett, *Christian Mass Movements in India*.
41. I. Kuhn, *Nests Above the Abyss*, 27–28.
42. I. Kuhn, *In the Arena*, 72.
43. Pak et al., *Singing the Lord's Song*, 36.
44. Tamez, *Scandalous Message of James*, 4.
45. Brown and Strawn, *Physical Nature of Christian Life*.
46. C. Taylor, *Sources of the Self*, 114.
47. Thomas, "Interiority and Christian Spirituality," 51.
48. Brown and Strawn, *Physical Nature of Christian Life*.
49. Thomas, "Interiority and Christian Spirituality," 52.
50. Ibid., 51.

Chapter 7

1. Xuejun Han, "Nujiangzhou jidujiao qingkuang diaocha baogao" [Report on Christianity in the Nujiang Valley], in *Zongjiao diaocha yu yanjiu* [Investigations and studies on religions] (1986), as cited in T'ien, *Peaks of Faith*, 129.
2. As cited in T'ien, *Peaks of Faith*, 129.
3. Morse, *Dogs May Bark*, 338.
4. Jie Jin, personal communication, March 26, 2014.
5. Shen and Qian, "Other in Education," 48.
6. Ibid.
7. Apple, *Ideology and Curriculum*, 2.
8. Ibid., 6.
9. "Geographic Distribution of Minorities," China Statistical Yearbook 2010, http://www.stats.gov.cn/tjsj/ndsj/2010/indexeh.htm.
10. Covell, "To Every Tribe," 26–29.
11. While one cannot discount the importance of J. O. Fraser and the succeeding missionaries to the Lisu, one must also give full credit to Lisu agency. As Jehu J. Hanciles has cogently stated, a people movement cannot happen without indigenous agency (*Beyond Christendom*).
12. Ward, "Hymn of Grace."

Chapter 8

1. Yan Chun Su, dir., *Treasure of the Lisu: Ah-Cheng and His Music* (Watertown, Mass.: Documentary Educational Resources, 2010), DVD.
2. Larsen, "Music of the Lisu," 44.
3. Mrs. A. B. Cooke, *Honey Two of Lisu-Land*, 30.

4. Mrs. H. Taylor, *Behind the Ranges*.
5. J. O. Fraser, Letter to Dr. and Mrs. Taylor, 31 October 1933, 2. Box 11, Papers of FHT, CIM Archive, SOAS Archives, University of London.
6. L. R. Cooke, *Fish Four*, x.
7. Ibid.
8. King, *Music in the Life*. See also Leaver, "Theological Dimensions of Mission Hymnody," 316–31.
9. Krabill, "Encounters," 73.
10. Charter and DeBernardi, "Towards a Chinese Christian Hymnody."
11. As cited in ibid., 93.
12. Brink, "Glimpses of Recent Chinese Hymnody."
13. As cited in Charter and DeBernardi, "Towards a Chinese Christian Hymnody," 93.
14. Hsieh, *History of Chinese Christian Hymnody*.
15. "Our Book Table," as cited in Charter and DeBernardi, "Towards a Chinese Christian Hymnody," 93.
16. "Chinese Music and Its Relation to Our Native Services," as cited in Charter and DeBernardi, "Towards a Chinese Christian Hymnody," 92.
17. G. Taylor, *Pastor Hsi*.
18. Austin, *China's Millions*, 378.
19. Wiant, "Oecumenical Hymnology in China," 429.
20. Brink, "Glimpses of Recent Chinese Hymnody." See also Selles, "Protestant Worship with Chinese Characteristics."
21. Larsen, "Music of the Lisu."
22. I. Kuhn, *In the Arena*, 51–52.
23. I. Kuhn, *Stones of Fire*, 103.
24. Hseih, *History of Chinese Christian Hymnody*, 88.
25. Crossman, *Mountain Rain*, 48.
26. J. O. Fraser, "Book Review," 141.
27. L. R. Cooke, *Fish Four*, 54.
28. Ibid.
29. Ibid., 30.
30. Ibid.
31. Ibid., 74.
32. Ibid., 94.
33. Leila R. Cooke, Circular Letter, March 10, 1937, 3. Collection 215, Records of OMF, Box 4, Folder 6. BGC Archives, Wheaton, Ill.
34. L. R. Cooke, *Fish Four*, 92.
35. David Morse, personal communication, January 12, 2014.
36. J. O. Fraser, Letter to Dr. and Mrs. Taylor, October 31, 1933, 2.
37. Crossman, *Mountain Rain*, 152.
38. I. Kuhn, *Nests Above the Abyss*, 176.
39. I. Kuhn, *Second-Mile People* (Kindle edition), chap. 1, para. 38.
40. L. R. Cooke, *Honey Two*, 74.
41. I. Kuhn, *Nests Above the Abyss*, 209–10.
42. Ibid., 158.
43. Ibid., 62.
44. Ibid., 72.
45. I. Kuhn, *Stones of Fire*, 63.
46. I. Kuhn, *Nests Above the Abyss*, 21–22. The hymn is #273 in the 2013 Yunnan Lisu hymnbook.
47. I. Kuhn, *In the Arena*, 120.
48. I. Kuhn, *Nests Above the Abyss*, 216.
49. Ibid., 205. "The Holy Spirit Is With Me" is #81 in the 2013 Yunnan Lisu hymnbook.
50. Ibid., 161.
51. Ibid., 41. The hymn is #272 in the 2013 Yunnan Lisu hymnbook.
52. David Morse, personal communication, January 12, 2014.
53. See Bays, "Chinese Protestant Christianity Today."
54. Turino, *Music as Social Life*, 26.
55. Ibid., 35.
56. Ibid., 29.
57. Van Heekeren, "Singing It 'Local.'"
58. Ong, *Orality and Literacy*, 72.
59. Watson, *English Hymn*, 18.
60. Ibid., 22.
61. King, *Music in the Life*.
62. Such as Chenoweth and Bee, "On Ethnic Music."
63. See, for example, Rees, *Echoes of History*.
64. Baily, "Role of Music in the Creation."
65. Westermeyer, *Te Deum*.
66. Watson, *English Hymn*, 1999.
67. Havelock, *Muse Learns to Write*, 74.
68. Wood and Wild-Wood, "'One Day We Will Sing,'" 145.
69. Fisher, *Human Communication as Narration*.

Chapter 9

1. Schreiter, *Constructing Local Theologies*, 35.
2. Ibid., 19.
3. See Hauerwas, "Story-Formed Community."
4. Hanciles, *Beyond Christendom*, 359–63.
5. Pak et al., *Singing the Lord's Song*.
6. Pachuau, *Being Mizo*.
7. Wenger, *Communities of Practice*, 89.
8. I. Kuhn, *Second-Mile People* (Kindle edition), chap. 1, para 10.
9. I. Kuhn, *Nests Above the Abyss*.
10. Witvliet, preface to *Christian Worship Worldwide*, xvi.
11. Ibid., xvii.
12. I. Kuhn, *Second-Mile People*, chap. 1, para. 38.
13. Johnson, *Body in the Mind*.

Postscript

1. Mrs. Roxie Fraser to Mrs. Howard Taylor, n.d., Box 11, Personal and Private Papers of Frederick Howard Taylor, China Inland Mission Archive, School of Oriental and African Studies (SOAS) Archives, University of London.

Bibliography

Allen, Roland. *Educational Principles and Missionary Methods: The Application of Educational Principles to Missionary Evangelism.* London: Robert Scott Roxburghe House, 1919.

———. *Missionary Methods: St. Paul's or Ours?* London: R. Scott, 1912.

———. *The Spontaneous Expansion of the Church and the Causes Which Hinder It.* London: The World Dominion Press, 1927.

Apple, Michael W. *Ideology and Curriculum.* 3rd ed. New York: Routledge Falmer, 2004.

Austin, Alvyn. *China's Millions: The China Inland Mission and Late Qing Society, 1832–1905.* Grand Rapids: Eerdmans, 2007.

Baily, John. "The Role of Music in the Creation of the Afghan National Identity, 1923–73." In *Ethnicity, Identity, and Music: The Musical Construction of Place,* edited by Martin Stokes, 45–60. Oxford: Berg, 1997.

Bartlo, Jenna. "Biola's *The Fundamentals* Still Relevant Today." *Biola News,* February 25, 2013. http://now.biola.edu/news/article/2013/feb/25/biolas-fundamentals-still-relevant-today.

Bates, Matthew W. *Salvation by Allegiance Alone: Rethinking Faith, Works, and the Gospel of Jesus the King.* Grand Rapids: Baker Academic, 2017.

Bays, Daniel H. "Chinese Protestant Christianity Today." *China Quarterly* 174 (2003): 488–504.

———. *A New History of Christianity in China.* Chichester, U.K.: Wiley-Blackwell, 2012.

Berger, Peter L. *The Sacred Canopy: Elements of a Sociological Theory of Religion.* New York: Anchor, 1967.

Bialecki, Jon, Naomi Haynes, and Joel Robbins. "The Anthropology of Christianity." *Religion Compass* 2, no. 6 (2008): 1139–58.

Boseto, Leslie. "The Gift of Community." *International Review of Mission* 72, no. 288 (1983): 581–83.

Bradley, David. "Birth-Order Terms in Lisu: Inheritance and Contact." *Anthropological Linguistics* 49 (2007): 54–69.

———. "Language Endangerment and Resilience Linguistics: Case Studies of Gong and Lisu." *Anthropological Linguistics* 52, no. 2 (2010): 123–40.

Bradshaw, Paul, and John Melloh. *Foundations in Ritual Studies: A Reader for Students of Christian Worship.* London: Society for Promoting Christian Knowledge, 2007.

Brink, Emily R. "Glimpses of Recent Chinese Hymnody: Including a Review of the 2006 Edition of Hymns of Universal Praise." *Hymn* 59, no. 2 (2008): 8–24.

Brown, Warren S., and Brad D. Strawn. *The Physical Nature of Christian Life: Neuroscience, Psychology, and the Church.* New York: Cambridge University Press, 2012.

Bush, Joseph E. "Land and Communal Faith: Methodist Belief and Ritual in Fiji." *Studies in World Christianity* 6, no. 1 (2000): 21–37.

Cable, Mildred. "Book Review." *China's Millions,* November–December 1944, 43.

Cabrita, Joel, and David Maxwell. Introduction to *Relocating World Christianity: Interdisciplinary Studies in Universal and Local Expressions of the Christian Faith,* edited by Joel Cabrita, David Maxwell, and Emma Wild-Wood, 1–44. Leiden: Brill, 2017.

BIBLIOGRAPHY

Canfield, Mrs. F. L. "In Memoriam: Mrs. Allyn B. Cooke." *China's Millions* (North American edition), July 1943, 109.

Chan, Simon. *Grassroots Asian Theology: Thinking the Faith from the Ground Up*. Downers Grove, Ill.: IVP Academic, 2014.

Charter, Vernon, and Jean DeBernardi. "Towards a Chinese Christian Hymnody: Processes of Musical and Cultural Synthesis." *Asian Music* 29, no. 2 (1998): 83–113.

Chenoweth, Vida, and Darlene Bee. "On Ethnic Music." *Practical Anthropology* 15 (1968): 205–12.

China and the Gospel: An Illustrated Report of the China Inland Mission 1908. London: CIM, 1908.

Comaroff, Jean, and John Comaroff. "Christianity and Colonialism in South Africa." *American Ethnologist* 13, no. 1 (1986): 1–22.

Cooke, Mrs. A. B. "Fish Four." *China's Millions*, November 1937, 212–13.

———. *Honey Two of Lisu-Land*. London: China Inland Mission, 1932.

Cooke, Leila R. [Mrs. A. B.]. *Fish Four and the Lisu New Testament*. Shanghai: China Inland Mission, 1947.

———. "A Missionary Mother Takes Furlough." *China's Millions*, April 1939, 59.

Covell, Ralph. "To Every Tribe." *Christian History and Biography* 98 (2008): 26–29.

Crossman, Eileen F. *Mountain Rain: A Biography of James O. Fraser*. Wheaton, Ill.: Harold Shaw Books, 1994.

D'Andrade, Roy. *The Development of Cognitive Anthropology*. Cambridge: Cambridge University Press, 1995.

DeSilva, David A. *Honor, Patronage, Kinship, and Purity: Unlocking New Testament Culture*. Downers Grove, Ill.: InterVarsity Press, 2000.

Diao, Ying. "Mediating Gospel Singing: Audiovisual Recording and the Transformation of Voice Among the Christian Lisu in Post-2000 Nujiang, China." *Yale Journal of Music and Religion* 4, no. 1 (2018): 60–75.

Donovan, Vincent J. *Christianity Rediscovered*. 1978. Reprint, Maryknoll, N.Y.: Orbis, 2003.

Douglas, Mary. *Natural Symbols: Explorations in Cosmology*. 2nd ed. London: Routledge, 1996.

———. *Purity and Danger: An Analysis of the Concepts of Pollution and Taboo*. London: Ark Paperbacks, 1966.

Dumont, Louis. *Essays on Individualism: Modern Ideology in Anthropological Perspective*. Chicago: University of Chicago Press, 1986.

Eddy, Paul Rhodes, James K. Beilby, and Steven E. Enderlein. "Justification in Historical Perspective." In *Justification: Five Views*, edited by James K. Beilby and Paul Rhodes Eddy, 13–52. Downers Grove, Ill.: IVP Academic, 2011.

Edersheim, Alfred. *The Life and Times of Jesus the Messiah*. 1883. Reprint, Peabody, Mass.: Hendrickson, 1993.

Fackre, Gabriel. "Narrative Theology: An Overview." *Interpretation* 37, no. 4 (1983): 340–52.

Farhadian, Charles E. Introduction to *Introducing World Christianity*, edited by Charles E. Farhadian, 1–4. Chichester, U.K.: Blackwell, 2012.

Fisher, Walter R. *Human Communication as Narration: Toward a Philosophy of Reason, Value, and Action*. Columbia: University of South Carolina Press, 1989.

Forrest, George. "Journey on Upper Salwin, October–December, 1905." *Geographical Journal* 32, no. 3 (September 1908): 244.

Fraser, James O. "The Aborigines of the Burma Border." *China's Millions*, March 1935, 42–43.

———. "Book Review." *China's Millions* (London edition), September 1924, 141.

———. "The Fruitfulness of Prayer." *China's Millions*, May 1917, 53.

———. *Handbook of the Lisu (Yawyin) Language*. Rangoon, Burma:

Superintendent, Government Printing, 1922.

———. "A Review of the Lisu Work." *China's Millions* (North American edition), May 1934, 70–71.

———. "Work Among Aborigines in the Tengyueh District." *China's Millions*, August 1913, 128.

Fraser, Mrs. J. O. *Fraser and Prayer*. London: OMF, 1963.

Giersch, C. Patterson. *Asian Borderlands: The Transformation of Qing China's Yunnan Frontier*. Cambridge: Harvard University Press, 2006.

Gowman, Carl G. "On the Burmese Border." *China's Millions*, October 1928, 154.

Graham-Harrison, Emma. "Christians in China Border Valley Keep Sweet Faith." *Reuters*, May 30, 2007. http://www.reuters.com/article/us-china-christians-honey-idUSPEK33242020070530.

Gross, Toomas. "Incompatible Worlds: Protestantism and *Costumbre* in the Zapotec Villages of Northern Oaxaca." *Electronic Journal of Folklore* 51 (2012): 191–218. http://www.folklore.ee/folklore/vol15/gross.pdf.

Hall, Edward T. *Beyond Culture*. New York: Anchor Books, 1976.

Hanciles, Jehu J. *Beyond Christendom: Globalization, African Migration, and the Transformation of the West*. Maryknoll, N.Y.: Orbis, 2012.

Hauerwas, Stanley. *A Community of Character: Toward a Constructive Christian Social Ethic*. Notre Dame: Notre Dame University Press, 1981.

Hauerwas, Stanley, and William H. Willimon. "Embarrassed by the Church: Congregations and the Seminary." *Christian Century* 103, no. 5 (1986):117–20.

Havelock, Eric A. *The Muse Learns to Write: Reflections on Orality and Literacy from Antiquity to the Present*. New Haven: Yale University Press, 1986.

Hayward, Douglas J. *Vernacular Christianity Among the Mulia Dani: An Ethnography of Religious Belief Among the Western Dani of Irian Jaya, Indonesia*. Lanham, Md.: University Press of America, 1997.

Heimer, Maria, and Stig Thøgersen, eds. *Doing Fieldwork in China*. Honolulu: University of Hawai'i Press, 2006.

Horton, Michael. *Justification*. 2 vols. Grand Rapids: Zondervan, 2018.

Hsieh, Fang-Lan. *A History of Chinese Christian Hymnody: From Its Missionary Origins to Contemporary Indigenous Productions*. Lewiston, N.Y.: The Edwin Mellen Press, 2009.

Hu, Yingshu 胡应舒. Preface to Shi, *Lisu-zu de gen yu yuan*.

Huang, Jianbo, and Qi Liu. "Faith as Lived in Private Life and Public Space: A Lisu Village Christian Church in Fugong." *Cultural Diversity in China* 1, no. 2 (2015).

Irvin, Dale T. "What Is World Christianity?" In *World Christianity: Perspectives and Insights*, edited by Jonathan Y. Tan and Anh Q. Tran, 3–26. Maryknoll, N.Y.: Orbis, 2016.

———. "World Christianity: A Genealogy." Paper presented at the conference "Currents, Perspectives, and Methodologies in World Christianity," Princeton Theological Seminary, Princeton, N.J., January 18, 2018.

Jenkins, Philip. *The Lost History of Christianity: The Thousand-Year Golden Age of the Church in the Middle East, Africa, and Asia—and How It Died*. New York: HarperOne, 2009.

Jin, Jie 金杰. "Jidujiao chuanbo dui Lisu-zu yuyan wenzi ji qi bian yong de yingxiang yanjiu 基督教传播对傈僳族语言文字及其使用的影响研究" [On Christian evangelization's influence on the Lisu language]. Doctoral dissertation, Yunnan University, Kunming, China, 2013.

Johnson, Mark. *The Body in the Mind: The Bodily Basis of Meaning, Imagination, and Reason*. 1987. Reprint, Chicago: University of Chicago Press, 2013.

Johnson, Todd M., Gina A. Zurlo, and Peter F. Crossing. "Religions by Continent." In *Yearbook of International Religious*

Demography 2017, edited by Brian J. Grim, Todd M. Johnson, Vegard Skirbekk, and Gina A. Zurlo, 85–97. Leiden: Brill, 2017.

Jonge, Christiaan de. "How Christianity Obtained a Central Position in Minehasa Culture and Society." In *A History of Christianity in Indonesia*, edited by Jan Sihar Aritonang and Karel Steenbrink, 419–54. Leiden: Brill, 2008.

Junio, Diana. *Patriotic Cooperation: The Border Services of the Church of Christ in China and Chinese Church-State Relations, 1920s to 1950s.* Leiden: Brill, 2017.

Juzwik, Mary M. "American Evangelical Biblicism as Literate Practice: A Critical Review." *Reading Research Quarterly* 49, no. 3 (2014): 335–49.

Kalusa, Walima T. "Elders, Young Men, and David Livingstone's 'Civilizing Mission': Revisiting the Disintegration of the Kololo Kingdom, 1851–1864." *International Journal of African Historical Studies* 42, no. 1 (2009): 55–80.

Keane, Webb. *Christian Moderns: Freedom and Fetish in the Mission Encounter.* Berkeley: University of California Press, 2007.

Kim, Heup Young. "An Asian Journey Seeking Christian Wholeness: Owning Up to Our Own Metaphors (*Theotao*)." In *Asian and Oceanic Christianities in Conversation: Exploring Theological Identities at Home and in Diaspora*, edited by Heup Young Kim, Fumitaka Matsuoka, and Anri Morimoto, 25–38. New York: Rodopi, 2011.

King, Roberta. *Music in the Life of the African Church.* Waco, Tex.: Baylor University Press, 2008.

Kipp, Rita S. "Conversion by Affiliation: The History of the Karo Batak Protestant Church." *American Ethnologist*, 22, no. 4 (1995): 868–82.

Krabill, James R. "Encounters: What Happens to Music When People Meet." In *Music in the Life of the African Church*, edited by Roberta King, 57–79. Waco: Baylor University Press, 2008.

Kuhn, Isobel. *By Searching: My Journey Through Doubt into Faith.* Chicago: Moody, 1959.

———. *In the Arena.* 1960. Reprint, Littleton, Colo.: OMF Books, 2006.

———. *Nests Above the Abyss.* 1947. Reprint, Singapore: Overseas Missionary Fellowship, 1995.

———. *Second-Mile People.* 1982. Kindle edition. Reprint, Singapore: OMF International, 2008.

———. *Stones of Fire.* 1951. Reprint, Littleton, Colo.: OMF Books, 2005.

Kuhn, Mrs. J. B. [Isobel Kuhn]. "Rainy Season Bible Classes in Lisuland." *China's Millions* (North American edition), November 1938, 167.

Kunhiyop, Samuel W. "Towards a Christian Communal Ethics: The African Contribution." *Cultural Encounters: A Journal for the Theology of Culture* 6, no. 2 (2010): 7–21.

Kustenbauder, Matthew. "Rediscovering the Eucharist as Communal Meal: African Contributions to the World Christian Church." *Other Journal*, August 8, 2005. http://theotherjournal.com/2005/08/08/rediscovering-the-eucharist-as-communal-meal-african-contributions-to-the-world-christian-church.

Larsen, Hans Peter. "The Music of the Lisu of Northern Thailand." *Asian Folklore Studies* 43, no. 1 (1984): 41–62.

Leaver, Robin A. "Theological Dimensions of Mission Hymnody: The Counterpoint of Cult and Culture." *Worship* 62, no. 4 (1988): 316–31.

Lee, Morgan. "Sorry, Tertullian: Recent Research Tests the Most Famous Adage About the Persecuted Church." *Christianity Today* 49, no. 10 (2014): 18.

Levine, Baruch A. *JPS Torah Commentary: Leviticus.* Philadelphia: Jewish Publication Society, 1989.

Lim, Francis K. G. "'To the Peoples': Christianity and Ethnicity in China's Minority Areas." In *Christianity in*

Contemporary China: Socio-cultural Perspectives, edited by Francis Khek Gee Lim, 105–20. London: Routledge, 2013.

Lin, Ci 林茨. *Fuyingu* 福音谷 [Gospel valley]. Shijiazhuang, China: Hebei Education Press, 2003.

Litton, George. *Report on a Journey in North- and Northwest Yunnan, Season 1902–1903*. Shanghai: Shanghai Mercury, 1903.

Luo, Xiaofeng, Song Duan, Qixiang Duan, Yongcheng Pu, Yuecheng Yang, Yingying Ding, Meiyang Gao, and Na He. "Alcohol Use and Subsequent Sex Among HIV-Infected Patients in an Ethnic Minority Area of Yunnan Province, China." *PlosONE* 8, no. 4 (2013): 1–8.

Ma, Jianxiong. *The Lahu Minority in Southwest China: A Response to Ethnic Marginalization on the Frontier*. New York: Routledge, 2013.

MacIntyre, Alasdair. *After Virtue: A Study in Moral Theory*. 3rd ed. Notre Dame: University of Notre Dame Press, 2007.

Maffly-Kipp, Laurie F., Leigh E. Schmidt, and Mark Valeri, eds. *Practicing Protestants: Histories of Christian Life in America, 1630–1965*. Baltimore: Johns Hopkins University Press, 2006.

Maggay, Melba Padilla, ed. *The Gospel in Culture: Contextualization Issues Through Asian Eyes*. Manila: OMF Literature, 2013.

Mannon, Susan E. *City of Flowers: An Ethnography of Social and Economic Change in Costa Rica's Central Valley*. New York: Oxford University Press, 2017.

Martin, Ralph P. *James*. Word Biblical Commentary. Waco, Tex.: Word Books, 1988.

Mbiti, John S. *African Religions and Philosophy*. 2nd ed. Oxford: Heinemann, 1990.

McConnell, Walter Leslie, III. "J. O. Fraser and Church Growth Among the Lisu of Southwest China." Master's thesis, Regent College, 1987.

McGavran, Donald. *Understanding Church Growth*. 3rd ed. Grand Rapids: Eerdmans, 1990.

McGrath, Alister E. *Iustitia Dei: A History of the Christian Doctrine of Justification*. 3rd ed. Cambridge: Cambridge University Press, 2005.

———. *Justification by Faith*. Grand Rapids: Academie Books, 1988.

Mills, C. Wright. *The Sociological Imagination*. New York: Oxford University Press, 1959.

Moemeka, Andrew A. "Communalism as a Fundamental Dimension of Culture." *Journal of Communication* 48, no. 4 (1998): 118–41.

Moo, Douglas J. *The Epistle of James: An Introduction and Commentary*. Grand Rapids: Eerdmans, 1985.

Morse, Gertrude. *The Dogs May Bark but the Caravan Moves On*. Joplin, Mo.: North Burma Christian Mission, 1998.

Mueggler, Erik. *The Age of Wild Ghosts: Memory, Violence, and Place in Southwest China*. Berkeley: University of California Press, 2001.

Mullaney, Thomas S. *Coming to Terms with the Nation: Ethnic Classification in Modern China*. Berkeley: University of California Press, 2011.

Nehrbass, Kenneth. *Christianity and Animism in Melanesia: Four Approaches to Gospel and Culture*. Pasadena, Calif.: William Carey Library, 2012.

Neyrey, Jerome H. "Body Language in 1 Corinthians: The Use of Anthropological Models for Understanding Paul and His Opponents." *Semeia* 35 (1986): 129–70.

———. "The Idea of Purity in Mark's Gospel." *Semeia* 35 (1986): 91–128.

Niditch, Susan. *Oral World and Written Word: Ancient Israelite Literature*. Louisville, Ky.: Westminster John Knox Press, 1996.

Nieman, James R. "Moves and Rhythms that Engage Local Wisdom." In *Christian Practical Wisdom: What It Is, Why It Matters*, edited by Dorothy C. Bass, Kathleen A. Cahalan, Bonnie J.

Miller-McLemore, James R. Nieman, and Christian B. Scharen, 88–118. Grand Rapids: Eerdmans, 2016.

Okonkwo, Izunna. "The Sacrament of the Eucharist (as *Koinonia*) and African Sense of Communalism: Toward a Synthesis." *Journal of Theology for Southern Africa* 137 (2010): 88–103.

Ong, Walter J. *Orality and Literacy: The Technologizing of the Word*. 1982. Reprint, New York: Routledge, 2002.

Opoku, Kofi Asare. "Communalism and Community in the African Heritage." *International Review of Mission* 79, no. 316 (1990): 487–92.

Pachuau, Joy L. K. *Being Mizo: Identity and Belonging in Northeast India*. New Delhi: Oxford University Press, 2014.

Pak, Su Yon, Unzu Lee, Jung Ha Kim, and Myung Ji Cho. *Singing the Lord's Song in a New Land: Korean American Practices of Faith*. Louisville, Ky.: Westminster John Knox Press, 2005.

Payne, T. DeW. "An Undermanned Field." *China's Millions* (North American edition), January 1934, 6.

Peterson, C. B. "Shepherding the Flock Among the Yunnan Hills." *China's Millions* (North American edition), November 1937, 166–67.

Pickett, J. Waskom. *Christian Mass Movements in India: A Study with Recommendations*. Lucknow, India: Lucknow Publishing House, 1933.

Piper, John. *The Future of Justification: A Response to N. T. Wright*. Wheaton, Ill.: Crossway Books, 2008.

Pocock, Michael. "The Influence of Premillennial Eschatology on Evangelical Missionary Theory and Praxis from the Late Nineteenth Century to the Present." *International Bulletin of Missionary Research* 33, no. 3 (2009): 129–36.

Ranger, Terence O. "Godly Medicine: The Ambiguities of Medical Mission in Southeast Tanzania, 1900–1945." *Social Science and Medicine, Part B: Medical Anthropology* 15, no. 3 (1981): 261–77.

Rees, Helen. *Echoes of History: Naxi Music in Modern China*. New York: Oxford University Press, 2000.

Robbins, Joel. *Becoming Sinners: Christianity and Moral Torment in a Papua New Guinea Society*. Berkeley: University of California Press, 2004.

Roberts, Neel. *No Solitary Effort: How the CIM Worked to Reach the Tribes of Southwest China*. Pasadena, Calif.: William Carey Library, 2013.

Rose, Archibald. "Chinese Frontiers of India." *Geographic Journal* 39, no. 3 (March 1912): 202.

Sanders, E. P. *Paul, the Law, and the Jewish People*. Philadelphia: Fortress, 1983.

Scharen, Christian, and Aana Marie Vigen. "What Is Ethnography?" In *Ethnography as Christian Theology and Ethics*, edited by Christian Scharen and Aana Marie Vigen, 3–27. New York: Continuum, 2011.

Schreiter, Robert J. *Constructing Local Theologies*. 1985. Reprint, Maryknoll, N.Y.: Orbis Books, 2015.

Scott, James C. *The Art of Not Being Governed: An Anarchist History of Upland Southeast Asia*. New Haven: Yale University Press, 2009.

Selles, Kurt. "Protestant Worship with Chinese Characteristics: Reflections on a Chinese Worship Service." *Exchange* 41 (2012): 1–18.

Selwyn, Jennifer D. *A Paradise Inhabited by Devils: The Jesuits' Civilizing Mission in Early Modern Naples*. London: Routledge, 2017.

Shen, Hongcheng, and Minhui Qian. "The Other in Education: The Distance Between School Education and Local Culture." *Chinese Education and Society* 43, no. 5 (2010): 47–61.

Shi, Fuxiang 史富相. *Lisu-zu de gen yu yuan* 傈僳族的根与源 LI-SU Xᴎ: C..MI [The roots and origin of the Lisu people]. Baoshan, China: Baoshan Daily News, 1995.

Smith, David I. "Reading Practices and Christian Pedagogy: Enacting Charity With Texts." In *Teaching and Christian*

Practices: Reshaping Faith and Learning, edited by David I. Smith and James K. A. Smith, 43–60. Grand Rapids: Eerdmans, 2011.

Soukup, Paul A. "Orality and Literacy 25 Years Later." *Communication Research Trends* 26, no. 4 (2007): 1–33.

Su, Yan Chun, dir. *Treasure of the Lisu: Ah-Cheng and His Music.* Watertown, Mass.: Documentary Educational Resources, 2010. DVD.

Tamez, Elsa. *The Scandalous Message of James: Faith Without Works is Dead*, translated by John Eagleson. New York: Crossroad, 2002.

Taylor, Charles. *Sources of the Self: The Making of Modern Identity.* Cambridge: Harvard University Press, 1989.

Taylor, Geraldine [Mrs. Howard]. *Pastor Hsi: A Struggle for Chinese Christianity.* 1903. Reprint, Fearn, U.K.: Christian Focus, 2000.

Taylor, Mrs. Howard. *Behind the Ranges: Fraser of Lisuland, Southwest China.* London: China Inland Mission, 1944.

Thomas, Owen C. "Interiority and Christian Spirituality." *Journal of Religion* 80, no. 1 (2000): 41–60.

T'ien, Ju-K'ang. *Peaks of Faith: Protestant Mission in Revolutionary China.* Leiden: Brill, 1993.

Tippett, Alan R. *Introduction to Missiology.* Pasadena, Calif.: William Carey Library, 1987.

———. *Solomon Islands Christianity: A Study of Growth and Obstruction.* London: Lutterworth Press, 1967.

Tomlinson, Matt. *In God's Image: The Metaculture of Fijian Christianity.* Berkeley: University of California Press, 2009.

Turino, Thomas. *Music as Social Life: The Politics of Participation.* Chicago: University of Chicago Press, 2008.

Van Heekeren, Deborah. "Singing It 'Local': The Appropriation of Christianity in Vula'a Villages of Papua New Guinea." *Asia Pacific Journal of Anthropology* 12, no. 1 (2011): 44–59.

Volf, Miroslav. "Theology for a Way of Life." In *Practicing Theology: Beliefs and Practices in Christian Life*, edited by Miroslav Volf and Dorothy C. Bass, 245–63. Grand Rapids: Eerdmans, 2002.

Walder, Andrew G. "Cultural Revolution Radicalism: Variations on a Stalinist Theme." In *New Perspectives on the Cultural Revolution*, edited by William A. Joseph, Christine P. W. Wong, and David Zweig, 41–61. Cambridge: Harvard University Asia Center, 1991.

Ward, Keith W. "A Hymn of Grace." *Journal of the Grace Evangelical Society* 9, no. 16 (1996). http://www.faithalone.org/journal/1996i/Ward.html.

Watson, J. R. *The English Hymn: A Critical and Historical Study.* New York: Oxford University Press, 1999.

Wenger, Etienne. *Communities of Practice: Learning, Meaning, and Identity.* Cambridge: Cambridge University Press, 1998.

Westermeyer, Paul. *Te Deum: The Church and Music.* Minneapolis: Augsburg Fortress, 1998.

Wiant, Bliss. "Oecumenical Hymnology in China." *International Review of Mission* 35, no. 4 (1946): 428–34.

Witvliet, John D. Preface to *Christian Worship Worldwide: Expanding Horizons, Deepening Practices*, edited by Charles E. Farhadian, xiii–xxi. Grand Rapids: Eerdmans, 2007.

Wolcott, Harry F. *Ethnography: A Way of Seeing.* 2nd ed. Lanham, Md.: Altamira, 2008.

Wood, Peter, and Emma Wild-Wood. "'One Day We Will Sing in God's Home': Hymns and Songs Sung in the Anglican Church in North-East Congo (DRC)." *Journal of Religion in Africa* 34 (2004): 145–89.

Wright, N. T. *Jesus and the Victory of God.* Vol. 2 of *Christian Origins and the Question of God.* Minneapolis, Minn.: Fortress Press, 1996.

Wu, Jackson. *Saving God's Face: A Chinese Contextualization of Salvation Through Honor and Shame.* EMS Dissertation

Series. Pasadena, Calif.: WCIU Press, 2012.

Yamamori, Tetsunao, and Kim-Kwong Chan. "Missiological Ramifications of the Social Impact of Christianity on the Lisu of China." *Missiology* 26, no. 4 (1998): 403–17.

Yang, Minkang. "Mainstreaming, Popularising, and Packaging: New Trends in the Christian Music of the Minorities in Yunnan." *Asian Musicology* 19 (2012): 117–41.

Yunnan Province Three-Self Patriotic Committee. Sl.. d: TⱯ DO, MU, DU M U: GW: [Hymns of praise]. Kunming, China: Yunnan Christian Association, 2013.

Zhu, Fade 朱发德, ed. *Dianxi jidujiao shi* 滇西基督教史 [History of Christianity in western Yunnan Province]. Kunming, China: Nuxin, 2008.

Index

Endnotes are referenced with "n" followed by the endnote number.

Allen, Roland, 34, 47
"Amazing Grace," 191
"And Are We Yet Alive," 117–18
Anderson, Rufus, 34
Anti-rightist Campaign, 7, 103, 108, 123, 124
"Are You Washed in the Blood?", 182

Ba Thaw
    biographical information, 31, 39
    creation of written script, 6, 32, 56
    translation work, 40, 43, 56
Bai (ethnic group), 46, 100, 161
Baoshan. See Paoshan
baptism, 40–41, 71, 104, 107, 114
Bible bags
    Christian identity, role in, 9, 24, 145, 149, 150, 185, 197, 199, 200
    history of, 9, 51, 56, 119, 167
    wearing of, xii, 1, 9, 49, 156, 169
Bible Institute of Los Angeles, xii, 66, 70
Bible, Lisu
    companion to hymnbook, xii, 2, 185, 190
    contribution to Lisu culture and social standing, 10
    copying by hand, 122, 158, 168, 172, 185, 191
    during the Quiet Years, 125, 127, 133, 151, 158, 171, 187
    hiding, 157–58, 171
    iconic nature, 61, 190
    knowledge of, 49, 168
    oral poetic forms, 57–59
    orally performed, xii, 61, 62, 187, 198, 201
    printing, 74, 80, 90, 158, 159, 187, 205
    reading, 60, 61, 62, 67, 148, 155, 163, 169, 185, 186, 191, 198, 201
    role in Lisu literacy, 47, 62, 163, 172, 186
    role in sustaining Lisu Christianity, 60, 62, 171–72
    study, 49, 62, 85, 140
    study Bible, 165
    transmitting doctrine, 150
    translation (*see* translation, Bible)
    use in missionary period, 35, 68, 73, 85, 88–89
Bible schools, short-term
    in the missionary era, 36, 43, 67–72, 84–85, 89, 91, 159, 175
    post-1980, 126, 159, 162, 167, 194, 196
Bible school for girls, 86, 183
Bible training centers, 159–67
    building faith, 126, 162
    curriculum, 164–66
    Chinese-language, 160, 161, 166
    communal nature of, 146
    development of Lisu literacy, 163, 187
    Gongshan Bible training center, 9–10, 37, 45–47, 53, 63, 116, 144, 159–61, 165, 186, 194
    hymn singing at, 145, 160, 169
    Liuku Bible training center, 10, 54, 63–64, 116, 159–62, 165, 194, 205
    means of cultural empowerment, 163–66
    training teachers, 164–65
Biola University, xii, 66, 70
"Blest Be the Tie That Binds," 135
Burma
    Ba Thaw, 31, 39, 56
    Bible translation, 158
    Fraser, J. O., and, 29, 32
    Lisu fleeing to, 89, 122–24, 126, 128, 133–34, 157, 167, 193–94
    Lisu returning from, 158, 167
    Morse family, 7, 89–91, 128
    missionary work in, 73, 182
    role in Lisu Christianity, 167
    See also Myanmar

catechism, Lisu, 7, 82, 119, 133, 206
    controversy over, 81–84
    development of, 32, 40, 43, 56
    missionary use of, 67–68, 73, 88, 90, 119, 175
    role in civilizing mission, 81
Chao, T.C., 176

INDEX

Chiang Mai, Thailand, xv–xvi, 11, 15, 129, 135
China Inland Mission (CIM), 84, 176
    Chefoo school, 74
    cooperation with other missions, 86, 88–89
    Fraser, J. O., and, xii, 25, 29, 31, 38, 43–44, 175, 208n3, 209n59
    hymnal, 177
    Lisu evangelization, 3, 15, 66, 76, 81
    single missionary women policy, 73
    withdrawal from China, 37, 125
    work in Yunnan Province, 26, 29, 31, 43–44, 175
Chinese language
    role in education, 60, 108, 163–65
    role in Lisu life, 21, 61, 93–94, 117
    use in Bible training centers, 53, 161
    use in church services, 63, 105
    Yunnan dialect, 211n50
"Christian Fellowship Song," 130
church, attending (as a Christian practice), 4, 14, 47, 60, 91, 131, 146, 147, 148, 153, 167, 199, 205
civilizing mission, 81, 86, 213n69
"Come Thou Fount," 45
communalism
    definition, 137–38
    difference with collectivism, 215n3
    nature of Lisu Christianity, 39, 45, 51, 62, 104, 107, 114, 116, 118, 128–29, 135–53, 159, 170, 196–203 (See also under Lisu people)
    orality, and, 51, 52
    tension with individualism, 55, 137–38, 140–44
    See also togetherness
community theology, 13
Cooke, Allyn B. xii, 50, 65–81, 103, 168, 181, 187
    departure from China, 6
    printing and producing the hymnbook, 90, 175, 177, 178, 181, 187
    work with J. O. Fraser, 6, 41–44
Cooke, Leila R., xii, 41–44, 45, 65–81, 84, 103, 119, 122, 168, 174
    death, 6, 90
    dispensationalism, 66–67
    hymns, 68, 175–87
    indigenous principles, 35, 72, 73
    translation work, 43, 74
    work with J.O. Fraser, 6, 35, 41
    work with Lisu poetry, 50, 57
    women in ministry, 73
Cultural Revolution, xii, 4, 7, 108, 124, 128, 168, 215n20

dispensationalism, xii, 66
Dulong (ethnic group), 46, 63, 94, 100, 111–12, 116, 126, 161

ethnographic imagination, 15–18
evangelizing (as a Christian practice), 14, 17, 36, 37, 43, 77, 85, 89, 105, 111, 126, 167, 186, 205.

faith/works debate, 13–14, 41, 71, 81, 84, 91, 150–51
festivals, attending (as a Christian practice), 14, 17, 69, 113–31, 136, 142, 169, 176
    Christmas, 41, 72, 88, 89, 116, 122, 157, 182–83, 198, 200
    Easter, 89, 113–31, 148, 157, 181, 198, 200
    Harvest, 69, 76, 79, 89, 157, 198, 200
    in the missionary period, 41, 43, 69, 71, 72, 76, 79, 88, 89, 91, 114, 182–83
    New Year's, 156–57
Fish Four. See Moses
Flagg, Herbert, 39, 43
Fraser, James Outram (J. O.) 25–44, 65, 66, 83, 88, 168, 181–82, 187, 205
    Bible translation, 43, 80
    Christian practices, encouragement of, 40–43, 81
    China Inland Mission, 25–26, 31, 208n3
    death, 205–6
    evangelization methods, 7, 21, 28–29, 33–34, 39–40, 42, 68, 83, 205 (see also indigenous principles, use of)
    festivals, 41, 114, 182
    Firs retreat center, The, 4
    Gansu province, 43
    group conversions, xii, 38–39
    hymns, 31, 40, 41, 174–75, 177, 182, 206
    indigenous principles, use of, 6, 34–37, 72–73, 75, 76, 80, 200, 205, 209n59
    linguistic work, xii, 5, 6, 32–33, 50, 56
    marriage, 43
    Morse family, relations with, 88
    musical abilities, xii, 6, 26, 181
    prayer circle, 6, 7, 32
    prayers, 28, 32
    Roland Allen, influence of, 34–35
    spiritual oppression, 32
    writing, 5, 7, 74
    youth, 25–26
Fraser, Roxie, 26, 43, 205–6
Fraser Script
    historical development, 56, 67, 68, 166
    orthographic features, xix, 32–33, 90, 163, 187

use in the Nujiang Valley, 7, 59, 92, 118
use with Christian literature, 47, 60–62
Fugong, Yunnan Province, 87, 126, 161, 193, 203
  churches and Christianity, 10, 19, 20, 54, 94, 161, 193–94
  culture, 8, 19, 126
  geography, 9, 24, 202–3
  linguistic situation, 7, 59–60
  mission history, 77, 86–87, 128
fundamentalism, 66
Fuyinshan (mission station). *See* Gospel Mountain

gender, 19, 120, 157
"Gloria, from the Twelfth Mass," 169
"God Be With You Until We Meet Again," 25
Gongshan, Yunnan Province, 148, 159, 161, 162, 171
  churches and Christianity, 9–10, 46, 93–94, 101, 102, 105, 111, 126, 159
  culture, 47, 63, 107, 121, 126
  geography, 24, 115, 117
  linguistic situation, 59–60
  mission history, 76, 86–90, 125, 127, 128, 133–34, 148, 159
Gongshan Bible School. *See* Bible training centers, Gongshan Bible training center
Gongshan Zion Church, 9, 45, 106, 145, 159, 196
Gospel Mountain (mission station), 30, 74, 75, 77–78, 80, 177
Gowman, Anna, 29, 31, 67, 69, 74, 80
Gowman, Carl, 69, 71, 74, 77, 80, 103
  death, 74
  short-term Bible schools, 67, 68–69, 71
  translation work, 74, 80
  wedding, 31
  work with Fraser, 29
  work with the Lisu church, 69, 76, 103, 213n60
"Great Is Thy Faithfulness," 195
Great Leap Forward, 7
grid (anthropological concept), 100

"Hallelujah Chorus," 80, 183
handshaking (as a Christian practice), 12, 23, 51, 85, 88, 131, 136, 145, 197–98, 199, 203
"Holy, Holy, Holy," 95
Hoste, D.E., 31, 209n59
Hsi, Pastor (Xi Shengmo), 176, 177
Hundred Flowers Campaign, 123
hymnbooks, 86, 92, 122, 125, 127, 129, 156, 157, 169, 170, 171, 175–92
  carried by Lisu Christians, 2, 9, 156, 185
  companion to Bible, xii, 185, 190
  copying of, 122, 158–59, 168, 171–72, 185, 191, 191
  in the missionary era, 80, 88, 90, 178
  literacy, relationship with, 10, 127, 187–88
  performance, role in, 129, 170
  printing of, 90, 187
  Quiet Years, 125, 127, 133, 157, 158, 187, 191
  spiritual role in Lisu Christianity, 60, 92, 186, 191
  translation of, xv, xix, 6, 47, 59, 68, 169, 175, 177–78, 187, 197
  use in Bible training centers, 161, 183, 205
hymns, 174–92
  "Amazing Grace," 191
  "And Are We Yet Alive," 117–18
  "Are You Washed in the Blood?", 182
  "Blest Be the Tie That Binds," 135
  Chinese, 29, 176
  "Christian Fellowship Song," 130
  "Come Thou Fount," 45
  compared with Lisu Christian pop, 118
  devotional, 186, 187–88, 192
  Fraser, J. O., taught by, 31, 40, 41, 174–75
  "Gloria, from the Twelfth Mass," 169
  "God Be With You Until We Meet Again," 25
  "Great Is Thy Faithfulness," 195
  "Hallelujah Chorus," 80, 183
  "Holy, Holy, Holy," 95
  "I Know Whom I Have Believed," 186
  indigenous Lisu, 177–79, 184
  "I Shall Be Whiter Than Snow," 191
  "I've Wandered Far From God," 41
  "Jesus Loves Me," 41, 145
  "Living for Jesus," 186
  "Lord Jesus, My Road," 178–79
  "Low in the Grave," 113, 121, 129
  "Man of Sorrows, What a Name," 206
  narrative nature, 17, 186–87, 197
  "Onward Christian Soldiers," 186
  "Our Great Savior," 173, 178
  poetic nature of, 57–59, 177–81
  "Since I Have Been Redeemed," 119
  "Sleep On Beloved," 184
  stability, 189–90
  "Take It to the Lord in Prayer," 186
  "Take Me As I Am," 194
  "The Heavens Are Telling," 205
  theological mediator, 40, 174, 185, 190–91
  "There is Power in the Blood," 191
  "Thou Didst Leave Thy Throne," 65, 68, 211n10
  togetherness/communal nature, 175, 188–89, 192

INDEX

hymns (*continued*)
  translation of, 68, 70, 77, 175–77, 181, 185
  "Trust and Obey," 186
  "To God Be the Glory," 127, 155, 170
  "Welcome to the Feast," 117
  "What a Friend We Have in Jesus," 2, 191
  "When I Survey the Wondrous Cross," 179–80
  "When My Life Work is Done," 181
  "When We All Get to Heaven," 186
  "Whosoever Will," 186
  "Win the One Next to You," 186
hymn singing (as a Christian practice), 171, 174–92
  a cappella, 166, 167, 174, 187
  Bible schools, 46, 70, 145, 160, 163, 164, 177, 183, 205
  Christian instruction, xii, 125, 156, 164
  cultural form, 166–67, 174, 200
  communal nature, 2, 136, 153, 159, 170, 201
  contrasted with Bible study, xii, 186
  expression of Lisu Christianity, 4, 15, 17, 43
  festivals, 114, 116, 117–18, 120, 127, 129–30, 182, 183
  four-part harmony, 2, 70, 91, 147, 166, 174, 175, 176, 177, 187, 192, 201
  funerals, 184
  intercessory prayer meetings, 2, 147
  in the missionary era, 51, 67, 68, 73, 75, 80, 86, 123, 175, 181–84
  Lisu Christian identity, 145, 183–84, 190, 191
  literacy, 47, 60, 187
  participatory nature of, 188–89
  rhythm of life, 182
  See also hymns

India
  Christianity, 143, 197
  Lisu ethnic group, xix, 5, 15, 46, 60, 123, 133–34
  World War II, 90
indigenous principles, 6, 34–37, 41, 72, 75, 80, 83, 88, 200, 205, 209n59
  self-evangelizing, 37
  self-governing, 35–36, 200
  self-supporting 35, 73, 80–81, 88
individualism, 136, 139, 140, 215n3
"I Know Whom I Have Believed," 186
"I Shall Be Whiter Than Snow," 191
"I've Wandered Far From God," 41

Jesse (Lisu pastor), xx, 9, 18, 46, 101, 104, 107, 158, 159, 162, 163–65, 166, 168, 171–72

"Jesus Loves Me," 41, 145
Job (Lisu evangelist) 43, 45, 76–77, 79, 184
justification (theological doctrine), 13–14, 48, 81, 150, 207n27

Kuhn, Isobel, xvi
  missionary work, 4, 36, 44, 45, 48, 65, 73, 77, 79, 83–85, 90, 168
  Rainy Season Bible School, 80, 84–86, 183
  observations about the Lisu, 33, 35–36, 70, 76, 130–31, 146, 176–77, 182, 183–84, 199, 201
  writing, 4, 5, 6, 33, 35
Kuhn, John
  catechism, 84
  departure from China, 90, 125
  missionary work, 65, 77, 182
  Rainy Season Bible School, 84–86, 183
  work with Fraser, 34, 37

Lahu ethnic group, 46, 72, 108, 117
leaven principle, 103–4
legalism, 43, 81–84, 91, 95, 96, 104, 109, 136
line dancing (as a Christian practice)
  bodily nature of, 12, 14
  communal nature of, 3, 46, 146, 147, 155, 156, 169, 201, 202
  festivals, at, 116, 118–20, 129
  performance, 200
Lisu (ethnic group)
  communal nature/group orientation, 39, 100, 103, 145, 151, 196–97, 200, 210n2
  ethnic identity, 5–6, 9, 28, 104–5, 114, 118, 121, 153, 163–63, 185, 187, 190, 199, 200, 202, 214n24
  early religion, 29
  independence, 17, 28, 33
  India, in, xix, 15, 60, 123, 133–34
  holistic nature, 36, 186, 202
  minority, as a, 5–6, 28, 46, 94, 96, 100, 108, 163, 165
  Myanmar, in, xix, 5, 11, 15, 21, 60, 66, 118, 156
  social structure, 38, 47, 62, 100, 108–9, 136, 146
  oral nature, xii, 8, 33, 40, 43, 47, 48, 49, 55–62, 136, 151, 162, 179, 184, 186, 190, 191, 192 (*see also* orality)
  Thailand, in, xix, 5, 11, 15, 60, 66, 91, 135, 158, 174
Lisu language, xix–xx, 46, 48, 93–94
  dialects, xix, 56–57, 59, 74, 80, 146, 190, 211n47
  four-word couplets, 2, 57–59, 177, 190

INDEX

literary Lisu, 59
oral language, 8
oral poetry, 57, 177–81, 190
poetry, 50, 57–59, 177–81
proverbs, 50
status, 10
written language, 23, 59, 60, 62 (*see also* Fraser Script)
See also translation, Bible
literacy
Bible schools, and, 84, 160, 162, 163
for the Lisu, 47, 56, 60, 61, 62, 145, 148, 168
traditional cultures, in, 52
promoted by hymn singing, 185, 186, 187, 190
promoted by missionaries, 34, 48
relationship with Christianity, xi, 13, 55
liturgical literacy, 61–62
Liuku Bible training center. *See* Bible training centers, Liuku Bible training center
Liuku, Yunnan Province, 30, 31, 60, 77, 78, 105, 159, 161, 162
"Living for Jesus," 186
"Lord Jesus, My Road," 178–79
"Low in the Grave," 113, 121, 129
Luda (mission station), 76–80, 86, 89, 90, 184

Mandarin Chinese. *See* Chinese Language
"Man of Sorrows, What a Name," 206
monumental function of writing, 52–54
Moses (Lisu Christian), 45, 68–70, 74, 80, 177–79, 185
Morse, David, xv, 11, 50, 88
Morse, Eugene, xv, 11, 87–91, 127, 128, 129, 187
Morse, J. Russell and Gertrude, and family, 6, 7, 65, 86–91, 123–24, 125, 127, 128, 148, 168, 171
Muchengpo (Stockade Hill), Yunnan Province, 28, 30, 41–43, 66–68, 72–77, 78, 80, 91, 177, 213n60
Myanmar, xix, 5, 11, 15, 21, 60, 66, 118, 156
See also Burma
Nevius, John, 34

Nu (ethnic group), 63, 94, 100, 111, 116, 161
Nujiang Valley
Christianity, 92, 95, 106, 108, 118, 123–25, 127–28, 157–59, 166, 173, 184, 187, 191, 197, 201, 205
culture, 48, 117, 146, 162, 173–74, 203
dialect, xix, 146
education, 162, 165
fieldwork in, xv, 7, 9, 10, 49, 115, 174, 187, 203, 205

geography, 5, 146
historical accounts, 28, 212n37
J. O. Fraser, and, 31
linguistics, 8, 55, 59–60, 79–80, 162, 177
missionary work, 4, 65, 76–84, 86, 91, 177–78, 183
Morse family, and, 86–90
persecution in, 122–24, 126–28, 149, 166

Oak Flat (mission station), 77, 78, 79, 83, 84, 85
"Onward Christian Soldiers," 186
opium, 40, 67, 71, 79, 81, 83, 104, 176
orality, 47, 49–55, 60–61
Christianity, and, xi, 13, 16, 40, 48, 51, 54, 55, 58, 61–62, 151, 191
impact on Christian practices, 43, 49, 51–52, 136, 151, 191–92
relationship with singing, 47, 184, 186, 190–92
synonymous parallelism, 179, 180
See also Lisu (ethnic group), oral nature
"Our Great Savior," 173, 178
Overseas Missionary Fellowship (OMF), xvi, 11, 125
See also China Inland Mission

Paoshan, 34, 83, 205–6
Payne, Talmadge, 81, 83
persecution, 18, 79, 103, 108, 123–24, 126, 128, 133, 149, 151, 166, 189, 196, 214–15n17
Peterson, Charlie, 81, 85, 86, 90, 125
practices, Christian. 3, 4, 11–14, 17, 21, 39, 40, 41, 43, 49, 60, 62, 167–68, 189, 192, 196–203
bodily nature of, 4, 11–14, 15, 103, 174
communal nature of, 11, 107, 109, 116, 118, 147 (*see also* Togetherness)
definition of, 11
history of, 12, 91
juxtaposed with belief, 11–13, 41, 43, 94, 101–2, 109, 125–27, 149–51, 202
theological significance, 12–14, 17
See also individual Christian practices
people movement, 3, 6, 34, 37–38, 43, 136, 140, 144, 151, 200, 216n11
praying (as a Christian practice), 21, 121, 148, 160, 171, 197, 201, 205
frequency, 62, 147–48, 156, 188, 201
individualistic nature of, 139–40, 142, 147, 160
intercessory, xiii, 2–3, 4, 10, 14, 19, 20, 146, 147, 167, 199, 202
communal nature of, 51, 128, 131, 136, 138–39, 147, 153, 157

231

INDEX

praying (*continued*)
  Quiet Years, 125, 127, 133, 149
  theology, 12
  in the missionary era, 31, 39, 40
purity and pollution, 95–109
  bodily nature of, 98, 103, 106
  distinctiveness, 97, 102
  external nature of, 97
  holiness, 99, 101, 102
  symbolic nature of, 97

Quiet Years (1958–1980), 124, 125–29, 151, 158, 159, 166, 184, 187, 191

radio broadcasts, 59
Rainy Season Bible School, 77, 80, 84–86, 89, 90, 91, 158, 177, 183
Reform and Opening Up, 7, 124, 157
sacraments, 15, 41, 141, 142

Salween Valley. *See* Nujiang Valley
"Since I Have Been Redeemed," 119
"Sleep On Beloved," 184
smoking and drinking, abstaining from (as a Christian practice), 17, 23, 43, 94, 95–109, 167, 197, 199, 205
  controversy over legalism, 83–84
  defining Christians, xii, 12, 23, 103, 125, 134, 145, 149, 153
  distinctiveness, 102
  holiness, commitment to, 102, 109
  marking boundaries, 102, 106–8
  redrawing the purity map, 105
  preserving community wholeness, 108
  use in missionary period, 40, 43, 67, 71, 83, 91, 92
Stockade Hill. *See* Muchengpo

"Take It to the Lord in Prayer," 186
"Take Me As I Am," 194
"The Heavens Are Telling," 205
Tengyueh (Tengchong), Yunnan Province 26, 27, 29, 30, 31, 34, 39, 41, 42, 43, 65, 78

Thailand, xv, xix, 5, 11, 15, 46, 60, 66, 91, 135, 158, 174
"There is Power in the Blood," 191
"Thou Didst Leave Thy Throne," 65, 68, 211n10
Three-self Principles. *See* Indigenous Principles
Tibetan (ethnic group), 63, 94, 100, 102, 105, 111–12, 163
togetherness, 11, 12, 92, 114, 129, 136, 146–48, 151, 153, 170, 185, 197–98
  See also communalism
"To God Be the Glory," 127, 155, 170
Torrey, R.A. 66, 70
translation, Bible
  coining new terms and grammatical structures, 57, 60, 74, 190
  dialects, use of, 59, 211n47
  four-word couplets, 2, 57–59, 177
  Fraser Script, xix, 47, 62
  in Burma, 40, 158, 167
  missionary translation effort, 6, 7, 34, 40, 43, 48, 56, 69–70, 77, 80–81, 91–92, 170, 175, 177, 205
  revitalization of Lisu language, 56
  role of Moses, 68–70, 74, 177
  unifying role, 57
"Trust and Obey," 186

Upper Salween. *See* Nujiang Valley

Venn, Henry, 34

Weixi, Yunnan Province, 8, 87–88
"Welcome to the Feast," 117
"What a Friend We Have in Jesus," 2, 191
"When I Survey the Wondrous Cross," 179–80
"When My Life Work is Done," 181
"When We All Get to Heaven," 186
"Whosoever Will," 186
"Win the One Next to You," 186
World Christianity, 14–15, 16, 17

www.ingramcontent.com/pod-product-compliance
Lightning Source LLC
Chambersburg PA
CBHW021941290426
44108CB00012B/924